What others say about "How to REALLY use LinkedIn"

"Jan and Bert, the networking experts in Belgium, have written the ultimate book on online business networking. *How to REALLY use LinkedIn* will benefit professionals wishing to enter the next era of networking. The book contains fascinating insights on the meaningful use of LinkedIn in a business environment; it familiarizes you with the unknown, interesting features of LinkedIn; and it deals with burning questions around this social network. In short, this book is an indispensable guide to discover the power of LinkedIn!"

Erik Van den Branden, HR Director, PriceWaterhouseCoopers Belgium, www.pwc.be

The importance of having a great team is one of my Success Principles—a team including colleagues, customers, suppliers, partners, and experts. *How to REALLY use LinkedIn* is your guide to find them—fast!

Jack Canfield, Co-author of The Success Principles™ and Co-Creator of the Chicken Soup for the Soul® series, www.jackcanfield.com

"*How to REALLY use LinkedIn* is a must-read for anyone who wants to grow their business through networking. Even if you're already a member of a referral or network organization, Jan Vermeiren and Bert Verdonck offer powerful, advanced strategies for how LinkedIn can help you get even more out of your participation in those sites as well."

Ivan Misner, NY Times Bestselling author and Founder of BNI, www.bni.com

"Finally, I learned why LinkedIn is useful—and from the experts. As a typical Gen Xer, I was starting to become frustrated to hear more and more people talking about the advantages and the fun of being Linked In. I immediately made a profile and started connecting. If I can do it, so can anybody."

Hubert Vanhoe, President, USG People Belgium, www.usgpeople.com

"I have been using LinkedIn only for connecting to people I personally know. This book gives you well-structured insights and tips to increase the effectiveness of your network—to reach your goals easier and quicker. Thanks for sharing your expertise, Jan and Bert!"

Frank Opsomer, Channel Partner Manager Hitachi Data Systems, www.hds.com

"It is great to read a book that is this practical and gives examp--- -- ---networking goal. Thanks, Jan and Bert!"

Mary Roll, Career Services Manager International MBA Prog Management School, www.vlerick.com

"If you take networking seriously, use LinkedIn. If you take Lin book."

Edgar Valdmanis, Marketing & Projects Director at the Norwegian Computer Society, www.dataforeningen.no

"*How to REALLY use LinkedIn* provides excellent insights in the fundamentals, then describes a basic strategy for everyone, and finally an advanced strategy to use with several profiles. A most worthwhile for every professional!"

Bill Cates, Author of "Get More Referrals Now!", www.referralcoach.com

"Everyone who understands the value of networking and building the right connections should read this informative and well-structured book. Put it at the top of your reading list this year!"

Paul Bridle, Leadership Methodologist, www.paulbridle.com

"Jan Vermeiren and Bert Verdonck have done it! They have written a LinkedIn guide in accessible language that is a godsend for neophytes and a boon for veteran users as well. Readers around the world will polish their online presence to build more internal and external credibility and learn how to turn connections into more sales and career success."

Lillian D. Bjorseth, author Breakthrough Networking: Building Relationships That Last, www.duoforce.com

"After reading *How to REALLY use LinkedIn* I'm able to better manage my list of professional business contacts. Also, I can find potential business more easily and achieve better contact with experienced professionals worldwide. I met Jan for the first time during a sponsorship seminar and since then I have read his interesting online networking publications. This type of networking will become ever more important in the future. It opens a lot of doors for my daily professional communication work."

Philiep Caryn, International Communication & Sponsorship Quick-Step Cycling Team, www.qsi-cycling.com

"If you buy just one book this year, it should be this one. Social networking is the new marketing medium and LinkedIn is at the forefront. Jan and Bert share their expertise and strategies in a concise and simple manner—they are undoubtedly the masters of LinkedIn. Whatever your business, this book has all the tools to enable you to make more connections and increase your productivity."

Frank Furness, Bestselling Author and International Speaker, www.frankfurness.com

"*How to REALLY use LinkedIn* explores every function and process in a simple step-by-step process. Jan and Bert, being two people who are also experts on 'live' networking, have been able to link the networking systems and principles—both online and offline—to ensure this book will be prized by those who wish to become modern all-around networkers."

Will Kintish, UK authority on business networking skills, www.kintish.co.uk

"*How to REALLY use LinkedIn* is a powerhouse book of tips, tactics, and approaches for raising your personal profile. LinkedIn is the buzzword in business networking these days and this book shows how to REALLY use its potential."

Dr. Tony Alessandra, author of The Platinum Rule and The NEW Art of Managing People, www.alessandra.com

"As a LinkedIn user with more than 600 connections, and an active blogger since 2004, I can recognize real value. You will find more good, quick, easy answers in this book than any of its competition. I've read the others and learned from them, but this book was written by people like me: professional speakers and authors, subject experts whose main product are themselves and the talent they offer. Every page is easy to read and apply. Buy this book and keep it on your desktop until your thousands of high-value connections cover it with money."

Jim Cathcart, author of Relationship Intelligence®: Who's Glad To Know You?
http://cathcart.com

"I find myself asked more and more about how to use LinkedIn effectively. People are becoming increasingly aware of its power and importance, to both individuals and to businesses. Jan and Bert have yet again succeeded in providing a clear, concise, and very readable guide. *How to REALLY use LinkedIn* will move people from beginning to advanced networkers. Read the book, follow the steps, and watch the benefits flow your way!"

Andy Lopata, Business Networking Strategist and co-author of '...and Death Came Third! The Definitive Guide to Networking and Speaking in Public, www.lopata.co.uk

"Native English speakers will know the saying, 'Cometh the hour, cometh the man'. In the case of this book we could correctly say, 'Cometh the technology, cometh the book'. *How to REALLY use LinkedIn* is an essential reference work for any business person seriously interested in the power of social networking. It's far more than just an operating manual. Here you'll find excellent strategies for how to gain from this technology and the benefits available through the different levels of membership. There is no doubt in my mind that LinkedIn itself has developed very fast and this book is being published at just the right time to help people maximize their use of the technology."

Chris Davidson, Managing Editor, www.ProfessionalSpeakersJournal.com

"This book is a essential reading for those wanting to enhance their networking skills and to leverage online networking tools, especially on LinkedIn. Jan and Bert have provided a practical, comprehensive resource with a large number of strategies. As an international productivity expert I look for valuable resources to recommend to my clients to boost their personal and professional productivity—I highly recommend this book. Based on the foundation of the Golden Triangle of Networking, Jan and Bert emphasize a need to give, ask, and thank. Do yourself a favor, invest your time and energy in reading and applying the principles in this book!"

Neen James, International Productivity Expert, www.neenjames.com

How to really use LinkedIn really opened my eyes to the possibilities within LinkedIn and how to use it efficiently and effectively. I am a member of LinkedIn, but I didn't intend to spend a lot of time on it. This book, however, changed my mind regarding the possibilities and opportunities; I will start to spend more time on networking with this book as my guide."

Menno Siebinga, Entrepreneur, martial artist, organizer of the Body & Brain Festival (The Netherlands) and founder of the Siebinga method, www.teamsiebinga.com

"Online business networking is a very hot topic. However, many people don't know how to really benefit from websites like LinkedIn. *How to REALLY use LinkedIn* guides you through the opportunities and benefits of connecting. Highly recommended! "

Astrid De Lathauwer, Chief Human Resources Officer, Belgacom, www.belgacom.com

"As a how-to guide, this book contains everything you may need to know about LinkedIn. I've personally found it very useful indeed."

Mike Southon, Financial Times columnist and co-author of 'The Beermat Entrepreneur," www.beermat.biz

"I have read many books about networking and most seem to rehash the same information. Jan and Bert, however, expand the possibilities in this book by examining one of the most underutilized tools that networkers have today: LinkedIn. As the relationship-networking revolution continues to capture attention worldwide, online networking systems like Linked-In continue to move to the forefront. Jan and Bert outline some really helpful strategies to show us how we can take advantage of this powerful utility."

Adam J. Kovitz, CEO, Founder & Publisher, The National Networker, http://thenationalnetworker.com

"Getting your head around an advanced networking tool like LinkedIn can be quite daunting. Jan Vermeiren and Bert Verdonck have simplified it— by explaining in easy steps how LinkedIn works as an effective tool to create the right contacts and clients for your business. They also provide priceless wisdom on the fundamentals of intelligent networking. Reading this informative book will save you literally hours online—and benefit your business quickly and positively."

Paul du Toit, Certified Speaking Professional, MD of the Congruence Group, South Africa, www.pauldutoit.net

"I love hands-on and practical books. This is one of those rare gems one can put next to one's keyboard as a how-to manual and immediately make progress. By providing clear insights and a simple, but effective strategy, Jan and Bert show how everybody can tap into the power of online business networking in general, and LinkedIn in particular."

Guido Thys, Corporate Midwife, www.guidothys.nl

"Great results come from simple and pragmatic methods! Jan Vermeiren and Bert Verdonck succeeded with their latest book. *How to REALLY use LinkedIn* will give you clear strategies to increase your network efficiency with the use of LinkedIn, and it will also explain the sense and purpose of networking. Required reading for every professional!"

Vincent De Waele, Business Transformation Director, Mobistar, www.mobistar.be

How to REALLY use LinkedIn

use LinkedIn

Second Edition - Entirely Revised

Discover the true power of LinkedIn
and how to leverage it for your business and career.

"How to REALLY Use LinkedIn" Second Edition - Entirely Revised

Jan Vermeiren & Bert Verdonck

ISBN: 9781466347601

NUR: 800, 802, 809

Networking Coach: www.networking-coach.com

Website of the book: www.how-to-really-use-linkedin.com

Printed in Belgium.

Lay-out and Print: Pages, Ghent, Belgium.

Cover: Graffito, Ghent, Belgium.

Photography: Ioannis Tsouloulis, www.purephotography.be

Library of Congress Control Number: 2009901615

Contents

Answers to Hot Discussion Topics and Burning Questions

Little Known, But Interesting Features and Behavior of LinkedIn

Go to the
"Video & Tools Library"
for **FREE** up-to-date LinkedIn
video tips, self-assessments,
worksheets and updates
of this book:

www.how-to-really-use-linkedin.com

Prologue

LinkedIn and other social and business networking websites have found their place in our society. In recent years we have seen an explosive and exponential growth of many networks. In the beginning, most people were very skeptical of their value, but now agree they are not only here to stay, but that they offer opportunities never available before.

In our roles as speaker, trainer and coach concerning networking and referrals, we have seen the value of these networks since their tipping point in 2003. As entrepreneurs who are continuously looking for customers, clients, suppliers, employees, partners, media contacts, expert's opinions and other help we personally also have experienced the tremendous power of these networks.

Our team at Networking Coach (www.networking-coach.com) receives an ever-increasing stream of questions from participants in our training courses, or members from the audience during our presentations about the value of online business networks and how to exploit them—especially LinkedIn. Many people expressed their resistance and skepticism about this new way of interacting, but the obstacle was primarily fear of the unknown. Once we explained how they, too, could benefit from LinkedIn, and how to start using it immediately, some of them became raving fans!

Before we explain the power of networking and how to use LinkedIn as a tool with tremendous leveraging capacity, we wish to make a few disclaimers:

- The disadvantage of writing a book about things that happen on the web is that some functionality might be different from our description. Some things might have changed or even been deleted. Certainly, more functionality will have been added. For example, during November 2008 when Jan was writing the first edition of this book, LinkedIn added *Applications* and introduced a new search function in only one week time. Such changes are the reason we will avoid using screenshots. Nevertheless, we want you to get as much out of your LinkedIn membership as possible. To receive your free Profile Self-Assessment and worksheets—and if you want to stay current with added functionality and new strategies, go to the *FREE Video & Tools Library* at www. how-to-really-use-linkedin.com.

- For your convenience, the links to all the tools and websites we describe in this book will be shortened. For example, the link for the Global Networking Group on LinkedIn (http://www.linkedin.com/groups?home=&gid=1393777) will be shortened to http://linkd.in/li-book11.

- Our explanations of LinkedIn won't discuss basic details. If you need lots of screenshots and basic explanations, there are more basic books to help you, such as *How to Succeed in Business using LinkedIn* (http://amzn.to/li-book2) by Eric Butow and Kathleen Taylor or *LinkedIn for Dummies* (http://amzn.to/li-book3) by Joel Elad. However, the tips from this book and the video's in the *Video & Tool Library* will take you a long way.

- We are not LinkedIn employees. We, and our company *Networking Coach* are independent from LinkedIn and any similar websites.

- Although we might be able to answer your questions about LinkedIn, LinkedIn offers good Customer Service. They have FAQ pages where you can find almost all answers to questions (these are the pages we also turn to), and they also have a help desk with real people who respond to questions if you don't find answers in their large Knowledge Base. You can click "Help Center" is at the bottom of each page, or you can go to: https://help.linkedin.com/

What are the key features of this book? It gives you insights in the value of networking and how to apply the fantastic tool of LinkedIn to tap into the power of your network. This enables you to reach your professional goals whatever career or business you might have in whatever industry. We begin with your current situation and how you can improve (better results in less time) by tapping into the power of your LinkedIn network.

From the First Edition to the Second Edition: What a Ride!

Since the book's first publication in March 2009, much has happened with us and with our team at Networking Coach.

Here are a few examples:

- LinkedIn has invited us to organize their worldwide training program pilot—LinkedIn Live, making us the first LinkedIn Certified Training Company in the world!

- The book has been featured in over a hundred magazines, newspapers, television, and radio shows.

- Requests for proposals for presentations, workshops and training courses about the use of LinkedIn led to a growth rate of 283% for our company.

Today, because of the success of the book, some people now look to us only for LinkedIn workshops, while we still offer offline networking courses. Meeting each other face-to-face will remain crucial in our professional lives. LinkedIn is a super tool to prepare us for a meeting, and to keep in touch afterward. Many people have difficulties making contact at an event or presenting themselves in a way they will be remembered (Sticky Stories© instead of Elevator Pitches that fail most of the time) or how to end a conversation with respect. In other words: it is the combination of LinkedIn and offline networking that will bring you the best results.

During our referral training courses, we teach account managers, sales managers and representatives, business owners and development managers, how to be introduced to prequalified prospects so they won't need to cold call ever again. LinkedIn is a fantastic tool to support this (and thus is an important part of our courses), but the real value lies in how you USE the knowledge you get from LinkedIn: how to approach people, how to set up a conversation about referrals, and how to ask for referrals in the way you will be the most successful. In short: LinkedIn is a super tool to gain insight in networks and to prepare yourself for a meeting or telephone call, but it won't help you much if you don't integrate it in a larger strategy or refrain from "normal" contact.

LinkedIn is enjoying its Second Wave

We have seen some changes in the last few years and believe this is the situation in June 2011:

1. LinkedIn is in its second wave.

    a. The first wave comprised people **getting to know** online networking in general and making a Profile on LinkedIn—the **passive phase**. We believe that many parts of the world (especially the Western world and India) are over the top of this wave (the late majority, see the Rogers Adoption/ Innovation Curve below).

    b. The second wave requires understanding how LinkedIn works, how, as a tool, it can REALLY benefit us professionally. This is the **proactive phase**. In parts of the Western World and India we are in the second phase of the curve: the early adopters.

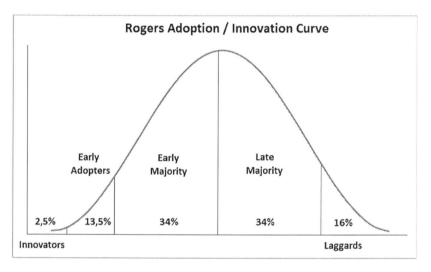

2. Our belief that LinkedIn is in its second wave is confirmed by the different kind of questions we receive in our workshops from individuals, and the different requests we get from companies.

    In the past, we received requests for workshops and presentations directed toward sales teams and recruiters. Today, we get more and more requests to do presentations for the management teams and boards of companies. This results in a company-wide approach instead of a partial one. Finally, the higher echelons understand that online networks are here to stay and that they need to incorporate them in their organizational strategies.

    We also see differences between countries in the way they adopt LinkedIn. For example, the Netherlands is far ahead of Belgium. As a country, the Netherlands is already in the beginning of the early majority phase of the second wave (being proactive), while Belgium has just started (innovators).

I, Jan Vermeiren, asked Bert Verdonck, our Master Trainer, to join me in writing the second edition. Bert knows LinkedIn very well, and as a "lifehacker" he has a vast knowledge of tools to make our personal and professional lives easier. Some of the tools mentioned in the book are free; some are not (and for some we are affiliates). The denominator: we have found them to be very useful in combination with LinkedIn.

Much is new in this second edition. These are some of the updates:

- 5-step basic general strategy to be successful on LinkedIn.

- New chapters with passive, active and proactive strategies for people looking for new customers, a new job, or new employees.

- A chapter about raising your visibility and credibility by personal branding.

- A chapter for Group Managers with tips to attract more members, stimulate interaction, and deal with spammers.

- A chapter about the power of combining online and offline networking: how to get the most out of the events as an organizer and as a participant.

- Probably the most important additional chapter is for organizations: how can they benefit from LinkedIn *company-wide*.

- Video clips showing you how to apply certain tips, constantly updated.

- And many more tips concerning your personal Profile, how to build your LinkedIn network, how to fine-tune LinkedIn (settings), and new tools and features (Applications, News. Labs, and Plugins).

Enjoy!

Jan & Bert

PS: You will realize the greatest value of this book when you **apply** the information, tips and wisdom. Our advice: read this book first to understand the ideas and strategies. Then, read it again and start applying the tips at your own pace. Pick three ideas that you can use immediately, and when you have integrated them move on to three more.

PPS: To help you get even more value out of this book:

1. We have created a *Video & Tools Library* with a free Profile Self- Assessment, video clips related to the tips in the book, and worksheets to support you. Download them from www.how-to-really-use-linkedin.com

2. We have started the *Global Networking Group* on LinkedIn (http://linkd. in/li-book11). It is open to anyone who wants to abide by the rules of this Group and is looking to give and receive support. We look forward to meeting you there!

Chapter 1: What is the Value of Networking?

Two remarks we hear the most in our training courses and presentations are:

1. "Why do I have to network? What is in it for me?"

2. Especially when discussing online networking: "Those people with thousands of connections, are they not just name collectors? I don't want to be like that."

It is important to understand the value and fundamentals of networking before diving into how you can use LinkedIn for your benefit.

In Jan's book, *Let's Connect!* (http://bit.ly/li-book1) he already explained the dynamics that form the foundation of networking and any networking strategy. In this chapter, we will revisit some of them briefly so you understand why and what we do in the following chapters. Please read this chapter attentively because understanding and applying these fundamental principles will make a huge difference in benefiting from LinkedIn.

First, let's look at some benefits of networking and then we will go deeper into fundamental principles of networking online and offline.

What are the Benefits of Networking?

Many people have already heard people say networking is important. But if someone explains how it helps in sales and you are not responsible for sales —you probably won't listen.

Here is a list of 26 reasons why networking is important for everybody, gleaned from the thousands of participants in our presentations, and networking and referral training courses.

Sales

1) Maintaining relationships with current customers.

2) Meeting new prospects.

3) Getting referrals to new prequalified prospects.

4) Receiving referrals to other departments.

5) Word-of-mouth publicity.

6) Creating ambassadors who will recommend you and connect you with potential prospects.

Non- Sales

7) Finding a new job.

8) Finding a new employee or colleague.

9) Getting to know people who can help you with your career.

10) Attracting the right organizations to form partnerships.

11) Notifications of important changes (for example, new legislation).

12) Up-to-date information for work-related topics.

13) Learning about new trends.

14) Receiving more visibility as a person or an organization.

15) Attracting more opportunities.

16) Getting new ideas, new insights, and new wisdom.

17) Gaining another perspective.

18) Connections for reaching people you don't have access to yourself.

19) Enrichment in unexpected ways.

20) Having more fun.

21) Developing as an individual.

22) Developing as an organization.

23) Attracting the best mentors for you.

24) Having a filter (= people within your network) to screen the massive amounts of information on the Internet and elsewhere.

25) Receiving more invitations to relevant events as a participant, speaker or co-host.

26) Security net when something happens such as

26 a. – When you are without a job.

26 b. – When you have too much work.

26 c. – Personal challenges (getting the kids out of school, help when renovating your house, finding a babysitter, etc.).

The rest of this book will show you how LinkedIn can help you have all these benefits. But let's first look at the foundation of networking: the 2 biggest problems, the 5 fundamental principles, and the challenge facing us all.

The 2 Biggest Problems With Online Networking

Many people, after giving some thought to networking, start going to events, make a profile on a website, and begin connecting with people.

Then comes a moment when they might say something like: "I have the feeling I don't get much out of my time and effort."

The reason is that they have never defined:

1. Their goal.

2. Who is in the best position to help them to reach that goal.

These are the 2 biggest reasons why networking seems to disappoint many people.

However, when set your goals first, and then look for the people who are in the best position to help you reach them, networking becomes more rewarding. It becomes clear which organizations, online networks, and Groups on those online networks you should join. You will know whom to reach out to and whom to ask for help.

Your networking success depends on how you approach them and how you will be perceived. Understanding and applying the 5 fundamental principles of networking will make sure you get results.

Fundamental Principle 1: Networking Attitude

In Jan's networking book, *Let's Connect!* (http://bit.ly/li-book1), he defines the ideal networking attitude as:

> **"Sharing information in a reactive and proactive way**
>
> **without expecting anything immediately in return."**

Let's look at this definition in more detail:

- **Information**: in his definition "information" refers to both general and specific knowledge. For example, how to record a television program with a video recorder, or finding the specific code for a software program. "Information" includes both business issues, like sales leads, and simple day-to-day matters (such as the hours of the supermarket). In a professional environment, "information" can be a job opening, a sales lead, a new supplier or employee, opportunities for partnerships, interesting training courses, or tips to work more efficiently.

- **Sharing** involves at least two parties. Networking is not a one-way street, but a two-or more way boulevard. The desired outcome is always a win-win situation in which all parties are satisfied. You need to be comfortable both giving help and making requests.

- **In a reactive and pro-active way**: First, this means you offer information or help when you are asked (reactive). But you can do more. Sending people information and connecting them, without their asking is being pro-active (without any spamming of course). A soft approach could consist of letting them know you have information of value that you are willing to share. This is especially useful when you don't know people well.

- **Without expecting anything immediately in return**: in this era of short-term benefits this is an extremely important concept. Let us also stress it is NOT about giving your own products or services away for free. It is your attitude when connecting with people. An attitude that builds trust and makes you more interesting to other people, works best.

By giving without expecting anything in return, you will actually receive much more than your initial "investment." But you never know from whom or when and this is a challenge for many people. In our training courses a lively discussion ensues because few people see how they can realize this without investing lots of time and money.

We'll discuss later in this book how we can overcome that challenge and use LinkedIn to help us.

Remember that networking is a **long-term** game that **always involves 2 or more players**. You reap what you've sown. Also, remember that **when you share something you still have it, so you don't lose anything.** So start sowing (sharing) so you can reap more, and faster!

Failure to understand and apply the right networking attitude is the number one reason why people feel that LinkedIn doesn't work for them. Since they are focused only on themselves, they don't receive help from others and become frustrated with the lack of positive responses.

Fundamental Principle 2: The Golden Triangle of Networking

The Golden Triangle of Networking is an easy and effective way to build relationships.

Give

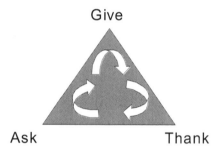

Ask   Thank

Let's look at the three angles of the Golden Triangle:

Give or Share

This underlies the networking attitude. What can we give or share with other people? By giving and sharing we improve our relationships with others.

For many, this is an unfamiliar concept because they think in terms of need instead of abundance. They also think if they give something away they no longer have it. That might be true for physical objects but not with knowledge in an information society (especially in the Western world). When you share information or knowledge (as we are doing with you) it is never lost. We both have it.

Ask

Asking for help from your network is also important. The power of the network resides in obtaining help from other people.

However, many people have difficulties asking for help. In her book *People Power* (http://amzn.to/li-book4) networking expert Donna Fisher explains the mental barriers many people impose on themselves. She explores 7 types of conditioning that can influence your networking effectiveness—without your even realizing it. Thus we often spend too much time figuring things out ourselves when we could ask for help.

Let's look at it from a different perspective. Do you remember the last time someone asked you for some information or for your help and you were able to assist this person? What feeling did you get? The answer is typically: a good, positive feeling.

Now, consider this: the next time you have a question or need help, and go it alone for whatever reason, you prevent other people of enjoying this good, positive and nice feeling!

When they look at it this way many people now see exchanging help from a different perspective; for some it is almost a paradigm shift.

While it might be obvious that we improve OUR relationships when giving and sharing, **asking** is important and necessary to give other people the opportunity to improve THEIR relationship with us.

However, past negative experiences have made many of us reluctant to ask questions. How can we turn that around?

Prepare yourself to ask a specific question.

This approach doesn't seem extraordinary and in fact it isn't. But most of the times we see the opposite: we have a problem or idea in our minds, don't voice it and we don't only expect other people to guess it, but also to provide a solution. Isn't that insane?

The good news is that it doesn't take that much time to stop, think about your question and then voice it in a way that people understand it.

The result? When you are prepared, people will love to help you because they experience you take responsibility, take action and don't waste their time with vague questions like so many other people.

> **Networking success tip:** if you want to move ahead in your professional and personal life *and* give your network the opportunity to assist you, it is important to ask regularly and respectfully!

LinkedIn provides several tools to ask your questions in the "Answers" and "Discussions" functionality. Also use the "Status Update" feature.
How to use these tools will be described in "Chapter 6: The Heart of LinkedIn: Groups" and "Chapter 10: Personal Branding, Raising Your Visibility and Credibility on LinkedIn".

Thank

Most of us do express thanks when someone delivers a solution to a problem. But do we always thank people if we did NOT get something? Do you always thank someone when she took the time to look for a solution, but didn't find one? Or when she took the time just to listen to you?

One of the things that continue to challenge us is remembering to thank people who introduced or referred us a long time ago. In January 2008 we were given the name of a contact person at company X from a networking contact regarding a networking training program. Time went by and there were a few contacts, but still no course was arranged. Finally in December we got the phone call from Company X, asking for a course.

We are ashamed to admit that we forgot to thank the initiator of this contact. Gratitude is important, no matter how many months go by with other projects and events intervening. This small effort will strengthen the relationship and keep your contacts involved in your network. As they learn of your successes, they are encouraged to help you even more. We learned from our experience and now keep track of all the introductions we received and send a small gift when a project finally begins.

Fundamental Principle 3: The Real Power of the Network lies in the Second Degree of Connection

Your own network is called your first-degree network (on LinkedIn you also see the number 1 next to the name of a person to whom you are connected yourself).

Thinking that the power of the network lies in the first degree is one of the largest barriers for people to really achieve their goals.

The real power of the network is not in whom you know, but in whom they know. There are many more opportunities in the second-degree network.

Of course, you need the first degree to reach the second degree, so the first degree remains an important foundation.

Understanding the power of the network in the second degree helps to connect differently with your network and the people you meet online. You only need to build a relationship **with** them instead of selling yourself or your products **to** them.

Understanding the power of the network in the second degree also leads to different conversations. Taking the time to get to know each other better will give more insights in how you can help each other with your own network. This applies to both offline and online networking, on LinkedIn and other websites.

How often do you think: "No matter how nice this person is, I will never do business with him or her because we have no industry, location or function in common. Let's end this conversation quickly so I can start talking to someone who really interests me."

If you take time to have a longer conversation, ask them what or whom they are looking for and share your goals—you might be very surprised at whom they know.

Also by getting any direct or hard selling out of the way (not only for sales people, but also for those looking for a new job or a new employee) networking becomes more relaxed and more fun.

A big advantage of LinkedIn is the leverage of this power of the second degree. LinkedIn shows you the network of your network. You see the second and third degree contacts, together with ALL the connections you have with them. Fantastic!

Understanding and applying this concept will be the single most important factor for your success on LinkedIn. To help you grasp this concept we will do a small exercise in "Chapter 3: How to REALLY Use LinkedIn: a 5 Step Basic Strategy".

Fundamental Principle 4: Quality and Diversity are Both Important

What is most important in networking: quality or quantity?

Actually the comparison is incorrect. It is not quantity that is important, but diversity. However, diversity brings along quantity. The more diverse your network is, the more people within it.

Let's look more closely at both quality and diversity.

The Importance of Quality

What is quality? How do you define it?

Many people perceive people with a high position in a large and well-known company as being of "high quality". Let's call such a person Ms. Big Shot. They do everything they can to make contact with her when they see her at an event. But when they get a few minutes of this person's attention they don't know what to say and focus on exchanging business cards. Afterward, they send emails and call Ms. Big Shot, only to be blocked by her secretary. And then they are disappointed in Ms. Big Shot, in the event they attended, and in networking in general.

If you recognize this situation from your own or another's experience it might be a good idea to look differently at the meaning of "quality".

For us "quality" can be measured only when compared to your goals. A person is of "high quality" if she (or her network) can help you to reach your goals faster. Ms. Big Shot could be a high quality lead, but she might also be very busy. So look for other people of equal quality who are easier to approach and who might have more time for you.

Quality is definitely important in networking. But so is diversity.

The Importance of Diversity

There are 4 major reasons why diversity is important.

Your goals change over time

As your goals change over time, the "quality" of people changes too. Somebody who was of "low quality" a year ago could be number one for you today. This is another reason why everybody is important!

For example: a former product manager of a large telecom company told us that he was never interested in meeting accountants and lawyers at the Chamber of Commerce events. Moreover, he avoided them. But the moment he started his own company, he regretted the fact that he had no connections in those two fields.

More opportunities

A more diverse network gives you more opportunities to find the "high quality" people. But you have to know your goals. We do not recommend collecting as many contacts as possible. At events and on the Internet you will see many people expanding their (virtual) address books. For some of them it's a kind of sport, to brag: "look at how many people I know." But when one of these contacts wants to deepen the relationship, they probably don't answer emails or phone calls.

There is nothing wrong with a huge address book as long as you are available to your network. On the other hand if you're just collecting people like collecting stamps, it might be good to tell them that. This way there are no wrong expectations. Wrong expectations can harm your reputation. And that's dangerous in networking.

More opportunities mean that you rely less on luck or coincidence for good happenings in your life. Lots of contacts combined with knowing your goals will help you experience more synchronicity in your life, too.

Value for your network

Somebody might be of "low quality" for you, but of "high quality" for someone else in your network. A good networking action is connecting people to strengthen your relationship with both. Creating goodwill and motivation helps you to find the right "high quality" people for you.

In fact, connecting people is one of the best networking actions. It is free, doesn't take much time and you help two people at the same time. To be remembered as a great help increases the likelihood that they will think of you when there is an opportunity in your field of expertise or when you reach out for help.

Diversity creates a larger safety net when circumstances change

We all have the tendency to prioritize people who share our interests, background, and education. Wayne Baker calls this the "similarity principle." In his book *Networking Smart* (http://amzn.to/li-book5) you find many examples of this principle. Sometimes it is a disadvantage. For example, when you are looking for a new job, it is better to have a large, diversified network —"the strength of weak links". Your small core group will probably limit you to the same sources of information or job opportunities that you already know.

Find your Balance between Quality and Diversity

You now know that diversity and quality are both important.

What should you do next? It's a cliché, but our advice is:

Find your own balance between quality and diversity.

Remember that a person who is not "interesting" for you today might become very helpful toward a future goal. You never know whom this person knows or how he could help somebody from your network.

For example: when Jan was gathering input for the first edition of this book many people who will never be customers or suppliers helped him to post his requests on LinkedIn Groups. They helped him to get input from people he wouldn't have been able to reach himself. The diversity of his network helped him to reach that specific goal.

Fundamental Principle 5: Your "Know, Like and Trust" Factor

Networking and referral expert Bob Burg is famous for his quote (from his excellent book *Endless Referrals*, http://amzn.to/li-book6): "**All things being equal, people do business with, and refer business to people they know, like and trust.**"

So in order to build relationships it is important to raise your Know factor, your Like factor and your Trust factor with the people from your network.

What does this mean in practice?

- **Know factor**: what do people know about you? What is your background? What are your interests on a professional and personal level? Which organizations do you belong to? To raise your Know factor it is important to complete your Profile on LinkedIn as much as you can.

- **Like factor**: people like people who are helpful, kind, and not pushy. Applying the networking attitude, thinking about what you can share with other people and answering questions in Discussions and Answers helps to raise your Like factor.

- **Trust factor**: there are two kinds of trust:

   o **Trust that you are an expert**. This part of the trust factor can be raised when answering questions in Answers and Group Discussions in your field of expertise. By giving solid answers you will be perceived as an expert. Also, having recommendations from other people describing your *professional expertise* will increase your Trust factor.

   o **Trust that you will behave in a decent way** when you get an introduction or referral. This is a consequence of your behavior described in the Like factor. Receiving recommendations from other people describing your *attitude* when working with them will also raise this part of the Trust factor.

LinkedIn helps to raise your Know, Like, and Trust factor in many ways. As Stephen M.R. Covey wrote in his book, *The Speed of Trust* (http://amzn.to/li-book7): trust can also be transferred via an intermediary. Therefore, it is good to ask for introductions and to pass on messages of trusted connections; this is one of the best and easiest networking actions to take. It works both ways, too: trust (and your reputation) can be damaged very quickly. So be a good advocate as well as a good filter!

The Challenge

On the one hand you now know that starting with your goals makes (online) networking easier and allows you to get results via the power of your network. On the other hand you learned the 5 fundamental principles that underlie networking.

The challenge now is to combine both. If you focus only on your goals and don't use all 5 fundamental principles results will be elusive. You also will get many negative reactions if you only use your network without reciprocating.

Your efforts to help people and to connect your contacts to each other might appear as time consuming. But if you start expanding your network with your goals in mind, and use LinkedIn as a tool in the way it is described in this book, this strategy will achieve faster results and actually save you lots of time.

Conclusion of this Chapter

(Online) networking is the most powerful and free resource for everybody. Starting from a goal is the key. Understanding and applying the fundamental principles of networking leads to success in both networking online, on the phone, and in all your face-to-face contacts. As a reminder, these are the 5 fundamental principles:

1. Networking attitude: sharing information in a reactive and proactive way without expecting anything immediately in return.

2. The Golden Triangle of Networking: Give (or Share), Ask, and Thank.

3. The Real Power of the Network is in the Second Degree.

4. Quality and Diversity are both important.

5. Your Know, Like and Trust Factor will be considered when dealing with people. Make sure all three factors are high.

In the next chapters you will learn how to build a successful LinkedIn networking strategy based on these 5 fundamental principles.

Chapter 2: The Benefits of LinkedIn

Since you are reading this book chances are you already have a Profile on LinkedIn and some experiences with this online business networking platform. Or you might be using LinkedIn on a regular basis and want to get more out of it.

For either situation it is a good idea to take a moment and look at what LinkedIn is and what it is not, its single most important benefit and how it can improve your (business) life as well.

What is LinkedIn?

As of August 2011 LinkedIn was the largest online **business** network website in the world, with more than 120 million users and growing fast (from December 2008 to December 2010 33 million users increased to 85 million). People from all industries are represented with a large variety of job titles and profiles of high-level executives of all Fortune 500 companies. The average age of a member is 45. LinkedIn serves *professional* networking, which makes it different from Facebook, MySpace, Netlog and many others that are focused more on *personal* networking.

Although some people think LinkedIn is a *sales* tool, for us it is a *networking* platform to start and maintain relationships. The consequence of building relationships might be a sale, but also a new job, a new employee, supplier, partner or expertise.

Some people have a sales or recruiting goal and they use LinkedIn and other networking websites just for that. Sure, they get results. But not as many as they could. By overlooking fundamental principles 1, 2 and 5 (networking attitude, Golden Triangle of Networking, and the Know, Like and Trust factor) they lose many opportunities spending lots of time without getting the results they could.

LinkedIn is a powerful tool to build and maintain relationships. A tool is something you use for support; it is not a goal. The amount of connections some people have might present a different interpretation (sometimes it seems their goal is to have as many connections as possible), but for us LinkedIn is only a tool, although a very powerful one.

It is one of the many tools we have nowadays at our disposal in the whole Social Media spectrum. Other tools are blogs, wikis (Wikipedia), microblogging (Twitter), photosharing (Flickr), videosharing (Youtube), social bookmarking (Delicious), slidesharing (SlideShare); interestingly, they all grow toward each other as well. LinkedIn started this integration in November 2008 when they launched Applications which, for example, allows your blog posts or slideshows to be visible in your Profile.

Erwin Van Lun, futurist and trend analyst, goes even a step further when describing LinkedIn:

"LinkedIn is an essential part of the new economy. LinkedIn is not just a handy website or a tool to leverage your business, communicate with other people or find contacts. No, LinkedIn shows the foundation of an open, networked system that arises when we have cleaned up the capitalistic, closed system. In such a world new companies help people as a virtual coach in several domains. LinkedIn specializes in the "work" domain.

This evolution in the new economy started with contacts, jobs and events. Then followed education, job orientation, and mediation. As these developments are assimi-

lated in LinkedIn, this platform will evolve to become a reliable worldwide companion. For now, LinkedIn is just at the beginning."

Just like Erwin, we are very curious about the evolution of LinkedIn and its increasing benefits in our (business) lives. Read Erwin's blog for his view on LinkedIn and other trends: http://bit.ly/li-book8 .

The Single Most Important Benefit of LinkedIn

For us the most powerful concept behind LinkedIn is that it **finds the right people AND the connections you have with them**. It reveals the networks of the people we know. LinkedIn's remarkable value is making our second and third degree networks visible, as well as the connecting paths.

Why is this so valuable?

Many people already have difficulty keeping track of their own (first degree) network. LinkedIn shows us whom our network knows. This is extremely powerful especially if you start with the end or goal in mind. You limit yourself if you look only in your own network when searching for help.

What if we start with defining the best person to meet our needs, find them and then discover via whom we can get introduced to them?

For example, let's suppose you are looking for a job at Coca Cola in your country (or you want to do business with them as a supplier or partner).

Most people then think of whom they might know at Coca Cola. They can't think of anyone and give up. Or they call the front desk, ask for the HR Manager and are stalled by the receptionist. Or the HR Manager says she will call back, but never does. Frustration!

Let's now start with the goal in mind. You define the HR Manager as the person who can best help you to reach your goal (a job, a contract, or expertise). Then you use LinkedIn and do a search with "HR Manager, Coca Cola, and *your country*". The result is that you find the exact name of the person, and also the connections you both share.

When you look at your mutual connections, you might discover that one of these connections is your neighbor. You didn't know this because Coca Cola never was a topic in your conversations. He has never mentioned anything about it and you never told him that you were interested in working for, or with, Coca Cola. After discovering and discussing your connection on LinkedIn with your neighbor, you learn that he has worked with the HR Manager in the past. When he hears your goal he agrees to write an introductory email. Five days later you are invited to have a talk with the HR Manager and get the job or contract.

Without LinkedIn you might never have known that they knew each other!

Of course, not everybody is on LinkedIn yet, so you won't find every person or function you need. However, LinkedIn being a website focused on business networking means we are able to find many people and gain access to most organizations. The large majority of organizations is represented on LinkedIn (as already mentioned, all of the Fortune 500 companies in the USA have an executive level presence). Maybe you don't find the Marketing Manager of a company, but you might find the IT Manager. The Marketing Manager is only one step away. And remember: LinkedIn is growing at an incredible rate (one new user per second), so business people who might not be on LinkedIn yet will be tomorrow or next week.

An extra advantage of being connected on LinkedIn that many users have reported is that you always have people's most recent email address. Since people are changing jobs faster than ever before, this might become even more valuable in the coming years.

How Could LinkedIn Benefit You?

LinkedIn is a tool that supports the networking process, including all the benefits we already mentioned in the previous chapter.

Of course, it depends on your professional role and situation whether you get results sooner or later.

Roles that might benefit in the very short term are:

- Sales people
- Recruiters and HR managers
- People looking for a new job, or internship

In addition, everybody else might benefit as well.

Think of:

- **Finding and identifying the right people** via one of the 10 ways LinkedIn offers.
- **Discovering information** that can help in a conversation, meeting or network event by reading their LinkedIn Profile beforehand.
- **Maintaining relationships** with your network via personal messages, sharing ideas in Discussions and helping people out in Answers.
- **Getting Recommendations** which are visible to anyone, but in particular to the people who are important in your job or for your goals.
- **Receiving introductions and referrals** to the people who matter to you via the introductions tool or a regular email.
- **Discovering the relationships between people** by looking at your mutual connections. (Doesn't the rapport always improve when you discover a mutual contact?) This might also avoid regrettable situations when sales people from the same company call the same prospect or customer without knowing their colleagues were already connected with them.
- **Raising your visibility, reputation, personal brand, and company brand** via your LinkedIn Profile, your contributions in Answers and Discussions and on the web via search engines.

- **Word of mouth publicity** by receiving Recommendations, or from people recommending you in Discussions or mentioning you as the expert in Answers.
- **Getting notifications via Network Updates when someone changes jobs**. This might be a good reminder to reconnect with them and review the possibility of their becoming a customer, supplier or partner (which they might not have been before). This might also provide an excuse if you are in sales to get introduced to the successor of your contact!
- **Picking up trends** in the marketplace via Discussions.
- **Finding the professional organizations** to join, both online and offline, via Groups, and via people's Profiles.

Extra benefits:
- **For sales**: Getting notifications via Network Updates when your customers link with sales representatives from a company that offers the same products or services as yours. This might be a time to contact your customers again.
- **For job seekers**: LinkedIn offers extra tools to help. For example, you can respond easily and quickly to job postings, and use an extra job tool in your browser when surfing any website.
- **For recruiters**: LinkedIn offers extra tools to help you, too. For example posting a job on LinkedIn and doing a search for references.

Do Your Project or Job More Effectively and Efficiently

If the above topics don't apply to you, you have probably an "internal function". Or you may "wear several hats" and have both external and internal roles at the same time.

Although many people who have only an internal function don't consider networking in general, and LinkedIn specifically, as useful to them, LinkedIn can bring many benefits. Many larger organizations have their own telephone and email directories, but most of them only contain basic information. In contrast, when people complete their Profile on LinkedIn their colleagues will discover more about them and see their connections.

As far as we know, there is no organization in the world that has such knowledge in an internal system. They would need to ask every employee to list their connections and also to update them when something changes. Since most people don't have enough time to do their normal work, this would be the first thing they will stop doing. The basic principle behind LinkedIn—and any other social or business network—is that everybody updates their own profile. It would be impossible to keep asking them to update the company's database with the contact details of their connections and their connections' connections.

From a different perspective people who get things done achieve more visibility, become promoted faster and will be the last ones to be fired. Getting things done means only that the job needs to be done, not that you have to complete everything yourself. Finding the right people to assist you is crucial in this new economy of specialists.

If you have an "internal function", LinkedIn can bring almost the same benefits to you as described before. Return to that list and "translate" the tips by adding to each one: "inside the organization I work for". For example: Finding and identifying the right people *inside the organization I work for* via one of the 10 ways LinkedIn offers.

Increase the Amount of Members of Your Professional Organization

The challenge for many organizations is keeping the interest of their members and attracting new members.

Starting your own LinkedIn Group can both add to the value of the membership and attract more members in many ways:

1. An online presence next to events will help members to keep in touch between meetings.

2. Members who can't attend many meetings will still be able to contact each other.

3. The LinkedIn Group is an extra platform to help each other and to discuss trends.

4. Some potential members might have never heard of your organization. They can get in touch with you and become a member of your organization after finding the LinkedIn Group.

5. It is a good, and free, alternative to a forum on your own website. Many organizations fail at building a successful community because they don't have a critical mass of people to participate in discussions. As a result, people won't visit the forum anymore, the downward spiral continues and they might visit the website infrequently. Since people use LinkedIn to connect with other people, and to build their network with other people in addition to the members of your organization, they will keep using LinkedIn and once in a while visit the LinkedIn Group of your organization.
    LinkedIn now also offers a Group API so this can be integrated in your own organization's website or in the website of an event you are organizing!

6. Free membership of the LinkedIn Group might generate interest in a (paid) membership or increase attendance at (paid) events.

Conclusion of this Chapter

LinkedIn is a business network that has grown exponentially over the past few years. The single most important reason to use LinkedIn is that it helps you find the people who can help you reach your goals, and also the mutual contacts who can introduce you to them.

LinkedIn offers benefits for every profile: finding new customers, a new job, new employees, suppliers, partners, expertise internal or external to your company, and other information to get your job done faster.

LinkedIn helps us to discover relationships between people, to get access, introductions and referrals to the people you need to meet, to provide answers to your questions, to raise your visibility, to explore the right groups to join both on LinkedIn and in real life, to receive notifications when someone changes jobs, to discuss issues and pick up trends in the market place.

Also, for people who run professional organizations or associations LinkedIn helps to stimulate the interaction between members and thus attract more members.

So now you know what LinkedIn can do for you, let's look at the first strategy for success with LinkedIn.

Chapter 3: How to REALLY Use LinkedIn: a 5 Step Basic Strategy

Frequently, we see people (including so-called "LinkedIn Experts") believe that they need only a great LinkedIn Profile and then the rest will automatically and magically happen: new customers, a new job, new employees, etc.

This is not what occurs in reality!

How many times do you use LinkedIn to find someone to offer them a job, hire them as a consultant or buy their products? Not often, right?

The problem for such people is failing to start from their goals; moreover most people fail to set goals at all.

To REALLY benefit from LinkedIn this needs to change. A passive presence needs to be transformed into a proactive approach. We help by giving you our 5 step basic strategy for success.

In later chapters you will find more details about each step, and many more strategies.

5 Step Basic Strategy for LinkedIn Success

In this chapter, as in the rest of the book we will share only tips that can be applied with a basic (free) LinkedIn account. If you are required to upgrade your account to apply a tip, it will be explicitly mentioned. Of course, LinkedIn can change its functionality at any time, so always check for yourself.

Step 1: Clearly define a Specific Goal

Take a piece of paper (or whatever you use to write—Word, Notepad, your IPad). Write a goal that can relate to finding new customers, a new job, new employees, partners, suppliers, advertisers, sponsors, volunteers, experts…make it as specific as possible.

This is the first step in our G.A.I.N. exercise© (Goals Achieving via the Immense power of your Network). If you want to do this exercise with lots more tips to help specify your goal, download this exercise from the "Video & Tools Library" at www.how-to-really-use-linkedin.com.

Step 2: Think of the People who can Help You Reach Your Goal

Review your written goal and reflect on "who are the people in the best position to help me reach my goal?"

Expand beyond the people you already know! You can reach anyone in the world via 6 steps, maximum, so keep an open mind and list the people who are in the best position even if you don't know them or even their name.

Remark: as advised above, if you want extra tips on how to actually do this, download the G.A.I.N. exercise© from the "Video & Tools Library" at www.how-to-really-use-linkedin.com.

Step 3: Use LinkedIn's "Advanced Search"

Log in to LinkedIn and go to "Advanced Search" (this is the word "Advanced" next to the search bar on top of your Home Page).

Use the parameters of step 1 and 2 in the fields available on this page. Looking at these fields might cause you to think of some more parameters for step 1 and 2 or to change them.

An explanation of all the fields you can use can be found in "Chapter 7: 10 Strategies to Find People Using LinkedIn", but most of them are self-explanatory.

Now you can have two results: you either find the person or you do not. If you have found the person, go to the next step.

If you haven't found this person, the reason might be that he doesn't have a Profile on LinkedIn. However, there can be other reasons:

- They filed with a different function from the one you are looking for. For example, maybe you typed in Human Resources Director while this person is profiled as HR Manager. You might need to use different descriptions of a function for a successful search.

- You used other parameters in your search than those in their Profile. Experiment with the options by refining your search on the left-hand side (or change the sort options at the top of the search results). Perhaps they no longer hold the same position anymore (change the "current & past" option for Title) or moved to another company (change the "current & past" option for Company). Or maybe they listed themselves under a different industry from the one you chose.

> **Tip:** Cast a wide net and fine-tune later on. When applying different parameters, start with the major ones first (e.g. country, function, company). If you find any results (big or small), add extra parameters (e.g. postal code, industry, language, relationship). This way you can see the effect of some of the parameters you are using. More tips about searching and finding can be downloaded for free from the "Video & Tools Library" at www.how-to-really-use-linkedin.com.

Step 4: Find People who can Help You

If you have too many or too few results of your search, change your parameters on the left hand side.

Then choose the most interesting Profile and look whom you know in common. You can do this by clicking on "x shared connections" in the result list (only for 2nd degree connections) or you can click on someone's name to read their Profile first and then look at whom you have in common on the right hand side (you have to scroll down).

If the Profile you are looking at is not what you want, or you are looking for more people, repeat this step.

Remark: if you don't find many 2nd degree connections (those are the ones you are looking for!), that probably means you don't have a big enough LinkedIn network yet or don't have the RIGHT LinkedIn network yet. In "Chapter 5: How to Build Your Network ... Fast" you will receive some tips to build your LinkedIn network quickly.

Step 5: Get Introduced to People who Can Help You

Once you have found the people who can help you reach your goal and your mutual connections, it is time to leave LinkedIn to ask for an introduction.

Although you can also use the "Get introduced through" option on LinkedIn, we don't recommend using it because you don't know how well they know each other.

They might have once met at a conference or even just connected with each other without knowing each other personally. If you ask for an introduction via the "Get introduced through" option, you might wait for a very long time for a reaction, if you get one at all!

Tip: if you insist on using the "Get introduced through" option, you should know that both the person who introduces you as well as the one being introduced can read both messages! Most people are unaware of this and write something (too) personal in the message to the person who will introduce them. For example: let's assume you want to be introduced to the Marketing Manager of Microsoft and you notice that a friend from university is connected to both of you. In your message accompanying your request to be introduced, you mention some of your "extra-curricular" (going out, drinking, etc.) activities because that's what you have in common. However, your first impression to the Marketing Manager, who can also read those words, will (probably) be your last one!

What's the alternative to the "Get introduced through" function?

Pick up the phone, explain your goal to your mutual connection, and ask how well they know the person you want to reach.

If they don't know them well enough, thank them for their time.

If they DO know them and want to help you, ask them to connect you by introducing you to each other via a NORMAL EMAIL (not via LinkedIn).

We call this the Magic Mail. Why? Because the results can be magical!

Tip: if you want extra tips and examples of a Magic Mail, download them from the "Video & Tools Library at www.how-to-really-use-linkedin.com.

Let us clarify this by showing you the difference between using the "Get Introduced Through" function and an email outside LinkedIn.

If you use the "Get Introduced Through" option, YOU need to write a message that can be forwarded by your contact. This is a cold message that is warmed up a bit by your contact. But it is still you, a stranger, who wrote the message.

On the other hand, when the person you want to reach on LinkedIn, receives an email from your mutual contact, someone they already KNOW, LIKE and TRUST to a certain level, they will be much more open to the message. At the least this person will be more open for a conversation with you; at best you are already "presold" by your mutual contact!

☞ **Assignment:** try the "Advanced Search" on LinkedIn.

> If you want to look at a video explaining these 5 steps, go to the
> "Video & Tools Library" at www.how-to-really-use-linkedin.com

Conclusion of this Chapter

You have learned the 5 step basic strategy for success on LinkedIn:

- Step 1: Clearly define a Specific Goal
- Step 2: Think of People who Can Help You Reach Your Goal
- Step 3: Use LinkedIn's Advanced Search
- Step 4: Find People who Can Help You
- Step 5: Get Introduced to People who Can Help You

You also learned what the most powerful tool is to use next to LinkedIn: the Magic Mail.

We truly hope you use this strategy since only taking action will bring you results!

Chapter 4: How to Craft an Attractive Profile

In this chapter we will look at the different aspects of your personal LinkedIn Profile.

Log in to LinkedIn so you can watch the next steps for yourself on your computer screen.

Although we mentioned in the previous chapter that the biggest "mistake" people make, is to focus only on their LinkedIn Profile instead of being proactive via the 5 step basic strategy, it nevertheless important to have an attractive Profile to support the 5 step basic strategy!

Someone who is introduced to you via a mutual contact, but has never heard of or from you, will look for you on LinkedIn or via a search engine like Google. If they then find out that you are indeed the expert you say you are (remember the Trust factor?), they might become VERY interested in talking to you.

Another benefit of having an appealing LinkedIn Profile is that it allows you to increase your visibility, which supports your personal branding and online reputation. This will make it easier to attract the right people.

A good Profile increases your visibility on LinkedIn and also on the web. Google and other search engines index the information from your Public Profile on LinkedIn. Since LinkedIn has a high Page Ranking in Google (indicating that LinkedIn is a very popular website) the Profiles will also appear high in search results.

Remember: LinkedIn is a business networking website. The focus is on the business side of people (with a small part for personal interests). More and more people use LinkedIn to look someone up before they have a meeting with them. This means that LinkedIn is the first professional impression you make on someone. Make it a good one!

Let's look at what you can do to increase your Profile on LinkedIn and on the web.

Tip: when you are going to **make several changes** to your LinkedIn Profile over one or two days, it is best to **turn off the updates for your network**. Otherwise they are notified every time you click "save" and that might annoy them (and even hide your updates, or worse—remove you from their connections).

This is how you turn the notifications off:

- On top of the page, click on the arrow in front of your name and click on "Settings".
- Usually you now have to give your password since LinkedIn wants to be sure it is you making the changes.
- Under the title "Privacy Settings", click on "Turn on/off your activity broadcasts".

- Then check off the box "Let people know when you change your profile, make recommendations, or follow companies".

> If you want to look at a video that shows how to do this, go to the "Video & Tools Library" at www.how-to-really-use-linkedin.com

Your "Teaser": Picture, Name, Professional Headline, Location and Industry, Status Update

Why do we call this part the "teaser"? Because this is what people will see when you end up in a search result or when you contribute to a Discussion. This part should encourage them to read the rest of your Profile.

1. **Your Profile Photo**: use a professional photo.

   a. Students tend to post holiday photos on their LinkedIn Profile as they do on Facebook. Since LinkedIn is a professional website it is better to have an appropriate photo.

   b. There is not much space for your photo—your head will be enough. Although it is not necessary to upload a photo, this makes it easier for others to remember and recognize you. It also helps before a meeting if the face is familiar. You help other people to feel more comfortable with you by uploading a professional, up-to-date photo and make it visible to everybody who visits your Profile (if you don't want to do that, you can make it visible only to your first degree connections or to your network = degree 1, 2 and 3).

   c. You can click on someone's picture to enlarge it, which helps later recognition. This means you can upload a higher-resolution image (up to 4 MB).

   d. Since you now can upload a high-resolution photo, you might want to have it taken by a professional. Afterward, you might want to print it, make a poster or a portfolio, as well. Take a look at this website to make prints: http://bit.ly/li-book26.

2. **Name:**

   a. If you want to be found by other people who know you, use the name you use in a professional environment—no nicknames.

   b. If you are married and have taken the name of your partner, people who knew you before (for example in college) won't be able to find you. So add your former/maiden name.

   c. If you want only your first-degree contacts to see your last name, you can choose to only show your first name and the first letter of your last name.

3. **Professional Headline:** by default it is your current function. However, we advise changing it. Use words that trigger a response when someone is looking for your area of expertise. Give more detail than on your business card! For example: "environmental consultant specialized in nuclear waste solutions" is much clearer than "consultant". Describe how what you do helps people, i.e., instead of "Owner, Vanity Press" choose, "Helping writers to self-publish".

Many people don't dare to make their Professional Headline specific because they might miss out. Someone important might not find them. Actually, it works the other way: the people you REALLY want to connect with will find you more easily if they are drawn to your headline! Of course, most people never consider to whom they want to appeal (remember the 5 step basic strategy and the G.A.I.N. exercise©) and as a consequence don't get results either.

Your headline is critical because this are the first words people see when you show up in their search results, or what is shown when you answer a question in Answers or in a Discussion. The headline will encourage or discourage people to read your Profile. So polish its appeal!

Remarks:

- When changing your professional headline the information in the "current" field won't change.

- In order to stand out, add a personal element (e.g. happy chocoholic like Bert) to initiate a response from others. LinkedIn is a platform for individuals, and people tend to like others who share their common interests. If you are looking for a "Quality Manager" and get 1.5 million results, who stands out? On which profile do you click and why?

4. **Location:** Although you have to provide your postal code, this is not shared on LinkedIn. For privacy reasons, LinkedIn works with geographic areas instead of exact addresses.

5. **Primary industry of expertise**: Complete this field to find colleagues in other companies in your industry, and to be findable by them.

6. **Status Update**: tell other people what you are doing. Actually, this is not really part of the "teaser", but helps to raise your visibility and credibility and hence is good for your personal branding.

If you want to look at a video that shows how to do this, go to the "Video & Tools Library" at www.how-to-really-use-linkedin.com

Short Overview: Current, Past, Education, Recommendations, Connections, Websites, Twitter and Public Profile

1. **Current & Past**: current and past position(s). This is matched with the field "title" when people use the "Advanced Search" option.

    a. If you want to be found by other people, use words that other people use to search for people with your expertise. If the title on your business card is Marcum Director, but people search using Vice President Marketing or Communication Manager, chances are small that you will be found.

    b. It is important to use this field when you want LinkedIn to help you find (former) colleagues and to be found by them. You will find more details in "Chapter 5: How to build your network ... Fast".

    c. If you want to edit this part (add a position or edit a past one), you need to go further down the page, under "Experience".

2. **Education**: the schools, colleges, universities, and post-graduate programs you attended.

    a. It is important to use this field when you want LinkedIn to help you find (former) fellow students and to be found by them. You will find more details in "Chapter 5: How to Build Your Network ... Fast".

    b. If you want to edit this part, you need to go further down the page under "Education".

3. **Recommendations**: by clicking on "edit" you can show/hide recommendations, ask for recommendations, and provide recommendations for other people. Since many people don't exploit this option in the best way, extra tips are provided in "Chapter 10: Personal Branding, Raising Your Visibility and Credibility on LinkedIn".

4. **Connections**: although many people go for as many connections as possible, that's not always the best strategy. Think about the Know, Like, Trust factor: if you have lots of connections, but nobody is willing to make an introduction or to write a Magic Mail for you because they don't know you well enough, nothing is going to happen. It is more important to grow your network in the right direction for you.

5. **Websites**: you can list three websites. Take advantage of them!

    a. Instead of the standard "Company website" or "Personal website", choose "Other" and then write some compelling text. This will help to get more clicks!

    b. Adding websites might help the websites you are linking to rank higher in search engines (because LinkedIn is an important website for search engines). However, we have seen in the last couple of years that LinkedIn has been changing the permissions on these settings. So don't count on it.

6. **Twitter**: if you have a Twitter account, list it here so people who are interested in you can easily follow you. However make sure that only your professional tweets reach your LinkedIn network (one of the biggest complaints in our ses-

sions is that people feel they are spammed with unprofessional messages on their LinkedIn Home Page!). You can use LinkedIn's suggestion of posting only tweets containing #li or #in, but we recommend using another tool like HootSuite (http://bit.ly/li-book9) or Tweetdeck (http://bit.ly/li-book10) so you can **consciously** post your message to multiple networks at the same time.

7. **Public Profile**:

    a. **Your Public Profile URL**: personalize your LinkedIn Profile page by using your name in the URL. This will boost your online presence on the web: when someone searches on your name in Google, Yahoo, Bing, or another search engine, your LinkedIn page will be in the top rankings. The URLs are unique so be the first to have a LinkedIn URL with your name.

        Tip: In case you are not the first, put your last name first, then your first name. This way, your full name is still in the public profile URL. If that doesn't help, you will need to add a number or an extra initial.

    b. You can also choose which details of your Profile are visible to people who are not logged in to LinkedIn. This means you control when someone does a search on the web with your name and finds your LinkedIn page, which details they may see.

If you want to look at a video that shows how to do this, go to the "Video & Tools Library" at www.how-to-really-use-linkedin.com

---

The Core: Summary and Specialties

Here you can add something more about the organization you work for and about yourself. However, many people get a writer's block when they face this empty space. So here are some tips for you.

1. **Summary**:

    a. Since our lives consist of many levels and dimensions we advise to reflect that in your summary. Use three blocks or text: information about the organization, some professional information about yourself, and some personal information.

        i. **Block 1**: Short overview of what the organization does. We also call this the "**company branding**" part. It makes sense that everybody who works for the same organization puts the same copy here.

        ii. **Block 2:** short description of your role or function in the organization. We call this the "**personal branding**" part. Indicate your responsibilities.

iii. **Block 3:** some **personal information**. Although LinkedIn is a professional networking website, people tend to find common things much faster on a personal level than on a professional one. If you share some personal interests, you make it easier for other people to relate to you when you have a conversation on LinkedIn, on the telephone, or face-to-face.

b. **Tone of voice** is important. If you talk about yourself, use "I" and not "He" or "She". The use of the third person pronoun puts people off. You don't talk about yourself in this form when you engage in a normal conversation. Treat your Profile as a "virtual you" who responds on your behalf to such questions as, "What do you do? What is your expertise? What do you have to offer (without expecting anything immediately in return)?" when someone visits the page.

c. **No selling in your Profile.** Many will resent being sold to at someone's page or in a normal conversation. A quick tip to solve this problem is to rewrite: "What I can do for you" as "What we do for our customers". Your Profile is an excellent way to increase your Know, Like, and Trust factor, but this works only if you share information, not when you market to the visitor.

d. Another pitfall is using too much **jargon** and too many **abbreviations** that people outside your industry don't understand. Use the "Specialties" field and the "Skills" section for that, not the "Summary".

e. **Readability tip**: create some space between the blocks by using "dividers" (horizontal lines). Just press the underscore key 72 times and then you have a straight line.

2. **Specialties**: this is the place to share the skills and knowledge you have accumulated in all your past jobs. This is the place to explain your expertise.

a. Jargon, acronyms, and abbreviations that are relevant to you and the people with whom you want to connect can be put here.

b. If you have a certification like Microsoft Certified Systems Engineer, mention it here. Also, use the abbreviation if it is commonly-used, MCSE.

If you want to look at a video that shows how to do this, go to the "Video & Tools Library" at www.how-to-really-use-linkedin.com

The Specifics: Experience, Education and Sections

In the Summary and Specialties part you have limited room. Fortunately, there are some other "areas" in your Profile to describe your past jobs.

1. **Experience**: for all your current and past positions you can add some more details. Be specific and goal-oriented.

    a. Your results are more interesting than your function. For example: instead of writing "I was sales manager for this company" you can write "During my time as sales manager the company's sales increased by 23% and grew from the 5th largest supplier of widgets X to the 2nd largest one".

    b. As already mentioned: if the title on your business card is Marcom Director, but people search with Vice President Marketing or Communication Manager, chances are small that you will be found. To solve that problem (partially), use some of the synonyms in the description under Experience. When people use "Keywords" to search (or the general search box on top of the page) you will be found. If you have lots of meaningful synonyms, make use of a combination of the Professional Headline, your Title, Summary, Specialties and Experience.

2. **Education:** add the schools, colleges, universities and postgraduate programs you attended. If relevant to your current or future job, you can add some more details.

3. **Sections:** Add them to your Profile.

    a. These are the sections that apply to **everybody**:

        i. **Skills**: you can list some skills and your level of competence.

        ii. **Languages**: you can add the languages you speak and your level of fluency.

    b. These are the sections in the LinkedIn Profile that are relevant **for some people**:

        i. **Courses:** if you have followed some extra courses that are relevant to your professional life, list them here instead of in "Education".

        ii. **Projects:** sometimes you have worked on projects as a student, volunteer or alongside your normal job.

        iii. **Organizations:** list here when you are/were member of a board, a professional or trade organization or another kind of relevant association.

        iv. **Certifications:** for many jobs you need to be certified in a skill. Use the "Certifications" section to show that you are indeed certified which can make you stand out from other providers of the same service, or can show people that you conform to quality guidelines.

        v. **Publications**: if you have written a book or published articles, use the "Publications" section in your Profile.

        vi. **Patents:** if you have a patent, share that as well.

vii. **Volunteer Experiences and causes:** passively: causes you care about and organizations you support. Actively: volunteer work. This helps to show another kind of work related experiences and how much you care. It is recommended to add this field to your Profile, especially when you don't have much work experience (like students) or are un-employed. It shows how proactive you are and your involvement. Two characteristics everybody loves in a professional environment as well!

c. **Remark:** LinkedIn has been adding a lot of possibilities to the "sections", so keep checking LinkedIn to find the latest new add-ons.

> If you want to look at a video that shows how to do this, go to the "Video & Tools Library" at www.how-to-really-use-linkedin.com

The Details: Additional Information, Personal Information, and Contact Settings

1. **Additional information:**

   a. **Interests:** list some of your personal interests here. They help other peo-ple to get a better image of you as a whole person. Many times, common interests are found in this small box, which facilitates online and offline conversations.

   b. **Groups and Associations:** list here the groups and associations you have joined outside LinkedIn. This is different from the Groups on Linked-In. Of course, some of these organizations will also have a presence on LinkedIn, but the LinkedIn Groups you joined are automatically added to your Profile.

   c. **Honors and awards:** if you have received relevant awards or honors, list them here. If they help other people to have a better idea of you as a person or of your special expertise—list them. Otherwise, it is better not to mention them to avoid confusion.

2. **Personal information:** you can add a telephone number, Instant Messaging (IM) name, address, birthday and marital status. Remember that LinkedIn is a professional networking website so add only the parts that are relevant for your professional network. A telephone number is useful if someone finds your Profile and wants to get in touch with you, but your marital status might not be of any interest.

3. **Contact settings:** there is a link to this item on the Settings page. If you receive tens of Invitations a week, discriminate between direct contacts of interest and those that are not. For example: we got lots of questions about LinkedIn functionality, so we have added that people can ask those ques-tions in our Global Networking Group (http://linkd.in/li-book11). This approach makes sure that we get fewer of those requests via our LinkedIn Profiles, and furthermore, people are helped much faster since our trainers are also part of this Group. Many other members also gladly give advice.

> If you want to look at a video that shows how to do this, go to the "Video & Tools Library" at www.how-to-really-use-linkedin.com

Extra Profile Tips

1. **Content tip for all fields**: if you want to be found on LinkedIn, use the words people will use when they look for your expertise or the topics you might have in common. Use variations (for example, Marketing Manager in your title and Marketing Director in the description) and both abbreviations and full names (for example, UCLA and University of California, Los Angeles).

    If you are not sure what exactly to write: LinkedIn offers examples for most parts of the Profile. Look at other Profiles. Use the ones you like as a model for your own. Get opinions about your Profile. Some skills, experiences or characteristics are so obvious to us that we forget to mention them, or we don't regard them as skills or strengths. Others will be more objective.

    Use the Google Keyword tool to find more synonyms or alternative words. This tool is primarily used for Google ads, but you can also use it to find the right words for your Profile. Find this free tool at: http://bit.ly/li-book12. However, don't stuff your Profile with keywords—you want others to be able to read it.

2. You can **drag and drop parts** of your Profile. For example: by default "Skills" and "Languages" are placed below "Applications". But you can drag and drop them below "Summary" if you prefer.

3. Your Profile can boost your visibility, increase your Know, Like and Trust factor, and become a lead generation tool by tapping the power of "**Applications**". Their many possibilities are discussed in "Chapter 9: Lead Generation Tools & Visibility Boosters: Applications".

4. You can **create a Profile in more than one language** (when you are in "Edit" mode this option is on the top right). This makes sense if you are doing business or work in regions or countries with more than one language, or when you do business in several countries. However, for the moment this is only beneficial for languages that are officially supported by LinkedIn (English, French, Spanish, German, Italian, Portuguese, Turkish, Russian and Romanian). For example, Dutch is still not a supported language.

    The supported languages allow you to have an English (primary) and French (secondary) Profile, for example. Someone who uses the French interface will automatically see your French Profile. If someone uses the interface in another language, they will see your English Profile.

5. If you want to **"spice up" your Profile** within the limits of LinkedIn (you can't use HTML tags, for example), write your copy in MS Word and then copy/paste it. In that way you can use some special characters to replace bullet points, for example.

Tip: you can also copy/paste special characters from another Profile instead of switching to MS Word or similar program to add them.

☞ **Assignment:** update your Profile on LinkedIn. Remember to turn off the updates when you are going to make a lot of changes in one go!

Conclusion of this Chapter

In this chapter you learned how to create an attractive LinkedIn Profile:

1. Your "Teaser": Picture, Name, Professional Headline, Location and Industry.

2. Short Overview: Current, Past, Education, Recommendations, Connections, Websites, Twitter, and Public Profile.

3. The Core: Summary and Specialties.

4. The Specifics: Experience, Education, and Sections.

5. The Details: Additional Information, Personal Information, and Contact Settings.

You also got some extra tips regarding crafting your LinkedIn Profile.

Chapter 5: The Fast Way to Build Your Network.

In Jan's network book, *Let's Connect!* (http://bit.ly/li-book1) he wrote about the 6 degrees of proximity (also known as the theory of the 6 degrees of separation): indeed we live in a small world. LinkedIn helps us to discover these links by presenting us ALL mutual contacts and is hence a powerful tool.

The only disadvantage is that LinkedIn shows only your network until the third degree. Fourth degrees and further are not in your LinkedIn network anymore.

To benefit from the far-reaching power of LinkedIn, it is necessary to build your own first-degree network. The real power of the network is in the second degree, but to be able to reach second and third degrees we need to begin with first degree contacts.

Let's look at a strategy for building a network on LinkedIn. And moreover how we can build it quickly. We are going to use the tools LinkedIn provides us for free. Importantly, we are going to connect with people we already know outside LinkedIn. The Know, Like, Trust factor already exists with them to a certain extent. This will be the foundation of your network.

Phase 1: The First Layer of Your LinkedIn Network

1. **Upload your contacts from Outlook, webmail like Hotmail, Gmail, and Yahoo. AOL or other address books.** You can do this via "Contacts" and then "Add Connections" in the top menu. You are automatically positioned in the first "tab", Add Connections.

   The easiest way is to give LinkedIn permission to access your webmail account.

   For most desktop email programs it works differently: you need to export your contacts to a .csv file (comma separated value file), a text file (.txt) or vcf (vCard File). Then import that file into LinkedIn. On the import page, LinkedIn provides step-by-step instructions for several email programs.

   Notes:

   - On the same page where you can log in to your webmail, you can also add one or more email addresses. We don't recommend using this option since the standard invitation message "Hi, I'd like to add you to my network" is used. The message is in English (not everybody's native language), and more importantly, it is impersonal.

   - When you upload these contacts they are visible only to you. There is also no automatic invitation message sent by LinkedIn.

Warning: some people receive an error when they try to import contacts from Gmail or when they use Windows Vista and Internet Explorer 7. To find the solution, go to the Help Center (at the bottom of each page on LinkedIn).

2. **Look at the contacts, which are now available in "Imported Contacts"** (under "Contacts", top menu, and then "My Connections", second tab page)

The people who are already on LinkedIn (with the email address you have in your address book) have a small blue icon with the letters "In". Since they are already using LinkedIn they will be the most open to a connection with you.

Select the people who are already on LinkedIn and whom you actually know (with some people you may have merely exchanged business cards with 10 years ago which decreases the chance either party will remember the other).

Warning: if you have imported hundreds of contacts you might get an error message: "Address book is not available". Our experience is that when you click a few times on the "Imported Contacts" list it will come through. Apparently, it needs more time to fetch all data.

3. **Send an invitation to the people you have selected.**

   a. **Send a mass invitation.**
      Unfortunately, LinkedIn removed the box for a personal message more than a year ago. The reason was that some people abused this option to spam LinkedIn users. Although we fully support anti-spam measures by any website, we feel eliminating a written personal message was not the best solution. Many non-native English speakers want to send a personal message in their own language. But now they are stuck with the impersonal "Hi, I'd like to add you to my network". It is a pity since LinkedIn advocates connecting with people you already know. We guess that if the box returns, membership in non-English speaking countries would increase even faster than it does now.

   b. **Workaround.** If you don't want to send the impersonal "Hi, I'd like to add you to my network" message, there is another option: invite them one-by-one. Of course, this is more time-consuming, but you can send a personal message in the language you prefer.

      How to do this?

      • Click on someone's name. You will arrive at their Profile.

      • Click "Add *name* to your network" (right upper corner).

      • Choose the relationship you have with them and write a personal message.

After doing these 3 steps people will respond to you. They will accept your invitation and your network will start to grow.

Phase 2: A Second Layer for Your Network.

While you are waiting for people to accept the invitations you sent in phase 1, you can add more people to your network. Again, focus first on the people who are already on LinkedIn because they will be more open to accepting your invitation.

We will use the tools LinkedIn provides for retrieving colleagues and classmates. Since LinkedIn works with the information in your Profile, it is important that you have listed the companies you have worked for and the schools and universities where you studied. See "Chapter 4: How To Craft an Attractive Profile".

Let's start with current and past colleagues.

1. **Look for current and past colleagues.** Do this via "Contacts/Add Connections" in the top menu and then the "Colleagues" tab.
   You will see all the companies that you yourself have listed in your Profile. You will also see how many people from each company are already LinkedIn members (with a maximum of 50).

2. **Click on a company** you are working for or have worked for. You will get a list of people you might know. Select the people you actually know. They end up on the box on the right side.

3. **Invite them to connect**. The good news is that here you have the option to "add a personal note with your invitation". Use it!

   a. Option 1: Write a **personal message** to them if you are going to invite them one by one.

   b. Option 2: Write a **semi-personal message** when you are going to invite a group of people. You can't make it too personal when you use this method because you have selected several people. To give you an idea what this might look like, this is an example of a message that Jan used recently:

   > *I see you are a member of LinkedIn as well.*
   >
   > *Let's Connect! :-)*
   >
   > *By the way did you know that LinkedIn has Labs? They are testing interesting new tools.*
   >
   > *Just put LinkedIn Labs in your favorite search engine and you will find them.*
   >
   > *Have a great networking day!*
   >
   > *Jan*

   A few remarks:

   - **You don't see any name at the beginning of the message**. The reason is that LinkedIn automatically adds the first name of the person to the message. Since there is no preview function, few people know this!

   - You see that Jan's **message in itself is not personal, but he makes it less impersonal by including a tip**. Jan got many good responses after connecting with people using this message. Many people told him they didn't know about the Labs. This tip doesn't have to be related to

LinkedIn. If you connect with people with the same function you might share a trend or anything else that is of value to the recipients (However, you can't send links since LinkedIn refuses them as an anti-spam measure).

Remember, this is an extra contact possibility with someone. The better you do this, the faster you get results. People who have received the invitation with the tip might remember you and get back in touch with you to see if you can work together in some way.

- If you work for a large company and have lots of contacts you will need to go through this process several times. But **you don't want to type your message again and again**. Of course, you can use notepad or Word to store your text and do copy/paste. However, there are also "genius shortcuts" that you can use for many repeating tasks, which can help you with this. The choices are "Texter" (for Windows, http://tinyurl.com/texter) and "TextExpander" (for Mac, http://tinyurl.com/text-exp). More tools can be found in "Chapter 21: Tools to Save You Time When Working with LinkedIn".

Once you have done this for one company, repeat steps 2 and 3 for others.

In this way your network grows with both current and past colleagues.

Now, we are going to do the same for the people with whom you studied (or are studying). While you might share fewer contacts or current interests on a professional or personal level, old classmates might be very valuable for your network. Remember the importance of a diverse network.

1. **Look for classmates.** You can do this via "Contacts-Add Connections" in the top menu and then the "Classmates" tab.
   You will see all the schools that you yourself have listed in your Profile.

2. **Click on a school**. You will get a list of people you might know. Select the people you actually know. You can select only one classmate at the time.

3. Write a **personal message** to them.

4. Repeat steps 2 and 3 for every classmate of that same school.

5. Repeat steps 2, 3 and 4 for every school where you enrolled.

In this way your network grows with current and past classmates.

Phase 3: Discover People You May Know

Every time you log in to LinkedIn, you see on the right three people you may know.

There is another place on LinkedIn where you can find those people you may know.

Go to "Contacts/Add Connections" and then the fourth tab page "People You May Know".

Click on the "Connect" link from people you actually know, add a personal message, and send your invitation.

> **Tip:** You will get a list of 10 "People You May Know". At the bottom of this page you will see a button Next. If you click on it, LinkedIn suggests even more people you may know!

> **Note:** you may wonder, "How does LinkedIn know that I know these people?" (Or sometimes: "I don't know these people at all, why is LinkedIn suggesting that I do?") LinkedIn uses 18 parameters to make the matches. Although the algorithm is a secret, it probably contains: mutual connections, Groups you are both member of, schools you both went to, companies you both have worked for and so on.

Phase 4: Grow Your Network Passively

In the first three phases you took action to invite other people by sending them an invitation. In phase 4 you will set up some tools that will passively invite people to connect with you, which means you set them up once and then don't have to invest time in them anymore.

1. **Mention your LinkedIn Profile in your email signature.** How?
   a. Scroll to the bottom of a page on LinkedIn. Click "Tools".
   b. In the middle of the page, you see "Email signature". Click on the "Try it now" button.
   c. Create your LinkedIn email signature.

2. **Mention your LinkedIn Profile on your website or blog.**
   a. Click on "Profile/Edit Profile" in the top menu.
   b. Scroll down to "Public Profile" and click on "edit".
   c. Scroll down and on the right hand side and below "Profile Badges" click on "Create a profile badge".
   d. Choose the button and code you want to use on your website or blog.
   e. You can also use this approach for an email signature in some email programs.

When you are going to use these email signatures and buttons some people will click on them and invite you to connect. In this way THEY take action, not you, that's why we call phase 4 a passive phase.

By going through the first 3 phases you will proactively lay the foundation of your network. It is good advice to repeat phases 1 and 2 two or three times a year. Phase 3 (People You May Know) can be done every week if you like. Over time phase 4 will bring you some extra connections.

One of the frequent mistakes we see people make in networking is that they start to build their network only when they need it: such as looking for a new job or when they need new customers. You need time to build your network and you may not have this time. An even greater danger is that you will contact people out of a need. In such a situation it is hard to network without expecting something immediately in return. People will sense that. As a consequence, many will be reluctant to connect with you and make introductions for you.

So start building your network right now!

In a next chapter you will learn some extra strategies for expanding your network further. Start now to build its foundation.

You will experience your network expanding automatically. Other LinkedIn members will find you and invite you to connect. People from your offline network will also discover LinkedIn, become a member and then invite you to connect. The larger your network grows, the more people will be interested in connecting with you. Even people you don't know. How to deal with them will be discussed in "Chapter 19: Hot Discussion Topics and Burning Questions".

☞ **Assignment**: build the foundation of your network on LinkedIn.

> If you want to look at a video that shows the 4 phases of building your network, go to the "Video & Tools Library" at www.how-to-really-use-linkedin.com

Conclusion of this Chapter

In this chapter you learned the 4 phases for building the foundation of your LinkedIn network:

1. Phase 1: Upload your email contacts and connect with the ones already on LinkedIn

2. Phase 2: Find current and former colleagues and classmates and connect with them

3. Phase 3: Discover people you may know and connect with the ones you actually know

4. Phase 4: Promote your LinkedIn Profile with a LinkedIn Email Signature and LinkedIn Profile Badge for your website and blog

Chapter 6: The Heart of LinkedIn: Groups

Why do we call the Groups the heart of LinkedIn? Because that's where the most interaction is. Groups are THE place to help others and be helped by them, to apply the Golden Triangle of Networking (Give, Ask, Thank) and to raise your Know, Like, and Trust factor.

The Added Value of Groups

The trigger that caused Jan to write the first edition of this book was the introduction of Discussions in Groups.

Before the Discussions function was added to the Groups, LinkedIn was primarily a directory of people with the links between them. The Answers functionality brought more interaction on the website, but since the introduction of the Discussions function LinkedIn contains a collection of professional communities where people can exchange help.

Building relationships depends on the interactions between the members, not just the fact that their Profiles are linked. Discussions make connections easier, and they offer the opportunity to tap into the power of Groups—many experts exchanging help and ideas.

The Value of Being a Group Member

Interactions in Groups are also more intuitive than the Answers functionality. People are used to coming together in clubs and associations in real life. Sharing ideas is also one of the first uses of the Internet.

So we encourage you to become a member of one or more Groups or to start one yourself. Once you are a member these are the benefits of belonging to a Group:

- By asking questions in the Discussions-forum you are able to **receive help from the other members**.
- **You can see the Profiles of other members**. This gives you direct access to additional people who might not be in your first, second, or third degree network.
- **You can contact other members directly**. Many people don't allow direct contact via LinkedIn (they disable that option in their Settings). However, the standard option in every Group is that members may contact each other directly. Almost nobody knows this option can be turned off. Therefore normally you would be able to contact all other Group members.
- **By answering questions in the Discussions-forum you gain visibility, and you also have the opportunity to show your expertise**. This increases your "Know, Like and Trust" factor. Make sure you provide good answers and don't make your contribution a sales pitch.
- **By sharing articles you also raise your visibility**. Again, no sales pitch. It is OK to share links to your own website, blog, or article that features you as long as it gives other people more insights or help.

- **When responding to a question in the Discussions you can add the URL of your website**. This gives your website more visibility and helps to boost your ranking in Google and other search engines. However, don't overdo it. Just one line, maximum two lines.

- **Some extra advantages of being a member of a Group that also organizes face-to-face meetings**:

  o You can ask who else is attending so you decide if it is worthwhile for you. You can also make arrangements to meet other people there. This helps when you are not comfortable in new environments.

  o If you have never been to such a meeting, ask about the past experiences of other members so you have realistic expectations.

  o You can make arrangements to car pool so you save some money and gasoline, and maximize your networking time.

  o You can easily follow-up after the event, and in between future meetings.

  o Extra tips about how to combine the power of a LinkedIn Group with LinkedIn Events and offline networking can be found in "Chapter 11: The Power of Combining Online and Offline Networking: Events".

  o *Remark: tips about how to prepare for live networking events, what to do when you are there and how to follow-up, can be found on the networking CD, "Let's Connect at an Event" on the website of Networking Coach (www.networking-coach.com).*

We strongly encourage you to become a member of one or more Groups. Be an active member—help people and share insights. This will make you more interesting to other people. They will contact you and consult you for your expertise.

You can also use "Answers" for exchanging help. The advantage is that this not limited to a Group, so you can get help from potentially many more people and raise your visibility with them at the same time. However, the wide reach is also a disadvantage: many people who belong to your "target group" (meaning: the people to whom you want to be visible for whatever reason) will never see the questions and answers in "Answers", but they might follow closely the Group Discussions online or get notified by email. In other words, in many cases you will get better results in Groups than in Answers.

Which Groups to Join?

The biggest question for many people remains: which Groups do I have to join?

You can join up to 50 Groups on LinkedIn. However, we don't recommend being a Group Member of more than 10 Groups since you can't actively contribute in tens of Groups.

Our biggest tip about which Groups to join is simply the ones that relate to your goals.

For example:

- If you are looking for a new job, choose the Groups where recruiters might see your Profile or where your future colleagues and hiring managers are.

- If you are looking for new customers, choose Groups where you will find current customers, other suppliers to your target group and prospects.

- If you are looking for new employees, choose Groups that focus on the type of employees you want. Also become a member of your company Group and the alumni Group of your own company.

- If you are looking for partners, choose the Groups they have joined along with people who have access to them.

As well, there are also some Groups that are more independent from your goals:

- Alumni groups of schools (former students)

- Alumni groups of companies (former employees, and many times also current employees)

- Groups of the organization where you work

- Groups of organizations you belong to in the real world (professional organizations, trade organizations, Chambers of Commerce, local business clubs, referral clubs, service clubs and the like)

3 Types of Groups

LinkedIn offers 3 types of Groups:

1. **Private Groups**: the Group owner or one of the Group managers needs to approve the request to join. All posts in such a Group can NOT be found via search engines (you will notice a padlock next to the name of the Group).

2. **Member-Only Groups**: everybody who wants to join the Group is accepted automatically. All posts to the Group can NOT be found via search engines (you will notice a padlock next to the name of the Group).

3. **Open Groups:** everybody who wants to join the Group is accepted automatically. All posts to the Group CAN be found via search engines.

   Remark: at the time of writing Subgroups may not be open.

4 Ways to Find Groups on LinkedIn

There are 4 ways to find Groups on LinkedIn. Since the search functionality in Groups is still rather limited (there is no "Advanced Search" for Groups at the time of writing), you will probably need all of them to find the right Groups for you.

1. **Use the Groups Directory**.

   a. In the top menu, click "Groups/Groups Directory".

   b. You will be presented with randomly featured Groups.

   c. On the left hand side you can use the search box to search with one or more keywords. You can refine your search with the type of Group you are looking for or the language. Be careful with the last option since a Group might be local Dutch Group, but the language English.

d. When you click on the name of one of the Groups you will arrive at the entry page of that Group (if it is an open Group) or at the Group Profile page (if it is a private or member-only Group). In the latter case, you will get some information about the Group and 10 people from your first two degrees network who are already members (you can find the same information for open Groups by clicking on "More/Group Profile"). This may help you to choose the right Group for you.

2. **Groups You May Like.**

   a. In the top menu, click "Groups/Groups You May Like".

   b. You will be presented with Groups that are similar to ALL the ones you have already joined.

3. **Similar Groups.**

   a. When you are looking for Groups using the search functionality of the Groups directory or the "Groups You May Like" option you will notice the "Similar Groups" link for each Group on the right side. Clicking on it will bring up a whole new collection of Groups that you might not have found any other way.

   b. When you select "More/Group Profile" in one of the Groups you have joined, you can find similar Groups.

   c. In this overview of Groups you can click again on "Similar Groups" for each of the Groups presented.

4. **Look in someone's Profile.**

   a. This is a totally different approach. People have a natural tendency to form groups and clubs. LinkedIn shows that information on someone's Profile, which can be very useful information.

   b. Go to someone's Profile that is of interest to you (whether it is a new customer, employer, employee, partner, supplier, investor, expert or a current/former colleague or business contact) and scroll to the bottom of his or her Profile to see which Groups they joined.

   c. Although this is more time-consuming sometimes, it often delivers better results.

☞ **Assignment**: find some Groups you want to join.

If you want to look at a video that shows you the 4 ways of finding Groups, go to the "Video & Tools Library" at www.how-to-really-use-linkedin.com

Tip: If you and your sales team or your recruitment team have found more than 50 groups (the maximum number you may join) of interest in (e.g. 300 groups on engineering, 73 on .NET programmers, 144 on Fast Moving Consumer Goods in Spanish), you might consider dividing these groups among your team. Let's assume you have found 80 groups you think you (or your colleagues) should join and your team consists of 4 people, you can each take 20 different ones and thus cover all 80 groups.

Interactions in Groups

Since you have now found some interesting Groups, you can start to participate.

The best approach is to take it slowly, so you get sense of the communication style within that particular Group. Begin by reading the Group rules (on the top right side).

Then review the current Discussions and see how you can participate. An easy beginning is to click "**Like**" for the Discussions you find interesting.

Even better is to share a tip, experience, or a thought by clicking on "**comment**".

You can also choose to "**reply privately"** to someone if your contribution or comment is not suitable for the whole Group.

If you are not participating, but find the topic very interesting, you can "**follow**" the conversation. Every time a new comment is posted you will be notified via email (this is default when you write a comment).

Unfortunately, you will see some spam messages once in a while. You can "**flag**" that message so the Group owner and managers are notified. Depending on the rules they have set, posts with flags will be automatically removed. They can also remove them manually.

Some Groups have **Subgroups** where you can find more specific Discussions or Discussions relating to an event. These might be more beneficial to join. You can find them by clicking on "More/Subgroups".

After you have observed how people behave in the Group and how they interact, it is your turn to **start posting**. You can ask a question, share an opinion, or give a tip. Be aware that some Groups are moderated. This means that the Group owner first needs to approve your contribution before it is visible to all Group members.

Participation will raise your Know, Like, and Trust factor. Since group participation tends to be time-consuming, choose carefully which Groups you join. Also evaluate your memberships. Evaluate every three months whether a particular Group is still interesting. If not, leave the Group so you free your time to join another Group, or contribute more to the ones you really like.

Your Know, Like, and Trust factor might even increase more by contributing to Groups. Depending on the preferences of other Group members they receive a daily or weekly digest of the actual Group Discussions via email. So even if people don't go to the LinkedIn Group, they may know of you since your name might show up in the daily or weekly digest email.

☞ **Assignment**: post a (meaningful) comment in a Group.

What Else Can You Do with Groups?

As well as Discussions you can do more with Groups. Here is an overview:

1. Look for other Group Members via **Members**. You can browse through all Group Members and search inside the Group for people with the function, knowledge or expertise you need.

2. If you want to promote something, use **Promotions** (if enabled by the Group owner). Don't use the "normal" Discussions to promote something because people might perceive it as spam, the Group manager might delete it and even evict you from the Group. You can also search within promotions and easily retrieve your own promotions and the ones you follow.

3. If you have a job to offer, you can post it in **Jobs** (if enabled by the Group owner). Thus, a more targeted audience might see your job offering.

4. **Search** inside the Group. You can search in all Discussions or only the ones that the Group owner selected as "Manager's Choice". There are also overviews of the Discussions you started, joined, or followed.

5. You can also easily review your past contributions and actions in the Group via "More/**My Activity**".

6. Via "More/**Updates**" you see an overview of the activity of all members: who joined the Group, who started a Discussion, who posted a comment etc.

7. Look for **Subgroups**. Unfortunately, LinkedIn put them behind the "More/Subgroups" menu, so they might not have caught your attention. Especially in large Groups, the Subgroups deliver value by focusing on a specific topic or geographic area.

Group Settings

Most people never look at the Group Settings after they have joined a Group (and actually don't pay any attention to them the moment they join either), but it is good to know the settings and how you can change them.

- **Contact Mail**: you can choose to which email address communication from this Group is sent. If you want all the emails from all your Groups or from one particular Group to arrive at a different email address than your main one (for example to avoid email overload or for a special topic that is not related to your job), you can change that setting.

- **Activity**: send me an email for every new Discussion. If you really want to be on top of what is going on in this Group, you can check that box. For most people this option results in email overload.

- **Digest Email:** you can choose to receive a daily (default) or weekly digest email or no email at all. If you want to follow pretty closely what is going on in the Group, you can leave it as it is (daily). But if you receive too many emails and you are not very involved with a particular Group, change it to weekly or even turn it off. LinkedIn recently started to help with this: if your involvement in a Group is very low, they automatically change daily to weekly digest email (and send you an email to notify you about this change).

- **Announcements**: you can choose to allow (or not) the Group owner to send you an email (maximum one per week). Default = allow.
- **Member messages**: you can choose to allow (or not) the other Group members to send you messages even if they are not your first-degree contacts. Default = allow.

Become a Group Manager

Create your own Group? As a Group owner you have a special status, which raises your visibility. However, do this only if you have enough time to spend on managing a Group. This means inviting people to the Group, accepting Join Requests and—most importantly—keeping the conversation going. You have to post questions and answers. Although this might scare you, there is also good news: you don't have to do this alone. Up to 10 people can be the manager of a Group.

See "Chapter 12: The Heroes of LinkedIn: Group Managers" for many more tips.

Conclusion of this Chapter

In this chapter you have learned the value of LinkedIn Groups and 4 ways to find the right Groups for you.

You also learned how to interact in Groups, what more you can do to share ideas and build relationships in Discussions, and how to change your Group settings.

Chapter 7: 10 Strategies to Find People Using LinkedIn

LinkedIn is an excellent tool to find the right people. However most people don't use LinkedIn in a proactive way. They make a Profile, connect with some people and then wait for things to happen.

They are the ones who complain sometimes that LinkedIn doesn't work. Compare it with a car: if you just step into your car, but don't start the engine and drive to the place you want to be, a car is a useless tool as well. Thus, you have to be proactive, as we will explain in this chapter.

When we think about "proactive types," people come to mind who have short- term goals like sales people, recruiters or job seekers. But many people are also looking for suppliers, partnerships, investors, sponsors, volunteers and expertise.

LinkedIn is considered by many organizations as an external tool: to find people outside the organization. However LinkedIn is also an excellent tool to find internal expertise and is may be even better than internal directories.

The reasons why LinkedIn is a great tool to find internal and external expertise:

- LinkedIn has more elaborate Profiles than most internal directories (which are sometimes also limited to one country). So it is easier to find someone and to see at a glance if this is the person you need. It also tends to be more up-to-date than the internal directories, because people want to let the world know about their projects.

- LinkedIn shows Profiles from people in other large organizations and from freelance experts. Without LinkedIn they would be harder to find.

- LinkedIn shows the connections between people and also the Recommenda-tions they received. This will allow you to make a quick decision on whom to contact. This makes sense for someone working in another company, and also within large organizations where employees do not know each other. In other words, you can use LinkedIn to find internal and external references.

This chapter contains 10 strategies you can use when you are looking for the people who can help you achieve your professional goals or other help. Whether it's about new customers, employees, members, suppliers, partners, investors, sponsors, vol-unteers, experts or a new job, you can apply these strategies to each goal.

But before you use the strategies to find people you have to prepare yourself, and after you have found them you need to take action. By preparing you save time and by taking action you get results.

First Things First: Preparation

Define Your Target Group

To find new customers, employees, or a new job, etc., the first step is setting goals like we did in "Chapter 3: a 5 Step Basic LinkedIn Strategy". Remember the G.A.I.N. exercise© can be downloaded for free from the "Video & Tools Library" at www.how-to-really-use-linkedin.com

These are some parameters to consider:

- What type of industry are they in?
- Which geographic location?
- Which functions, roles, or titles do these people have?
- Which other parameters are important to you? Remember to use different words or phrases for the function or title you are looking for. Also, as well as noting the decision-makers write down the functions of the influencers.

Build Your Network

LinkedIn is a great tool to find the right people. But you need to have a minimum of connections before LinkedIn can work for you.

So start by building the foundation of your network as explained in "Chapter 5: Building Your LinkedIn Network...Fast".

Next, apply the 10 strategies from this chapter to find people and connect with them. You will notice that if you connect with a few people from the same industry in the same geographical area, all the people from that industry and geographical area will be in your second- and third-degree network very fast.

Or in other words: you don't need a network of thousands of people to get results on LinkedIn. One hundred connections might be enough if they are aligned with your goals.

Strategy 1: Search with Name

If you know the name of the person you want to reach, it is pretty easy: just type their name in the search box on top of the page.

However if it's someone with a very common name like Andy Johnson (more than 4.600 hits) you need another approach.

If you use the "Advanced Search" and put "Andy" in the First Name field and "Johnson" in the Last Name field, you get only 1.600 hits.

What's the reason for this big difference?

If you use the search box on top of the page, LinkedIn searches for those words throughout the whole Profile (this is the same as the "Keywords" field). If you use specific fields like First and Last Name, only these fields are searched.

Take care that you have not reversed your first name and last names. Though that seems a strange remark, we encounter that situation on a regular basis.

Strategy 2: Search with Parameters

When you have started from your goals and made them specific, you will have some parameters that can be used in the "Advanced Search" screen (the "Advanced" link can be found on your Home Page next to the search box).

These fields are available to you in "Advanced Search" at the time of writing:

- **Keywords:** here you can type anything you want. LinkedIn then searches all fields (free text and lists).

- **First Name and Last Name**: self-explanatory.

- **Location**: anywhere (in the world) or "located near" followed by your country.

- **Postal code**: you can search in a radius around a specific postal code. This helps to fine-tune the results if that is helpful for your goal.

- **Title**: function. You can choose to receive only people who are currently holding that position, people who once had that position, or both (default). Remark: this search is based on the function, not the Professional Headline (= description under your picture on your Profile, by default this is your function, but we recommend changing it)

- **Company**: You can choose to receive only people who are currently working for this company, people who worked for that company in the past, or both (default).

- **School**: self-explanatory.

- **Industry**: you can search all industries or individual ones.

- **Relationship**: you can search all LinkedIn members or limit your search to people in your first-, second-, third-degree networks or beyond, or to people who belong to the same Groups as you.

- **Language**: you can limit your search to people speaking a specific language. However we don't recommend that option because you might miss a lot of people who haven't used it yet.

When you upgrade your Profile, you will have these extra options:

- **Company Size:** several options, from 1-10 to 10.000+

- **Seniority Level:** several options, at the moment: Manager, Owner, Partner, CXO, VP, Director, Senior, Entry, Students & Interns, and Volunteer.

- **Interested In**: any user (default) or the specific kind of profile this person listed he is interested in to connect with (see your own Profile at the bottom of the page for the options).

- **Fortune 1000**: you can limit your search to the Fortune top 50, top 100, top 250, top 500 and top 1000.

- **Search only other openlink members**: people who upgrade their account can send messages to each other for free when they are not in each other's first-degree network. If you have a basic (free) account you have to buy In-Mails to be able to do that. Selecting this box means that you can limit your search to people to whom you can send a free message (provided they permit that).

You can also sort your search results

Sort by:

- o **Relevance** (default): listed matches are ranked using logistics based on the keywords you have entered, and your network of connections.

- o **Relationship:** your first - and second-degree connections, and groups, are shown first (in that order). Third degree and out-of-network members are always combined. Use this option if you are not looking for someone in particular. Second-degree contacts are easier to reach (via Magic Mail) than third-degree contacts.

- o **Relationship + Recommendations:** matches shown first are based on your level of connection and amount of recommendations. Use this option if you are looking for a supplier or partner. The recommendations can give you a first impression.

- o **Connections**: the people with the most connections appear on top.

- o **Keywords:** displays the best match based solely on your query.

- o **Views:** how the search results are presented: basic (default) or expanded. The difference between the two is that the expanded view shows the amount of connections, the amount of recommendations, as well as current and past functions.

A special kind of search is "**Reference Search**". **Recruiters** can use this (paid) option to find people who have worked with a candidate.

On your Home Page, click on "Advanced" and then on the third tab "Reference Search".

On this page you can enter the name of a company and a time period (between year x and year y). LinkedIn will display everybody who worked for that company during those years.

You can then contact some of the people to find out more about a candidate.

> More tips about searching and finding can be downloaded from the "Video & Tools Library" at www.how-to-really-use-linkedin.com.

Strategy 3: Browse in the Network of Your Network

In the previous strategy we started from our goals and then considered the people who appeared in the search results.

In this strategy, we start from our current network and look in their networks to find the people who can help us achieve our goals.

1. Use the (Advanded) Search to go to the Profile of a first-degree connection whom you know rather well and who has the same function or role of the person you are looking for.

a. People tend to connect with their peers. Chances are high they are connected to people who might help you reach your goals.

b. The Know, Like, and Trust factor is already higher than with other people.

2. Scroll down until you see a box on the right side titled "*Name's* Connections". At the bottom click on "See all Connections".

3. Now you can browse through their networks and find the people who are of interest.

Extra benefits of browsing in someone's network include:

- You might discover some terms or titles you hadn't thought of yourself. For example: if you did a search on "Marketing Manager, Banking Industry, USA" when as a speaker you were looking for new customers, you might discover that people also call themselves "Marketing Director", "VP Marketing" or "Marcom Manager". They won't show up in your "Advanced Search" results from Strategy 2. And you might discover functions like "Event Coordinator" or "Events Manager", titles you might not have thought of yourself.

- You might stumble upon people who might be helpful to reach a different goal from the one on which you are presently focused. For example: when you are a HR Manager and looking for new employees you might come across a HR consultant who specializes in international compensation and benefits programs. Perhaps a perfect profile to help you with another project.

Can you browse everybody's network? No, some people don't allow access to their network. Of course, it is their choice, but we always wonder why: do they expect other people to open their networks to them without reciprocating?

Strategy 4: Look at "Viewers of this Profile also Viewed"

When you find someone who is in line with your parameters, you can't browse their network yet. They first need to be part of your first-degree contacts.

However, interesting information may be available to you. When you scroll down in someone's Profile, at the right side you will notice a box titled "Viewers of this Profile also viewed".

You will see that many of those people work for the same organization or have the same role in another one. So you might find some extra people of interest.

When you click on their Profile you will often notice a mutual contact popping up whom you hadn't thought of, next to people you had decided to ask for help. In other words, these possibilities give you more roads to success.

When you scroll down in this person's Profile you might discover new interesting people via "Viewers of this Profile also viewed" and new mutual connections. And the same applies to these people. The option "Viewers of this Profile also viewed" can be used for every new Profile you encounter (and for all your first-degree connections as well). What an enormous treasure chest!

Strategy 5: Use Groups that Your Target Group has Joined

People link with their peers and also look for ways to meet each other. On LinkedIn, people with the same profiles, backgrounds, and interests gather in Groups.

Starting from your goals, use the 4 ways from "Chapter 6: The Heart of LinkedIn, Discussions" to find the right Groups for you.

If you are in sales, it is very important NOT to sell in Groups. Groups are an excellent place to build your Know, Like and Trust factor and apply the Golden Triangle of Networking (Give, Ask, Thank)—not to post your promotional material. Actually, it may have the opposite effect: if people perceive it as spam they may get a negative feeling about you and your organization. In that case, it would have been better to do nothing!

Strategy 6: Use Groups of People with Access to Your Target Group

From our experience working with large international companies to solo entrepreneurs, we have noticed that not many people understand the power of the second degree.

For example: if they already consider the power of a network, they think only about their own network.

We suggest you reverse the exercise: think of the network of your target group: who are their peers, customers, suppliers, partners, media, government contacts, etc.

After you have listed those, look for LinkedIn Groups where you can meet the people who already have a relationship with the people you want to reach.

If you build a relationship with them, they can act as an intermediary or even your ambassador!

> **Tip:** This can also work for Groups you are not allowed to join. Some Groups require a certain skill, experience, or degree (e.g. civil engineer) in order to join. When someone in your first-degree network qualifies you could ask him/her to join the group for you and act as your ambassador. For example: in some Groups recruiters are not welcome. As a recruiter you can ask a colleague with the required Profile to join the Group and post a job offer.

Strategy 7: Use Companies

Another approach is to find the right people via the organization where they work or the company they own.

There are several ways to use the information in the Company Profiles to find the right people.

Step 1: Find the Right Organization

1. The simplest way is when you already **know the name** of the organization. Just go to "Companies" (top menu) and then type in the name of the organization you are looking for in the search box. For example, look at LinkedIn's Company Page: http://linkd.in/li-book69.

2. If you don't know the name of the organization, but you know some parameters, use the "**Search Companies**" function. This can be found under "Companies" (top menu) and then the second tab page. You immediately get a "result list" of all companies on LinkedIn. On the left side you can refine your search. These are the **parameters** you can use:

   a. **Keywords**: free text

   b. **Location**:

      i. Headquarters only: yes or no (default).

      ii. Locations: insert the name of a location or refine it afterward when you get the results from your search.

   c. **Job Opportunities**: choose whether you want to select only the companies with a job offer on LinkedIn (default), or not.

   d. **Industry:** write the name of an industry or refine it after you get the results from your search.

   e. **Relationship**: all LinkedIn members, only first-degree contacts, only second-degree contacts, only third degree and further. Or you can choose a combination.

   f. **Company size**: you can make a selection from the entire range from self-employed (1-10 employees) to very large organizations (10.000+).

   g. **Number of followers**: you can make a selection from the whole range between a few followers (1-50) to organizations with a lot of them (5.000+).

   h. **Fortune**: you can limit the search results to the Fortune top 50 up to 1000.

Note: if you have a basic (free) account, the Company search provides you with a workaround for the paid options in the "Advanced Search for People". In that "Advanced Search" you can't use Company Size or Fortune 1000 as a parameter unless you upgrade your account.

Tip: If you don't know what the actual name of the company is, you can also try a product or service in the search box. For example, type iPad and you will see that Apple will pop up in the search results. However, since not all companies have their products or services in their Company Page Overview, this tip will not always work.

Step 2: Useful Information from a Company Profile

The interesting part about LinkedIn Company Profiles is that most of the information comes from the Profiles of people who work for or have worked for this Company. The advantage is that a marketing or PR department does not tweak the information. The disadvantage is that not all data is current since it is up to all individuals to keep their personal LinkedIn Profile up-to-date.

> **Note:** *tips for creating an attractive Company Profile can be found in "Chapter 17: How Organizations Can Benefit from LinkedIn (versus Individuals)".*

What useful information can we find in a Company Profile?

1. The first page is the **Overview page**. In addition to some general information this might be useful:

   a. You see immediately the first 5 people you know inside that organization (under tab page "**Your Network**"). This gives instant insight into your connections. You may have forgotten about these people when setting your goals or perhaps someone changed companies without your knowing it.

   b. Tab page "**Your College Alumni**" provides you with people who went to the same school, college, or university (this comes from the "Education" field in both their and your Profile). Having an educational institution in common often creates a strong bond, even before you have met. A fellow alumnus may be more open to your request.

   c. Tab page "**New Hires**" gives you an overview of people who indicated in their Profile that they have started to work for this organization. This could be interesting information if you are looking for a new job or if you provide services regarding hiring, selecting, or training people. At the bottom of this box click on the "See all activity" link. You get an overview of what has happened with all people working for this Company on LinkedIn. You can filter this in many ways: Profile Changes, New Hires, Recent Departures, Promotions & Changes, Status Updates, Job Postings, and Products & Services.

2. **Follow a Company** (on the top right side you can click on the button to "follow" a Company). "Why would we want to do that?" was our first reaction until we clicked on the small arrow next to the "Following" button (= the same button as the "Follow" button once you have clicked on it). Then you see what will happen and you can fine-tune how you receive this information.

   a. **Content: "I want to be notified when":**

      i. **Employees join, leave or are promoted "in my network" or "all employees"**. This is pertinent information. For example, when you are in sales, if you are notified when your contact changes positions you can first congratulate them, of course, but you can also ask to be introduced to their successor. If they change organizations you may want to ask them for the introduction and stay connected to have an opportunity to be a supplier to their next company. Finally, when not having a personal click with the buyer was the only reason you never have done business—and this buyer changes positions—this might be a good opportunity to see if you have a chance with the new buyer.

    ii. **New Job opportunities.** If you are looking for a new job or helping someone to find a new job, this is an excellent way to be alerted. Instead of having to look every day on LinkedIn for new Job posts, you receive an overview for all Companies you are following.

    iii. **Company Profile Updates.** This option is for most people more for information than a direct benefit. However, it could be interesting to see which new products & services a Company adds to their Profile, to be "in the know" or to discover some partnership opportunities.

  b. **Delivery**:

    i. **I want to be notified by Network Updates**.

    ii. **Email digest: weekly or daily.** This will affect all Companies you are following.

    Modify these settings so they match your preferences. If you are looking for a Job you may want to receive this information on a daily basis, but if you are just curious you may want to receive this information only via Network Updates.

3. **Check out insightful statistics about** this Company (on the right side). When you click on this link you will arrive on a new page with information and statistics derived from people's personal LinkedIn Profiles and their activity on LinkedIn. There is quite some information available that might be useful:

  a. You can find statistics about **Job Functions, Years Experience, Educational Degree and University Attended.** The "University Attended" statistics might be useful for recruiters if they do campus recruitment: first you see which universities graduated the most employees (so the potential is present), and secondly, you can find colleagues who studied at the same institution and can help you with personal testimonials and connections. They also might want to join the campus recruitment team.

  b. Under "**People also viewed**" you get a selection of other Company Profiles that were visited by people who also looked at the Company you are viewing right now. Most of the time this will give you the direct "conculleagues" (we prefer that word to "competitors"). If you are in sales, these might be your next prospects or if you are looking for a job, these Companies might be interesting to add to your list.

  c. On the right side of the page you will see **where employees came from before they joined** the Company you are investigating and **where they go to afterward**. This could also be good information when you are a recruiter or when you are looking for a new job.

A potential disadvantage of using Companies to find the right people is that many Companies work in several countries or have several independent business units and don't have a clear strategy how to organize themselves on LinkedIn. For example: when you are looking for a job in France with a big international company headquartered in the USA, you might not find the right people in your own country because you get too many results or they are linked to a different Company Profile. This problem might also arise when you are using LinkedIn to find expertise inside your own organization.

Tips for how to deal with this for your own organization can be found in "Chapter 17: How Organizations Can Benefit from LinkedIn (versus Individuals)".

Strategy 8: Look at Network Updates

Another interesting source of information is the Network Activity or the Network Updates. You see them on your Home Page and you also receive them via email if you haven't disabled that option (tips about how to set the frequency of emails you receive and other settings can be found in "Chapter 13: Keep Control Over LinkedIn: Home Page & Settings").

There are lots of Network Updates you can turn on or off. These ones may be of particular interest:

- *New Connections in your Network*. For example, when you see that your customer is connected to your conculleagues, you might want to contact them to make sure you remain top of mind.

- *Status Updates from your Connections* and *Posts from your Connections*. By commenting or liking a post you keep yourself in front of others.

- *When connections change Profile information*. You can congratulate them for their new project or position. Especially in sales this can be useful. When your contact changes positions you can ask to be introduced to the successor. If contacts change organizations you want to ask for the introduction and stay connected to have an opportunity to be a supplier to their next company. Or, when a connection suddenly moves into a position in which they are able to buy your products or services, you might want to contact them. As a recruiter, you may discover that someone who was not suitable before (for example, because they lived in another country) is now an interesting candidate.

- *Groups your connections have joined or created*. Another way of finding interesting Groups to become member yourself.

Strategy 9: Change Your Profile Settings

When we ask our audiences who has already looked at the function "Who's Viewed Your Profile", most of them affirm that they did. With the next question, "Who wants to know who are those people with a description like "Someone from the Banking Industry in the Göteborg area, Sweden" almost all hands go up. And when asked how they can find this out, most people reply: "You have to pay and upgrade your account".

However, that is not true. You can never see someone's details unless they allow you to see them, whether you have a basic (free) account or an upgraded one.

Let's now reverse the situation: when you allow other people to see who you are when you visit their Profile, it could benefit you.

Our personal experience is that some potential customers call us after we have visited their Profile. They start the conversation, which is much more powerful than doing so yourself.

Does it happen a lot? No, but many small pieces can make a large pie.

This is not always a good strategy for everybody though. Sometimes, you might want to be anonymous. LinkedIn gives you the option to do that. However, if you are in that "mode", you miss seeing who has visited your Profile.

To change the settings that control what people may see, follow these steps:

1. On the top of the page, click on "Your Name/Settings".

2. Log in again (this is a security check).

3. Scroll down and in the middle of the page click on "Select what others see when you have viewed their Profile".

4. Choose "Your Name and Headline".

5. Click on "Save Changes".

In the default mode, you can see some Profile Statistics (when you click on "Who's viewed my Profile" on your Home Page or on your own Profile). What you will see depends on whether you have a free (basic) account or an upgraded one.

These are the different statistics:

Profile Stats - Available to free basic account holders only if you display your name and headline when selecting "What others see when you've viewed their profile". It shows:

- Up to 5 results of who has viewed your Profile.

- Number of visits to your Profile.

- Number of times you have appeared in search results.

Profile Stats Pro is available to all premium account holders. It shows:

- The full list of who has viewed your profile (Note: You won't see additional information about a profile viewer if they've chosen to remain anonymous).

- Trends.

- Total profile visits.

- Keywords used to find your profile.

- Number of times you have appeared in search results.

- Industries of people viewing your profile.

Strategy 10: Create Alerts

We kept the most powerful strategy for the end.

LinkedIn allows you to create alerts so you don't have to go on LinkedIn and search time and time again.

To create these alerts:

1. Go to "Advanced Search" and create a search with your desired parameters (like in strategy 2).

2. Look at the search results. When you have found the right people, go to step 3, otherwise refine your search till you are satisfied with the result.

3. Next to the number of results, click on "Save". When you save the search, you create an alert.

4. Name the "Saved Search".

5. Choose the frequency of your email alert: weekly, monthly or never. We suggest you select "weekly" and then press "save".

LinkedIn is going to run this search for you automatically and email you the results. You only need to click on the link, look at their Profile and find out whom you know in common!

With a basic (free) account you can have up to 3 saved searches. When you upgrade your account you can have more (depending on which subscription model you have, see question "Do I need to upgrade my account" in "Chapter 19: Answers to Hot Discussion Topics and Burning Questions").

If you want to look at the results of the searches you have saved or modify/delete them: you can find them via: "Advanced Search" (on your Home Page), and then tab page 4 "Saved Searches".

☞ **Assignment**: try at least 3 of these 10 strategies.

> **Remark:** when you apply these tips you might get a long list of people. You can store their names in print or In Word® or Notepad®. LinkedIn also offers a paid solution: Profile Organizer. You can save an interesting Profile and add some extra notes, contact information or find references.

4 Strategies to Contact People after You Have Found Them

After applying one or more of the 10 strategies above, you now have a list of people who can help you reach your goal. Some might be the ones who can help you with achieving your goals, others the ones who can give you information.

For example: if you are a job seeker you may have found people who can hire you (recruiters or hiring managers) or people who can give you more background information about the organization or the future job.

There are four options to contact someone:

1. **You know this person yourself.**

   a. Contact them directly.

2. **You don't know this person yourself and they are a 2nd degree contact.**

   a. Call one of your mutual contacts. Yes, on the phone!

   b. Explain your goal and mention that you have discovered that they know the person you want to reach. Ask them HOW they know each other. On LinkedIn you can see that they are connected, but neither how nor how well they know each other. If they don't know the other person well, thank them and call the next mutual contact. It is important for your result that the Know, Like, Trust factor is high!

   c. When your mutual contact agrees to help you, ask them to introduce you to the person you want to reach, and vice versa, in ONE email, what we call the Magic Mail.

   Tip: if you want extra tips and examples of a Magic Mail, download them from the "Video & Tools Library at www.how-to-really-use-linked-in.com.

3. **You don't know the person and they are a third-degree contact.**

   a. Go to that person's Profile.

   b. On the top right side click on "Get introduced through a connection".

   c. Choose the first- degree contact you have the best relationship with.

   d. Write a message to the end recipient why you want to get in touch and a note to your first- degree contact asking to forward the message.

   What happens next is that your first- degree contact receives both messages and then chooses to forward it or not. When they forward it, the person in 2nd degree also can choose to forward it or not. So this process is sequential. What many people don't know is that everybody in this "message chain" can read all previous messages. So you better be professional in your communication!

   For many people this approach doesn't work that well. The first reason is that they write a pushy message that turns off one of the people in the chain. The second reason is that you might have an excellent relationship with your first- degree contact, but they don't know the people in second-degree that well. Most of the time the result is that your message gets stuck somewhere along the way. So it is much better to spend more time looking for second-degree contacts instead of third-degree and to build your network first. That's why we advise building your network before you need it. Start the foundation of your network right now, with the tips of "Chapter 5: Build Your Network … Fast."

4. **You don't know this person and s/he is a fellow Group member.**

   a. You can send a direct message (if they haven't disabled that option). Make sure you have already built your Know, Like, Trust factor adequately in the Group, and with them personally. For example, by responding to their posts or comments.

   b. If your Know, Like, Trust factor is not sufficiently high, you may want to take a different approach from sending a "cold" message. Look for mutual connections and arrange to be introduced via a Magic Mail. If you lack a mutual contact, you may want to expand your network first. Since you both belong to the same Group it shouldn't be too hard to find connections.

Conclusion of this Chapter

By now you have a 5-step basic strategy to grow your network on LinkedIn and you know how to really tap the power of your network. You also have 10 extra strategies to find the right people to achieve your goal, and 4 strategies to contact them. If you have downloaded the document about the Magic Mail, you also have a better insight into how a Magic Mail works and how to request one.

Whether you are looking for new customers, a new job or internship, new employees, suppliers, partnerships, investors, experts or internal/external expertise, you can apply these strategies.

The best results happen after you prepare yourself first and take action once you have found the right people. Two crucial steps that are too often overlooked or minimized!

Chapter 8: Communicate With Your LinkedIn Network: Inbox & Contacts

Although LinkedIn is not always the best medium to have one-on-one contact (we see other people and ourselves still using telephone and email after a first LinkedIn contact), there are some tools LinkedIn offers.

Let's examine how you can use them.

LinkedIn Inbox

This is the place where you receive invitations and messages, and also where you send messages. This may seem contradictory, but that's the way it is set up.

Compose a Message

You can send a message to up to 50 first-degree contacts.

You can select them from your LinkedIn address book that pops up when you click on the LinkedIn icon. These are the filters you can use:

- The first letter of the last name
- Location
- Industry

If you want to use more filters or group your contacts, see the tips below in the subchapter about Contacts.

If you want to send a message to up to 200 people, you can use the "Answers" section of LinkedIn. See "Chapter 10: Personal Branding, Raising Your Visibility and Credibility on LinkedIn".

Warning: When you send a message to many people at once, by default the recipients see all the email addresses. Uncheck that box if they don't know each other.

Inbox

In your Inbox you can find both Invitations and Messages (= every other kind of message than an Invitation like introductions, Job offers, Recommendations, InMails, etc.).

Messages

- Actions
  - Archive
  - Delete
  - Mark Read
  - Mark Unread
- Sort options: newest or oldest first

- Filter options:
  - o All Messages
  - o Unread
  - o Flagged
  - o InMails
  - o Recommendations
  - o Introductions
  - o Profiles
  - o Jobs
  - o Blocked Messages

When you receive lots of messages, use the Archive and Delete function with the Filter options.

Invitations

When you receive an Invitation you can:

1. **Accept**

   If you know this person well enough (remember the Know, Like, Trust, factor) or if you plan to build the relationship, accept the Invitation.

2. **Reply (don't accept yet),** is the small arrow next to the Accept button.

   Use this option to explain you connect only with people you know well. We used to ignore impersonal messages, but were glad to switch to the "reply, don't accept" option. Many people are still learning how to work properly with LinkedIn. In several cases we were glad to have used the "reply" button because we might have missed important customers who contacted us with an impersonal "Hi, I'd like to add you to my network" message.

3. **Ignore**

   Clicking this button will move the invitation to your "Archived" folder without accepting it. The other person won't be notified that you've ignored their invitation, so they may try to connect with you again.

   After you have clicked on the "Ignore" button you can choose "I don't know *name*", "Report as Spam" or do nothing. When you choose "I don't know *name*" this is registered with LinkedIn. These people won't be able to send you another Invitation. If someone invokes too many "I don't know *name*" registrations, their account will be restricted. This means they will be able to send an Invitation only when they know the email address. Be aware that this might happen to you if you invite people who don't know you.

4. **Report as Spam**

   This is registered with LinkedIn. Those who gets too many "Report as Spam" registrations, will have their account restricted. This means that they will be able to send someone an Invitation only if they know their email address.

If you don't do anything with an Invitation, you will get one reminder (week later) from LinkedIn that you haven't taken any action yet.

Sent, Archived, Trash

These folders are self-explanatory.

LinkedIn Contacts

Since the part about adding connections has already been covered in "Chapter 5: How to Build Your Network … Fast" let's focus on "My Connections".

In this part of LinkedIn you can find your first-degree contacts, imported contacts, profile organizer, network statistics, and how to remove connections.

My Connections = First-Degree Contacts

There are three columns on this page:
- Column 1: Filter options

- Column 2: List of your first-degree contacts

- Column 3: Details and actions

Column 1: Filter Options

You can search with any word or use one of the tags.

LinkedIn automatically makes these tags:

- Tags: partners, group members, friends, classmates, colleagues, untagged (LinkedIn uses the relationship that was used when sending the invitation to populate these tags; the category "untagged" is a result from mass invitations)

- Last Name

- Companies

- Locations

- Industries

- Recent Activity

You can create up to 200 tags yourself. So use this option to assemble your own groups or mailing lists. However, remember that you can send a message to only as many as 50 people at the same time.

Column 2: List of your first-degree contacts

By default you find all your contacts in alphabetical order.

If you use a filter, the result is shown in this column.

Column 3: Details and actions

On top of this column, you see the actions that are available for the individual you have selected or for the selection you have made.

For individuals:

- Browse their network (if they allow you)
- Send a message via LinkedIn
- Edit their details
- Send an email
- Edit tags

For a selection of contacts:

- Send message (see below)
- Edit tags

Send a message to a selection of first-degree contacts

LinkedIn offers you an alternative to the Inbox for sending a message. In the Inbox you have only 3 filter options (first letter of last name, location and industry), while here you have more options using the default tags or tags you created.

This is how you do this:

- To choose the recipients you have two options:
  - o You go through the list and select people.
  - o Use one or more of the tag categories on the left side.
- Click "Send Message" (on top of the third column).
- Compose your message and click "Send Message".

Remember you can select up to 50 people only. If your list contains too many people, delete a few so you will have a list of maximum 50 people. Do this by clicking "all" in the second column. Names will appear in the third column where you will be able to delete some out of your selection for this message, (not from the tag or your contact list!).

If you want to watch a small video about how to send a message to a group of people, go to the "Video & Tools Library" at
www.how-to-really-use-linkedin.com.

Imported Contacts

As described in "Chapter 5: How to Build Your Network … Fast" this is the spot where people from your email address book are listed after you have imported them.

You can send a mass invitation, but remember that you can't personalize the message. A potential danger is that people will report this as spam, restricting your options to invite other people.

Profile Organizer

This is a paid feature on LinkedIn.

The Profile Organizer offers following options:

- Save LinkedIn Profiles in folders
- Add contact info
- Add a note
- Find references

This is a useful feature when you want to save LinkedIn Profiles (other than your first-degree contacts) so you can find them easily. You can also add information in addition to what they have provided themselves in their Profile.

In other words: you can use this feature as a simple CMS (Contact Management System).

The advantage over an in-house CMS is that members keep their own Profiles up-to-date. The disadvantage is that someone might not update his or her Profile or even worse, delete it. Then you lose the data. In that case an in-house CMS would have been better.

Many CMS providers (or consulting agencies) are starting to offer integration with LinkedIn, combining the best of both options.

Who might benefit from the Profile Organizer?

- Sales people without access to an integrated CMS to store prospects and current customers.
- Recruiters without access to an integrated CMS, or who don't use one of the Hiring Solutions that LinkedIn offers. They can store candidates.
- Job Seekers.

Network Statistics

On this page you get an overview of:

- The amount of connections of the first, second, and third degree.
- Top locations in your network (locations with the most people from your first three degrees).
- Fastest-growing locations in your network.

- Top industries in your network.
- Fastest-growing industries in your network.

Remove Connections

Sometimes you want to remove some of your contacts. The reasons might be that you are changing jobs or that you are reorienting yourself and don't want to be associated with a certain industry anymore, or some bad experience happened between you.

Only the last reason would be enough for us to remove a connection. In the other cases you never know whom they know or who can help you in your new situation.

If you want to remove someone from your first-degree network, go to "Contacts/My Connections", click "Remove Connections" (upper right side), choose the connections you want to remove and click the button "Remove connections".

The connections will not be notified that they have been removed.

They will be added to your list of "Imported Contacts" in case you want to re-invite them later.

Note: When you remove someone from your first-degree network, they will only notice that you are no longer in their first-degree network when they look at your Profile or when you appear in search results.

Conclusion of this Chapter

LinkedIn offers you tools to invite people and to stay in touch with them.

In the "Inbox" you find Invitations and other messages people have sent you. You can also send messages yourself. You now understand the actions you can take with Invitations and their consequences.

In "Contacts" you have on overview of your first-degree connections and another way to send messages to individuals and to groups. You can also remove people with whom you no longer wish to be connected.

For those in sales, recruiting, or job-hunting, an account upgrade will allow use of the Profile Organizer. More information about Premium accounts can be found in the response to the question, "Do I need to upgrade my account?" in "Chapter 19: Answers to Hot Discussion Topics and Burning Questions".

Chapter 9: Lead Generation Tools & Visibility Boosters: Applications

In the first chapter we talked about the Know, Like, Trust, factor. All three are crucial in building relationships and generating leads, whether it is to attract more customers, more employees, or a new job.

Fortunately, LinkedIn provides a whole range of tools to assist: Applications.

Applications are "plugins" for your personal LinkedIn Profile and can be found under "More/My Applications". Some can also be used on your Home Page.

Overview of Applications

In this part you will find tips about some Applications that are currently (August 2011) available and are applicable to everybody. There are many more (see top menu "More" and then "Get More Applications") and LinkedIn adds new applications on a regular basis. In this chapter you find an overview of the ones that have the most potential to increase visibility and generate leads.

SlideShare

SlideShare is an Application you can use to show PowerPoint presentations and other documents on your LinkedIn Profile.

Use the LinkedIn wizard to help set up a free account on SlideShare.net, upload a document (it doesn't have to be a slide show) and link it with your Profile.

For two reasons:

1. You can share interesting information with your network. This increases your "Know, Like, and Trust factor" as well as your personal branding, visibility, and credibility.

2. Google loves SlideShare. As a consequence, you can achieve a high rank in search results. Jan accidentally discovered this when he found one of our presentations in the second spot on Google! Many companies pay large sums of money to get their website ranked that high and fail. You might do better this way, without spending a cent!

Remarks:

*   It is crucial to share only insights and tips in your SlideShare documents. Conventional marketing material or a sales pitch has no place here.

*   Use different slideshows from your presentations to a live audience. Images and few words make the best impression when performing live. However, since people see only the documents on your Profile, without you explaining them, you might need to rework them before posting on SlideShare. (Tip: with extra effort you can add audio and create a SlideCast.)

*   You can add up to 4 SlideShare documents on your Profile although you can upload many more to SlideShare. Choose wisely the ones to integrate with your LinkedIn Profile.

Google Presentation

Google Presentation is comparable to SlideShare: you can use it to show PowerPoint slides and other documents in your LinkedIn Profile.

Although you might think: I won't need the Google Presentation Application if I already use the SlideShare application (and I can use 4 SlideShare presentations in my Profile but only one Google Presentation), you may want to reconsider.

The use of video is increasing on the Internet. However, on LinkedIn there is no place for a video UNLESS you use Google Presentation in combination with YouTube.

Yes, you can also use SlideShare for video, but when you do, you lose the potential benefit of ranking high in Google. So we recommend using SlideShare for documents and Google Presentation for video.

These are the 10 steps for using Google Presentation to add video to your Profile:

1. Make a SHORT video (2-3 minutes).

2. Upload it to YouTube.

3. Go to Google Docs (you might need to create a new account, such as a Gmail account).

4. Choose "Create New" and then "Presentation".

5. Choose "Insert" and then "Video".

6. Search for the video you just uploaded to YouTube, click on it and press the "Select Video" button.

7. Log in to LinkedIn and choose "Profile/Edit Profile".

8. Scroll down until you see Applications (left side) and Press "Add Application".

9. Choose "Google Presentation".

10. Select the presentation you have just made.

> If you want to watch a small video about adding video to your Profile, go to the "Video & Tools Library" at www.how-to-really-use-linkedin.com.

A word of caution regarding the content: always use videos (or slideshows or documents) to share tips and help people. Explicit sales messages have no place on your Profile. Encourage people to know and like you first by sharing and helping (remember the "Know, Like, Trust Factor"!).

This also applies to job seekers. In your video, share some tips from your expertise. This will show future employers your potential value. Video gives you an extra advantage. It endorses you as proactive and creative since almost nobody uses video in their LinkedIn Profiles.

Tip: We use Camtasia (http://bit.ly/li-book32) (Windows & Mac) or IshowU (www.ishowu.com) (Mac) to create videos.

Box.net

This application allows posting of all kinds of documents.

The difference between Box.net on the one hand ans SlideShare and Google Presentation on the other hand is the different layout. While SlideShare and Google Presentation are more visually attractive (they show the first slide), the Box.net files application offers just an icon or list view. So that may be a disadvantage.

Ease of use is an advantage of Box.net.

Two tips:

- Use a folder with an appealing title for more visibility.

- Make sure you use the list view (not the icon view) so people can read the complete title of your document. This way they will be more inclined to actually open the document and read more.

Box.net offers more features for file sharing on its website: http://box.net.

Tip: other websites for archiving documents and sharing them: **DropBox** (http://bit.ly/li-book31) and **Mozy** (http://bit.ly/li-book42)

WordPress

WordPress is a supplier of free blog software. You can either put your blog on the Wordpress website or on your own server.

If you have a personal or company blog at WordPress, you can link the blog to your LinkedIn Profile.

The advantage is that every time you post an article on your blog it is automatically updated in your LinkedIn Profile. So you need to make the link only once; no further action is needed.

Of course, keep in mind that the blog should be relevant to your professional activity. Thus, not all personal blogs should be linked.

Tip: You can do much with Wordpress. Many companies make their entire website using the Wordpress platform. We also use it for this book's website. If you would like to set up a "Video & Tools Library, " as we have, use the Wishlist plugin (http://bit.ly/li-book40).

Blog Link

If WordPress is not your blog platform, you need to use the Blog Link application. This is a bit trickier to use because it looks at the three websites in your LinkedIn Profile for content. If you want to use the Blog Link Application, put your blog's URL in one of the three websites in your Profile.

Events

In the Events directory (See top menu "More" and then "Events") you can indicate that you are going to attend an event, present or exhibit at an event, or are interested in an event.

You can also make visible on your Profile the events you will to attend (or have attended).

These are the reasons why you would want to do this:

- People can see use the information to meet you there in person. That's always preferable to meeting online. People can see the Events in your Profile or on their Home Page under Updates.

- You can help promote an event (organized by your or someone else). Your connections might discover interesting events they might otherwise miss by reading your Profile and updates on their LinkedIn Home Page.

- Likewise, you can learn about events by looking at your Home Page and people's Profiles to find where you could meet them.

Tip: if you are organizing your own events, take a look at **Eventbrite** (http://bit.ly/li-book25) to assist with registrations.

Amazon Reading List

If you like certain books and want other people to know about them, or if you want to show other people what kind of books you like so they get to know that part of you, use the Amazon Reading list.

Make a link to a book on Amazon.com and the books (maximum 2) appear in your Profile.

Tweets - Twitter

You can link Twitter to your LinkedIn account. However, review your strategy before integrating the two accounts.

This is a post from Jan's blog "The Networking Coach's Opinion" (www.janvermeiren. com).

Pros of Twitter integration:

- When someone looks at your Profile and likes it, they can click immediately on your Twitter ID and start following you. This is a benefit because sometimes it is hard to find someone on Twitter (despite the search engine). Not everybody uses their own name or when they do they don't always use the same photo as on LinkedIn (and then you try to figure out which John Smith he is). Shortcuts make life easier.

- You need to post something only once, instead of posting it on Twitter and then again on LinkedIn. This single step saves time.

Cons of the Twitter integration:

- Some topics posted on Twitter are personal. Members of a professional networking website may have no interest in them (and sometimes it is better that they don't know the content of personal posts). Be aware that everything you post online could be found by your professional contacts. Post prudently.

- Twitter has a different pace from LinkedIn. Some people tweet 20 times a day. LinkedIn goes much slower and people use it differently. This sometimes frustrates younger people who prefer the speed of Facebook and Twitter. LinkedIn is a website for *professional* networking where quality is more important.

To benefit from the advantages, while avoiding the disadvantages, use free services that allow you to post to different websites at the same time (LinkedIn, Twitter, Facebook, MySpace and many others). For every message you post, you can select the websites where you want it to appear, giving you more control and saving time. These are a few tools:

- HootSuite (http://bit.ly/li-book9)

- Tweetdeck (http://bit.ly/li-book10)

- Ping.fm (http://ping.fm)

So use these "meta tools" to save time and control which messages you send out to the world! For more assistance, see "Chapter 21: Tools To Save You Time When Working With LinkedIn".

Note: You could also setup a purely professional Twitter-account, where you send only occasional updates. This way, you can have the best of both worlds.

As well as these tips, the Tweets application offers:

- **Overview**: you get the stream of Twitter messages from the people you follow in the middle of the page. Your list and the people you follow appear on the left side. You can post a Tweet from this page as well.

- **MyTweets**: the stream of your own Tweets.

- **Connections**:

  o An overview from all your first-degree contacts who are also on Twitter. This can be handy to see whom you want to follow (and whom to unfollow).

  o Save as Twitter list: you can make a separate Twitter list of your LinkedIn connections. In our opinion it makes more sense to create your own lists on Twitter depending on your relationship with each Twitter user you are following, or depending on the topic. But on the other hand: this is another way LinkedIn helps with a free tool to keep up-to-date with your network.

- **Settings**:

  o Choose which Tweets to display on your Profile (thus not in MyTweets): all of them or only the ones containing #in or #li. As mentioned before we do not recommend choosing all.

  o Additional Twitter settings (will link to your Settings page):

    » Add more Twitter accounts.

    » Show rich-link display where possible (picture, page title, and short description).

LinkedIn Polls

Polls is a LinkedIn Application that helps answer your research questions using the LinkedIn network and your network of personal connections. You can create a poll with up to 5 multiple-choice answers. Members are limited to 10 open polls at one time. Those who participate in the poll see the (graphed) results, too.

More Applications

There are many more Applications. Maybe Huddle Workspaces, Manymoon Projects, and Teamspaces are of interest if you do lots of project work. If you are a frequent traveler, Tripit might be a favorite application. More creative workers may want to add Behance Portfolio Display. Real Estate agents might like Rofo Real Estate Pro. Explore the Applications to find those that could benefit you.

☞ **Assignment**: go the Application Directory on LinkedIn and install at least one Application.

Crucial Tips for Success with Applications

Being Congruent

As you know by now, it is important to build your Know, Like, and Trust factor via your Profile if you want success on LinkedIn.

But even if you don't want to make much effort nor want to use the Applications as a lead generation tool (see below), it is still important that your Profile is congruent.

Why? If your current network talks about you or refers you to someone, most of the time the third party will end up on your LinkedIn Profile. Your Profile then needs to confirm what they heard about you and preferably take them further (via Applications).

In other words, an attractive Profile with interesting Applications needs to support your offline networking and referral strategy.

The Two Key Elements When Using Applications as a Lead Generation Tool

Many people use Applications as a lead generation tool to attract new customers, employees, sponsors or volunteers but remain unsuccessful. Let's look at the two key elements that most people underuse.

1. They forget to **share good free content**. In the worst cases, they try to sell something right away. Giving away good tips helps to build the Know, Like, Trust factor:

   a. Know: the more they read, the more they get to know you.

   b. Like: the more they get for free, the more they like you.

   c. Trust: when good content reveals your expertise, the trust that you are the expert you claim to be, increases as well.

2. Then the most important part (which most people and organizations forget), is to **lead them to your website** where they can find more free information. In this way you increase the Know, Like, and Trust factor even more.
   On your website ask them to **sign up** to receive more free information from you in the future. Once they are in your database you can send them information on a regular basis (until they terminate).

Remark: a more powerful alternative to emailing, is hosting webinars in which people can see what you offer. Or talk to them using Skype (http://bit.ly/li-book44) or another telephone service.

Resources:

- If you don't have a website yet, look at **Godaddy** (http://x.co/Ycxt). They offer domain names and hosting at a low price, and in-house (not outsourced) tech support.

- To build your database and send automated emails (this is called autoresponders), **Kickstartcart** (http://bit.ly/li-book27), beyond the first outdated page is a very useful tool, or use **Aweber** (http://bit.ly/li-book24). These websites also offer integrated payment solutions.

- If you want to sell only on your website, use **PayPal** (http://bit.ly/li-book28).

- If you need expert help to create documents, slideshows, video or other forms of content, use the market place for freelancers, **Elance** (http://bit.ly/li-book43).

- If you want to host a webinar to share tips like we do in our free LinkedIn Fundamentals webinar and our (paid) LinkedIn Steps to Success webinar series, use a tool like **GoToWebinar** (www.gotowebinar.com) or GoToMeeting (www.GoToMeeting.com).

- To record tips to share on your computer screen (like we do in the "Video & Tools Library"), use **Camtasia** for Windows or Mac (http://bit.ly/li-book32) or **IShowU** for Mac (http://bit.ly/li-book39).

- If you want to self-publish a booklet or even a book or CD to send them (or to sell), look at **CreateSpace** (http://bit.ly/li-book41), a part of Amazon.

To Blog or Not to Blog

This may be your most difficult decision. After reading this book you might be enticed to start one using an application such as WordPress or Blog Link.

The benefits of blogging for your business include:

- It raises your Know, Like, and Trust factor:
  - o Know factor: readers get more insight into you as an individual or as (a representative of) an organization.
  - o Like factor: by sharing tips without wanting anything in return people start to like you more.
  - o Trust factor: if you write using your professional expertise it shows people you are the expert you claim to be.

- You become more referable: it is easier for other people to talk about you and refer people to you: "Jan Vermeiren is an expert in networking, LinkedIn and referrals, but you don't have to believe me, just check out his blog and you will find out for yourself."

- It might help you rank higher in Google and other search engines (Google loves content and prefers blogs over ordinary websites).

- It reinforces other facets of your career. Often, someone hears about us or reads an interview with Jan, then they find the blog, next they sign up for the free networking e-course, check our LinkedIn Profile and then call us to request a presentation or workshop.

A blog is part of a mix that reinforces your brand and supports your business in an indirect way.

When NOT to start blogging:

- If you are not committed to maintaining it.

- If the theme or purpose of the blog is unclear. This is very important as much for readers, as you, the writer. The clearer you can be, the easier it is to become inspired.

- If you want to only take or sell something and not want to give or share first.

- If you want immediate results. Blogging is a long term strategy.

- When you have insufficient time. A following is not built quickly. If you do not have the time to write, instead do a pod cast (= you talk instead of write) or record your tips and have someone transcribe them.

If you cannot overcome these obstacles, it is better not to start blogging. It could backfire on you: when people see that the last blog post is of 2003 or that you "gave up" after posting a few tips they might wonder whether you are still in business.

But if you do it the right way, it will help you to become more referable and you will attract more business.

Conclusion of this Chapter

LinkedIn offers you lead generation tools and visibility boosters through Applications:

- With SlideShare it is easy to share information (presentations, documents, etc.).

- Google Presentation helps you to integrate video into your Profile.

- Box.net facilitates downloading documents you want to share.

- Integrate your personal or company WordPress blog or use the Blog Link application to update your blogs automatically on your Profile.

- Use LinkedIn Events to promote your own events and network upfront.

- Recommend books through the Amazon Reading List application.

- (Carefully) combine the power of Twitter with your LinkedIn Profile.

- Find the right applications for your needs.

In order to get results it is important to be congruent and to keep the two key elements for lead generation in mind: sharing great content and leading people to your website. Use the extra resources we mentioned to get fast results.

Chapter 10: Personal Branding, Raising Your Visibility and Credibility on LinkedIn

Social media helps personal branding: making yourself visible, credible, and referable without much expense.

When you develop your professional brand—whether it is to find new customers, a new job, new employees, partnerships, investors, sponsors, volunteers or anyone else – LinkedIn offers a lot of opportunities.

In general, success is always a result of your Know, Like, Trust factor.

Since we already covered the details of how to do that on LinkedIn in former chapters, here we will give an overview of the important components, with some additional tips.

Raising Visibility and Credibility: the Ingredients

An attractive LinkedIn Profile is essential, but it is NOT enough if you really want results. You also need to take action. So let's divide the components into a passive, active and proactive strategy.

Passive Strategy

	Ingredients	Where to find pointers
1	**Having an attractive LinkedIn Profile**	Chapter 4: How To Craft an Attractive Profile
2	**For everybody: using Applications to build the Know, Like, Trust factor further**	Chapter 9: Lead Generation Tools & Visibility Boosters: Applications
3	**If you are in marketing, sales or recruiting: using Applications as a lead generation tool**	Chapter 9: Lead Generation Tools & Visibility Boosters: Applications
4	**Be a member of Groups that interest you**	Chapter 6: The Heart of LinkedIn: Groups
5	If you run your own company or are responsible for marketing or recruiting: **Create a Company page**, including your products/services	Chapter 17: How Organizations Can Benefit from LinkedIn (versus Individuals)

The benefits of implementing the "ingredients" of this passive strategy are:

o   To be found by other people via LinkedIn.

o   To be found via search engines.

o   To support your active and proactive strategies.

Active Strategy

	Ingredients	Where to find pointers
1	**Post Status Updates and "Like", "Share" or "Comment" on other people's Status Updates**	See below
2	**Share information via the Sharing Bookmarklet**	See below
3	**Ask for Recommendations**	See below
4	**Contribute to Answers**	See below
5	**Contribute to Groups**: start Discussions yourself and comment on other people's Discussions	Chapter 6: The Heart of LinkedIn: Groups
6	**Confirm your attendance via LinkedIn Events** when available	Chapter 11: The Power of Combining Online and Offline Networking: Events
7	**Start your own Group.** Make sure you consider the consequences before choosing this responsibility!	Chapter 12: The Heroes of LinkedIn: Group Managers

The benefits of implementing the "ingredients" of this active strategy are:

o   To increase your visibility to other people, hence your Know factor will increase.

o   To show you care about helping others (by contributing answers as well as asking questions), to increase your Like factor.

o   To show you are a specialist in your field of expertise—hence your Trust factor will increase.

Proactive Strategy

	Ingredients	Where to find pointers
1	**Use the 5 step basic strategy to find people who are of interest**	Chapter 3: How To REALLY Use LinkedIn: a 5 Step Basic Strategy
2	**Use the 10 strategies to find people who can help you reach your goals**	Chapter 7: 10 Strategies to Find People Using LinkedIn

	Ingredients	Where to find pointers
3	**Attend offline events,** whether or not connected with LinkedIn Events and Groups	Chapter 11: The Power of Combining Online and Offline Networking: Events

The benefits of implementing the "ingredients" of this proactive strategy are:

o People love to help each other, but need to know how. The more concise the question we receive the more effectively we can respond. So help other people to help you by preparing your question with care, and then explain how they could help you. Never assume they know how to be of assistance or that they are thinking of you.

o It is crucial to have an attractive LinkedIn Profile to support this proactive strategy. It is your first impression after the contact is made by your mutual contact—make it memorable.

The above passive, active, and proactive strategies apply to everybody. However, there are more elaborate strategies for particular situations:

- If you want **new customers**, read the strategies in "Chapter 14: How to REALLY Use LinkedIn to Find New Customers".

- If you are **looking for a new job**, read the strategies in "Chapter 15: How to REALLY Use LinkedIn to Find A New Job".

- If you need to **recruit new employees**, read the strategies in "Chapter 16: How to REALLY Use LinkedIn to Find New Employees".

Raising Your Visibility with Status Updates

Posting Status Updates once in a while keeps you "on the radar screen" of your first-degree contacts.

Status Updates are about your activities or opinions. This is comparable to Twitter or "What are you doing?" on Facebook or other websites.

These are some parameters of a Status Update:
- You may use up to 599 characters for the text.

- You can also add a link to a web page. LinkedIn then looks for more information about that link and presents you with a picture and/or text. This might make your status update more appealing. You will see a preview, allowing you to make changes before you post.

- You can also select who sees your status update: only your connections (first-degree) or anyone who visits your Profile.

When choosing content, remember that LinkedIn is a professional network. Keep your status updates professional as well (and avoid personal messages).

When you post your status update (besides being visible on your Profile), usually your first-degree contacts will be notified via Network Updates on their Home Page, and via a weekly Network Updates email.

However, this depends on your own "Profile settings" in the "Privacy Settings" part of the "Settings" page. It also depends on whether the people you allow to see these updates have included these updates on their "Home Page" via their "Settings" page.

Tips:

- A good strategy to remain the one your network will think of first, is to check other people's status updates and then choose "like" or make comment.

- If you have connections who share lots of content (perhaps too much… monopolizing?) in your homepage stream, you can easily hide those connections from the overview and keep your stream relevant to your professional interests. Just hover over an update and click 'Hide'. Unfortunately, uninformed people don't use this "Hide" function, but remove those who are updating too much from their network. In other words, if you post too many status updates that are not relevant to your network, they might remove you as a first-degree connection.

☞ **Assignment:** write a Status Update.
(If you don't know what to write, just mention that people can get free LinkedIn tips at www.how-to-really-use-linkedin.com ☺)

Raising Your Visibility with the Sharing Bookmarklet

The Sharing Bookmarklet is a tool to help you share interesting content, found under "Tools" (at the bottom of each page)

After you have installed it in your browser you have these options:

- **Post to Updates**: you share a current web page with a personal note, as a Status Update on LinkedIn.

- **Post to Groups**: post this web page (together with a note) to one or more LinkedIn Groups you have joined.

- **Send to Individuals**: send this web page via a (personalized) LinkedIn message to your first-degree contacts. You can also add the email addresses of other people.

The Sharing Bookmarklet helps you post interesting information in a minimum amount of time.

However, keep in mind that not all Groups apply the same criteria to regulate content in their Discussions. Always make a considered choice when you want to post to a Group.

If you only contribute to Groups and never answer a question, people might perceive you as a spammer. Then the negative Know, Like, Trust factor starts: instead of recommending you they warn people NOT to contact you. And that's to be avoided.

> If you want to watch a small video about the Sharing Bookmarklet, go to the "Video & Tools Library" at www.how-to-really-use-linkedin.com.

Raising Your Credibility with Recommendations

A positive, interesting recommendation always increases your personal branding and your Know, Like, and Trust factor.

However, there are two problems with recommendations on LinkedIn:

1. Most recommendations are:

    a. Too vague instead of focused on specific results you achieved.

    b. Written only by colleagues instead of by a variety of current and former customers, clients, partners, suppliers, managers, and team members.

2. Caution: LinkedIn works to devalue recommendations instead of increasing their value. When you recommend someone, the following message appears on their screen: "Would you like to return to favor by recommending *name*?" The words "return the favor" reduce the credibility of this action because most people reciprocate right away. Someone who really values recommendations will look at both Profiles and notice that they are submitted on the same day. The perception then becomes: "You scratch my back, I'll scratch yours"—gone is the value of the recommendation.

How to Ask for Recommendations

These are the steps we recommend:

1. In conversation (whether face-to-face or on the telephone) ask the other person if they use LinkedIn.

    • If they don't use it or have negative feelings about social media in general including LinkedIn, go no further. You may want to explain the benefits of LinkedIn first. Or you might want to back off if they are extremely negative.

2. Ask if the other person liked working with you. If their answer is positive, go to the next step. If they hesitate, you have to explore their reticence first.

3. Ask them if they will kindly write a recommendation for you on LinkedIn. Again, only if you get a positive answer, go to the next step.

4. IF they say you may send them a request to write a LinkedIn Recommendation, do so.

Impulsive people skip steps 1 to 3. Even worse they may send out an impersonal mass mailing requesting a Recommendation.

The result? Few responses and their first-degree contacts will feel spammed. This damages your reputation instead of helping building the Know, Like, and Trust factor.

What about the content? Unfortunately, people typically write a vague recommendation. You can always ask them to refine it before you make it visible on your LinkedIn Profile. If they want to help you, but don't know what to write, offer to write a **draft** they can use as a basis. The words in this last sentence are very important since you don't want to be perceived as commanding.

If the recommendation still is not satisfactory (or if you receive a recommendation from someone with whom you would rather not be associated), you can hide it. It won't be shown on your LinkedIn Profile.

What about the comment about reciprocating? If you genuinely want to write a recommendation for them as well, wait a couple of weeks to avoid the "you scratch my back, I'll scratch your back" perception.

How to Deal with Requests for Recommendations

Sometimes people will ask you for a Recommendation that will show up on their Profile page.

If you know them well, it's easy to write a specific recommendation. (Remark: you can choose who can see any recommendations you write for others. The options are: everybody, only your first-degree contacts, or nobody.)

But what if you don't know this person well? Unfortunately, there are people who will ask you to do this when you have never experienced their work or had any significant exchange with them.

This is a tip from Bob Burg, author of *Endless Referrals* (http://amzn.to/li-book6) and *The Go Giver* (http://amzn.to/li-book13):

I often discuss how to refuse a request that is either unreasonable or simply one you don't care to accept. The key is to do so in such a way that the other person is not offended and not made to feel ashamed for asking, while at the same time not "leaving the door open" for them to come back with an answer to your "objection."

In this uncomfortable situation you need to say "no" without embarrassing them (which might lead to their blaming and resenting you), and in such a way that they will understand and respect your decision. The following should be agreeable:

> *Hi xxx,*

> *Thank you so much for asking me to write a recommendation for you on LinkedIn. You seem like a great person and I'm sure your work is excellent. Of course, because I haven't experienced your work directly, it would be difficult for me to write a recommendation as though I have. But I truly do appreciate the fact that you thought highly enough of me to ask.*

Thank you for understanding. I have a feeling there are many people who have benefited from your fine work and will be delighted to provide a recommendation based on their actual experience with you.

With best regards,

Bob

☞ **Assignment**: write a Recommendation for someone else.

Raising Your Visibility and Credibility with Answers

A part of LinkedIn we have not mentioned until now is Answers (top menu "More/Answers").

We already explained that the value of Groups lies mainly in the interactions between people. Before the Discussions function was introduced, there was another tool that stimulated interaction: Answers.

The concept is simple: some people ask questions and others answer them.

Again, this allows you to receive help from the network as well as raise your visibility and credibility.

The Benefits of Answers

1. People will notice when you answer questions. The same may apply when you ask a question. "Answers" are open to all LinkedIn users, worldwide. This may provide exposure in countries other than your current location.

2. When responding to a question you can also add the URL of your website. Moderate use of this feature gives your website more visibility and helps to boost your ranking in Google and other search engines.

3. The person who posted the question may select the best answer. The person who provided it is awarded an expert point.

   Once you have gained some expert points you will also be listed in the expert's directory, which raises your Profile even more. The number of points required to be included in that list depends on the category. It is easier to get in the expert list of a category with few questions and few people who answer. But with fewer questions your visibility as an expert will be limited.

Expert points are a bonus, but your intent is to genuinely help other people and share good tips. By doing so you will be perceived as an expert and rewarded in this way for your effort.

Using Answers

Possibilities

- You can ask questions.
- You can answer questions.
- You can search through open and closed questions and their answers. In this way you can find an answer before you post the same or similar question. You can also find questions to which you know the answer.

Ask a question

LinkedIn allows you to ask 10 questions per month.

To help you get answers to your questions, LinkedIn provides a few options:

- You can choose an appropriate **category** for your question so chances are higher you will get a good result.
- You can indicate whether your question is related to a **specific geographic location**.
- You can post your question in every **officially-supported language** via the interface of that language. This might be easier if expressing your question in English is difficult. Of course, you can always ask your question in your own language via the English interface, but chances are higher to get a good response if you use the officially-supported languages interface.
- You can choose NOT to post your question to the "Answers" pages, but **only to (up to 200 of) your first-degree contacts**. This might be a good workaround if you want to send a message and want to reach more people in one attempt than the 50 you can select when you compose a message in your Inbox or via "My Connections".

Don't abuse the "worldwide" option when looking for a job, posting a job offer or promoting your services (you could use the "private" option to send it to only up to 200 contacts, but be aware that they may perceive it as spam!). We have described other places on the platform for those purposes. Both LinkedIn employees and members want to keep "Answers" as succinct as possible. A question that is inappropriate might get "flagged" and removed. There could be consequences for your Profile and connectivity if you keep doing this (although we don't know of an actual case).

Answer Questions

Answering questions may help to raise your visibility, credibility, and expert status.

LinkedIn provides you with the following options:

- "Answer Questions" page:
  - o   Browse through **categories**.
    - »   When you are in a category you can subscribe to its RSS feed. Then you will receive questions in your field of expertise in your RSS reader instead of having to go to LinkedIn to look for new questions.

- o Choose the **language interface** (officially-supported languages).
- o You can also look at **closed questions** and the **list of experts** (= people who have earned expert points by answering questions).
- • "Question" page:
  - o Share these answers by copying/pasting a **permalink** to this question or emailing it.
  - o You can choose to only **reply privately** or to add a private message to your public answer.
  - o You can add up to **3 URL's** to your answer and **suggest one or more experts**. In this case, the expert is not someone who has earned expert points, but someone you consider an expert. Give your network some visibility as well by sharing their web sites and suggesting they are experts. In time, they might even do the same for you.

☞ **Assignment**: go to Answer and answer a Question.

A Few Remarks about Answers

You know now that "Answers" may give you worldwide exposure. However, since you probably are not active professionally in the entire world and focus on a rather limited target group, "Answers" might not be the place to spend your time. Answering questions in your chosen Groups provides faster visibility and more credibility to the appropriate people. However, in Groups you can't earn expert points.

The advantage of Answers is that all the answers are stored and visible for everybody—months after you have answered a question. So this is another way to passively raise your visibility and credibility.

Also be aware of how others react to heavy contributors in "Answers". Some have 100 expert points spread across 7 categories! Our clients say: "These people apparently don't do anything else all day. I don't know if I would hire them or trust they are actually working." Of course that's their perspective and it says more about them than those who help others. From a personal branding perspective it might be wise to focus on fewer categories and a few select Groups than to answer all kinds of questions worldwide.

Note: if you ask a question yourself, whether in Answers or in a Group, people appreciate knowing what you did with the input you got. So take the time to respond.

Conclusion of this Chapter

Your Personal Branding strategy consists of three levels:

- Passive
- Active
- Proactive

As well as the reminder to (re)read the tips from preceding chapters, you also learned how to increase your visibility and credibility via Status Updates, Sharing Bookmarklet, Recommendations and Answers.

Always remember the intent is to increase your Know, Like, Trust factor.

Chapter 11: The Power of Combining Online and Offline Networking: Events

As already mentioned, the REAL power of networking lies in the combination of online and offline networking.

LinkedIn Events and LinkedIn Groups can stimulate networking before, during, and after an event—and vice versa.

In this chapter (and the rest of the book) the word "event" is used as a general term for receptions, conferences, trade fairs, mixers, and similar activities organized in a business environment.

Let's look at it from the point of view of an organizer first, and then from the point of view of a participant.

How to Use LinkedIn for a Successful Event

There are 5 parts:

1. Preparation
2. Facilitation Before the Event
3. Promotion
4. Facilitation During the Event
5. Facilitation After the Event

Step 1: Preparation

When you are organizing an event, the most time is spent in the preparation phase. If you are organizing year-round events, these tasks might be routine but most people organize an event only once in a while.

For a large event you need various suppliers. Some of them you already know, others you still need to find.

Whether you are looking for a venue, speakers, sponsors, partners, hosts, catering, audiovisual equipment, badges, hotel accommodation, flyers, handouts, banners, or anything else—LinkedIn is an extraordinary tool to help you find the right people.

How can you use LinkedIn to help you find suppliers?

Go to "Chapter 7: 10 Strategies to Find People on LinkedIn" and follow the three steps:

1. Preparation: define whom and what you need.
2. Use one or more of the 10 strategies to find the people need. Look at your mutual connections.
3. Ask them their opinion of the potential supplier and if it is positive, request an introduction via a Magic Mail. When you are looking for a supplier a Magic Mail is less necessary than when you are looking for a customer. You still may benefit from it since being introduced by a mutual connection might achieve or increase a discount.

If you need a platform for event registration, take a look at Eventbrite (http://bit.ly/li-book25). Their registration and payment solutions cost little.

Step 2: Facilitation before the Event

Many people don't feel comfortable attending events if they find it intimidating to make contact with strangers. Other people report they no longer go to events because they find them of low value.

You can use LinkedIn to facilitate both types of people and lay the foundation for the promotion of the event in one step.

1. **Create a LinkedIn Event for your event.**

The benefits are:

   a. People can indicate whether they are attending, presenting, exhibiting, or are just interested. Whatever the chosen option, their first-degree network is notified via Network Updates. When people have the LinkedIn Events Application installed, your event might be featured in their profile, too. Imagine several –or many—participants doing this!

   b. The event will get extra visibility in Google and other search engines. Since LinkedIn is a website with a lot of traffic its pages are ranked high in search engines.

2. **Create a Group or Subgroup for your event.**

   a. We prefer a Subgroup rather than a Group. An event is temporary and so is the forum for the event. The best solution is a Group that facilitates online networking all year round with one Subgroup for each event. This Subgroup can be started a few months or weeks before the event and closed a few months after.

   b. Use a Subgroup to facilitate networking up front and during the event.

      i. Start some Discussions yourself. For example:

         1. Car Pooling.

         2. Discussion about the main topic.

         3. More information about the event.

         4. Ask for advance questions from registrants so speakers can use them in their presentations.

    ii. Ask one or more of the speakers to start a Discussion.

        1. One time.

        2. Schedule it before the event. For example: 4 speakers at the event; every week another speaker starts a Discussion.

    iii. Behind the scenes: help connect participants ahead of the event. Maybe you know a good reason why they should connect that's not obvious to them yet. Magic Mails are a perfect tool to this end!

    iv. Read the tips about how to stimulate interaction in "Chapter 12: The Heroes of LinkedIn: Group Managers".

3. **Create a Twitter hashtag for your event**

   This Twitter tip is another form of communication to help people to promote the event and to facilitate networking during it.

4. **Make a Foursquare location for your event**

   Although most venues now have their own FourSquare (http://4sq.com/li-book36) location, also make one for your event to help people find each other much easier.

An extra tip outside LinkedIn: send participants some tips about how to network at the event before they arrive, or host a webinar for this purpose. For example: some organizations hire someone from our team at Networking Coach to speak about LinkedIn at the event itself and host a pre-conference webinar with tips for offline networking.

Step 3: Promotion

To promote your event, use two strategies: a first- degree and a second-degree approach.

First-degree approach

Most people are familiar with these straightforward actions on LinkedIn:

1. Send a message to your first-degree contacts.
2. If you are a Group manager, you can:
   o   Send an announcement to the Group members.
   o   Post a Discussion about the event.
3. Post Status Updates.
4. If you want to pay: use LinkedIn Ads (or work together with LinkedIn on a special project, see http://marketing.linkedin.com).

Second-degree approach

The second-degree approach doesn't focus on your target group, but on the people and organizations **having access** to the target group.

These may be basic tips but we have noticed that not many people use them.

1. **Get more access to <u>individual</u> potential participants**

   Go to "Chapter 7: 10 Strategies to Find People on LinkedIn" and follow the three steps:

   1. Prepare yourself: **who is your target audience**.

   2. Use one or more of the 10 strategies to find the people you want. Check mutual connections.

   3. Ask them for an introduction via a Magic Mail.

2. **Get more access to <u>groups</u> of potential participants**

   1. Go to "Chapter 7: 10 Strategies to Find People on LinkedIn" and follow the three steps:

      a. Prepare yourself: find who has **access to** your target audience. Think of other suppliers to the same target group (e.g., marketing managers), the various media related to the target audience (journalists), professional organizations (board members), trade organizations (chairman), etc.

      b. Use one or more of the 10 strategies to find the right people. Explore your mutual connections.

      c. Request an introduction via a Magic Mail.

   2. **Tap the power of your direct contacts**

      a. Ask your first-degree contacts to send a message to their connections.

      b. Ask your first-degree contacts to post a status update.

   3. **Tap the power of the participants who have already registered**

      a. Ask participants to confirm their attendance via the LinkedIn Event you have set up. Their first-degree contacts will be notified via Network Updates.

      b. Ask participants to join the (Sub) Group you created for this event. Their first-degree contacts will also be notified via Network Updates.

      c. Ask participants to send a message to their connections.

      d. Ask participants to post a status update or tweet about the event, using the hashtag you chose for the event.

      e. Note: few people are accustomed to helping you in this way; you need to encourage them. For example, request their help in the confirmation message about the event.

4. **Look for LinkedIn Groups with the same target audience** and ask to work together. Think how you can make it worthwhile for them as well. For example, free tickets to the event. You can ask Group managers of another Group to:

    a. Send an announcement to their Group members.

    b. Post Status Updates.

    c. Attend the event themselves.

    d. Post a Discussion in their Group about it. Of course you can do this yourself if you are a Group member. However, some Group managers want to be consulted. It is also preferable that Group managers or any third party rather than you promote an event. You want the post to be perceived as a notification rather than a sales pitch.

While strategies to get access to individual participants are more time consuming than strategies to get access to groups, they may be more effective. You make direct contact with potential participants, while the other strategies give your event visibility. When you run smaller events for a specific target audience the individual approach might bring more participants.

Step 4: Facilitation during the Event

We want to share a tip about the Twitter hashtag.

At the beginning of the event ask everybody who has a Twitter and LinkedIn account to tweet their LinkedIn name followed by the hashtag. The other participants can then find them to make contact during a break.

Of course you can't do this with a conference of 2000 people, but for smaller events this tip might really help participants find interesting people. As a result they will value your event more—and come again next time.

Step 5: Facilitation after the Event

The LinkedIn Subgroup you have set up for the event offers extra ways for participants to stay in touch.

Since most people don't expect this you need to direct them to the Subgroup and explain what they can find there. The best way to do that is in a follow-up email after the event.

Some examples of what you can do in the Group:
- Post some extra Discussions about topics raised or comments made during the event.

- Ask the guest speakers to start a new Discussion, to continue a Discussion they started before the event, or to comment on another relevant Discussion.

- Post links to photos of the event (unfortunately you can't share them in Groups yet).

- Post links to slides or other material (you can't share any other documents in Groups yet, but if you only have a few documents, you could post them in your LinkedIn Profile and direct people there. In this way you will get some extra exposure as well).

- Announce a post-event webinar with extra tips for using the ideas shared.

How to Use LinkedIn to Prepare Yourself for an Event as a Participant

If you are attending an event, LinkedIn should be a fantastic resource to prepare yourself to get the most out of the event.

Let's look at what you can do:

1. Before the event
2. During the event
3. After the event

Step 1: Before the Event

Many people feel uncomfortable at events because they don't know anybody. Others report that the event was a waste of time because they didn't meet any interesting people.

Let's look at how LinkedIn might help with both issues.

1. **Determine on LinkedIn if a LinkedIn Event has been created.**

    - If you can't find a LinkedIn Event, notify the organizer and ask them to make one.

    - If there is a LinkedIn Event:

        o Indicate you will be attending. This will help other people to contact you before the event.

        o Make sure that you have enabled the Event application on your LinkedIn Profile. This will show other people that you are attending the event. They may contact you.

        o Look at the LinkedIn Profiles of the other participants. You can make contact with some and arrange to meet each other before or during the event. Or if you are from the same location, you might suggest sharing transport to the event.

    Whether or not you make contact before the event, just looking at other people's Profiles gives you a feeling of being acquainted. This makes it easier to approach them at the event. It works the other way around as well, so make sure you have created an attractive Profile (including an up-to-date photo)!

> **Tip:** create a list of people you want to meet at an event and contact them. You may prefer to meet before, during or right after the event (a meal together?). More advice can be found on the CD *"Let's Connect at an Event"* that contains 30 tips to get the most out of any event (also available in MP3 format) via www.networking-coach.com.

2. **Look on LinkedIn for a LinkedIn Group or Subgroup for the event.**

   - If you can't find a Group or Subgroup, ask the organizer to make one.
   - If there is a (Sub) Group:
     - Look at the member list of the LinkedIn Subgroup. You can make contact to arrange a meeting at the venue.
     - Contribute to existing Discussions. This makes you visible to others. Your Know and Like factor will increase. Some people may also look for you at the event to talk face-to-face about your posts.
     - If you are interested in car pooling (whether you are wanting or offering a ride), look for a Discussion around car-pooling. If there is none, start one yourself.
     - Start a Discussion yourself about:
       - » One of the topics.
       - » A question you have.
       - » A statement.

3. **Let other people know about the event**

   - Use these options that LinkedIn Events provide you with:
     - "Recommend" the event. It will be shown in the Network Updates on the Home Page of your connections.
     - "Share" the event. This option allows you to choose which contacts you want to send the information about the event.
   - Post a Status Update about the event. Use the website and Twitter hashtag for the event.
   - Tweet about the event. Use the event's website and Twitter hashtag.

☞ **Assignments**:

1) Go to LinkedIn Events, look for an Event you are interested in and confirm your attendance/interest.
2) Join the (Sub)Group of the Event.
3) "Recommend" and "Share" the Event.
4) Send a Status Update about the Event.

If you want to watch a video about using LinkedIn to prepare yourself for an event, go to the "Video & Tools Library" at www.how-to-really-use-linkedin.com.

Step 2: During the Event

Since you have prepared yourself it should be more comfortable to make contact with the people who interest you, and the contact should be more valuable.

You can also tweet about the event with its hashtag included so other people know you are present. This also helps to make contact during breaks.

If you use FourSquare (http://4sq.com/li-book36), mention your arrival. This will allow other participants to find you. More background information on Foursquare and other tools can be found in "Chapter 21: Tools To Save You Time When Working With LinkedIn".

Step 3: After the Event

During an event we are limited by time to speak with only a few participants. Of course, there were many other interesting people in the room. Perhaps they will connect when you continue the conversation online, in the LinkedIn (Sub)Group for the event.

Benefits of returning to the LinkedIn (Sub) Group after the event:

- To find participants you haven't met face-to-face.

- To continue Discussions started before the event.

- To start a new Discussion about a topic, idea or statement that came up during the event.

- To post questions from people you have met so other people might become involved.

- To share your experiences of the event.

- To further build your Know, Like, Trust factor with the other members.

Conclusion of this Chapter

The real power of networking is in the combination of online and offline networking.

LinkedIn helps both organizers and participants to get the most out of their events.

Event organizers got tips for these 5 stages:

1. Preparation
2. Facilitation before the event
3. Promotion
4. Facilitation during the event
5. Facilitation after the event

Participants received tips to get more out of events:

1. Before the event
2. During the event
3. After the event

Chapter 12: The Heroes of LinkedIn: Group Managers

Groups are the heart of LinkedIn—their owners and managers are the heroes. They spend time and effort without being paid (at least not by LinkedIn) to build communities in which people can exchange mutual help.

Maybe you are a manager yourself of a thriving Group. Then you probably know most of this chapter. However, if you are a Group Manager with a slow or dormant Group, or if you aspire to start a Group, read the information carefully.

Benefits of Being a Group Manager

Why would someone want to become a Group manager since it involves time and commitment with no immediate return?

These are a few reasons:

- Passionate about sharing ideas.
- Passionate about helping people.
- Desire for increased visibility.
- Contacts with people they otherwise would never have met.
- Contacts with people they otherwise would never have accessed.

Pitfalls

One of the reasons why LinkedIn Groups (or other online communities) sometimes don't succeed is that the last 3 benefits are seen as the goal and not as a consequence.

For example:

- Companies start Groups around their organization or their brands to have better access to current and potential customers. They don't think about what they can share or how they can help their customers, only of ways to have easier access to them.
- Many companies don't give employees the time to think about a strategy for their Group and to manage communities because this doesn't pay off in the short term.

Solutions:

- Create Groups around a topic or a theme—not a brand.
- Think of ways members of this Group can be helped—consider their needs and interests.
- Give the Group managers enough time to be committed to success.

These solutions involve time and creative ways for the long term. As a consequence only few companies succeed in having interactive Groups. The Groups with Group managers who dedicate their spare time and who are focused on helping others tend to be the successful ones.

Challenges of a Group Manager

Let's assume you are still interested in becoming a Group Manager. What will be your main concerns?

1. There are too few members.

2. There is not enough interaction between the members.

3. Some members are active, but not in the way you want: for example, self-promoters or spammers.

Most people, including Group Managers, have never heard of the 1-9-90 rule of online communities (whether on Facebook, LinkedIn or any other network). Understanding this rule is crucial for success with LinkedIn Groups.

This is the 1-9-90 rule:

- **1%** of the members of a Group are very **proactive**: they post questions, share information, and start discussions.

- **9%** of the members of a Group are **reactive:** they answer questions and comment on discussion topics.

- **90%** of the members of a Group are **passive**: they only look or don't even visit the Group.

This is very important to know as a Group Manager. It means you need a critical mass for an active Group; you also need to be more proactive yourself, especially in the beginning.

Though this might be discouraging, the 1-9-90 rule can also have the opposite effect. It's not because there are not many responses to a Discussion that only a few people have seen it. From a contributor's point of view the first results might be disappointing, but more people might have seen it than you would think.

How to Get More Members for Your LinkedIn Group

What Do You Want for Your LinkedIn Group?

Before you start inviting people to your LinkedIn Group review your intentions for this Group:

- What is the goal?
- Who belongs in the target audience?
- What type of Group do you want: open, member-only or private (see "Chapter 6: The Heart of LinkedIn: Groups" for an explanation of those types)?

For example: you could set up a Group for HR Managers in Italy to stimulate the exchange of ideas. You could make it a member-only Group so the content is not shared on the web, but everybody is allowed to join the Group. You can also create Subgroups around specific topics like diversity, compensation, benefits, and recruiting. Another Subgroup could be a closed one for members of the trade organization of HR Managers in Italy. In this Subgroup they could discuss topics that are more sensitive or specific to the trade organization.

Setting up a Group like this might ensure enough contributions and an influx of potential new members for the trade organization while keeping sensitive information inside a smaller Subgroup.

Caution: if you don't pay enough attention to the purpose of the Group and the target audience, subsequent steps will be harder and more time-consuming!

Grow Your LinkedIn Group's Membership

If your LinkedIn Group is associated with a trade organization, an alumni program or another kind of professional organization, the logical first step is to invite all members or alumni via an email. If you have a private Group, but don't want to approve each person on your list manually, you can pre-approve them all (via the "Manage" tab in your Group).

Whether starting a group, or wanting to encourage new members, use these tips to attract more people to your LinkedIn Group:

1. **Build your network** using the tips from "Chapter 5: How to Build Your LinkedIn Network … Fast". This provides you with the foundation of people to invite to your Group, as well as people with connections to potential members.

2. **Invite the people from your own first-degree network** to join the Group.

3. Use the following **strategies to find potential members** from "Chapter 7: 10 Strategies to Find People Using LinkedIn":

   a. Search with parameters: define the characteristics of your target audience.

   b. Browse in the networks of your connections to look for people who have the profile of a potential member. Browse the network of current Group members first.

c. Look at "Viewers of this Profile also viewed": many times you will find peers.

d. Use Companies: if you focus on a specific industry in a specific country, this should provide you with some names.

e. Create alerts: once you have defined your target audience you can save your searches and be notified of new potential members.

4. **Ask your mutual connection for a Magic Mail** or to **point out the Group** to him or her. Asking for the Magic Mail and following-up is much more time-consuming, but if you focus on a smaller group of people with a well-defined profile—this approach could be of great benefit.

5. **Use the "Share Group" link** (right side in the Group Home page menu):

a. Share on LinkedIn: in one action you can post to a selection of sources including

    i. Status Updates

    ii. Discussions in other Groups

    iii. Messages to your LinkedIn connections or to people whose email address you have

    iv. Be careful when you use this approach: not all Group Managers of other Groups will be happy that you promote your Group in theirs. Other people might perceive your message as spam. Announcing a **free** event or webinar would work much better than a plain invitation to join the Group.

b. Invite others (use "Send Invitations" inside the "Manage" part of Groups):

    i. You can invite your connections to join the Group or people whose email address you have (you can even upload a list).

    ii. You can allow other members to use this option as well or disable it depending on what you want with the Group. If you want to keep the Group private, it is better to disable it.

6. **Create a Welcome message with an invitation to invite other people**. As a Group Manager you can create "Templates" (in the "Manage" section of a Group). One of these templates is a welcome message. You could invite new members to invite their network as well. However, until they have any experience with your Group they may be hesitant to do this.

Once you complete these actions, you will see a snowball effect. People are notified via the Network Updates on their Home Page, and via email, which Groups their connections have joined. This alert may arouse their interest.

The more members your Group has the higher it will rank in the search results of the Groups directory. That should attract extra members as well.

Of course, you need to keep repeating the above steps to achieve a continuous inflow of new members over time.

How to Stimulate Interaction between Group Members

Having members in your Group is one thing, having lots of activity is completely different. Many Groups start very enthusiastically, but die a silent death after a few months.

These tips stimulate interaction:

1. **Post interesting articles**. We advise making a list of topics while you are creating the theme and target audience of the Group. If you can't list at least 30 good topics, review your target group definition. You don't have to write these articles yourself. You can ask other people to do that or refer members to some interesting websites and blogs. The most important factor is that the content should interest the members.

2. **Post your questions in the Discussions**. In addition to your 30 topics for articles, you might want to make a list of questions that might interest or stimulate participation of the members. Also add relevant news that is important for the members and ask them to comment on it.

3. **Answer questions in the Discussions**.

4. Post a **preview of the next event** or a **review of a past event**. Encourage members who attended the event to add their opinion or share the ideas they found enlightening. Members who couldn't attend might also want to share their opinion via this channel.

5. Ask **an expert from the Group, or external to the Group,** to write an article and then post it to the Group. This should be interesting if you have an external guest speaker at your next event, perhaps a foreigner. Access to such a speaker is typically limited. However, when the speaker starts a Discussion and responds to comments, members may feel special because they now enjoy access and interaction.

6. **Ask members who might be an expert to respond to a question**. They may have not read the question in the Group.

7. If you want to stimulate (immediate) interaction, **send messages to a few people asking them to join the discussion**. Many people have set their notifications for "weekly digest" and are missing out on a timely topic. However, do this only when the discussion topic is really interesting.

8. **Post in the Discussions the name of the expert** who might know the solution, especially if this person is a Group member. Public praise is always appreciated.

9. **Avoid clutter in the Discussions.** When members post messages that are outside your established rules, you can explain that the Discussions are not the place for such messages. Keep in mind that most people who post "inappropriate" messages often need help to interact in forums. Removing undesirable messages and replacing them with pertinent ones will also help keep the other members happy.

10. **Help connect members**. When you meet someone online or offline who might be interesting to another member, connect the two via a Magic Mail.

This action alone will create a happy community of members who will keep extending their membership year after year.

11. Extra action for outside the Group: **suggest your members as experts in the "Answers" section** of LinkedIn.

12. **Send a periodic announcement.** As a LinkedIn Group manager you can send an email to all Group members (only 1 per week). Since many members don't visit the Group, receiving an extra email might rekindle their interest. However, avoid being perceived as a spammer since they probably already receive the daily or weekly digest. Make the content worthwhile.

13. **Set up News Feeds**. As a Group manager you can set up feeds from interesting blogs and websites with RSS functionality. Once set up, they run automatically. You can do this via the "Manage" tab in your Group.

14. **Feature an interesting Discussion**. A Group Manager can select a Discussion as the Manager's Choice. The title of the chosen Discussion will be shown on the top right side of the Home Page of a Group.

15. **If possible: organize events**. The full power of networking can be found in the combination of online and offline networking. If you have the time and the resources (and your Group is located around a specific geographic area), consider organizing a local event so members can meet each other. (For more tips about events: "Chapter 11: The Power of Combining Online and Offline Networking: Events").

16. **Integrate your LinkedIn Group in your own website.** If you are responsible for a professional organization or for an event, look at the Group API. This software code allows you to integrate some LinkedIn Group functionality with your website. It doesn't really stimulate conversation, but it makes the Discussions visible at more places and increases the chances that someone will contribute.

17. **Involve more people in a "leadership function".** As a Group owner you can add up to 10 Group managers. When people have an official role, they feel more involved and will contribute more. You can divide all the previous tips over 11 people. This decreases the workload and increases your leverage. Ask them to stimulate interaction, and to invite new members.

☞ **Assignment**: Apply one of the tips to stimulate interaction.

How to Deal with Group Spammers and Other Unwanted Actions

LinkedIn has received many requests from Group owners and managers for tools to support them in keeping their Groups clean from spammers. As a result LinkedIn now provides tools to do this under the "Manage" tab in your Group.

Group Rules

The Discussions sections in some Groups get cluttered with messages, which are not relevant or are shameless sales pitches. Defining rules for all members helps prevent this behavior or justifies corrective action when it happens.

The Group Rules link can be found on the top right side of each Group page. However, don't expect your Group members to read them!

Why is it important then to set Group rules?

You need an objective frame of reference when you remove someone's Discussion or move it to Promotions or Jobs. Then they understand that there is no personal attack—these rules apply to everybody.

Group Settings

In Group Settings you can balance more allowed actions by members (and more potential spam) with less potential spam (but fewer actions).

Options:

- **Enable/Disable Discussions and News Features.** When you disable this feature, you won't get any spam, but also no interactions.
  - o Enable/Disable Promotions tab.
    - » Allow/Disallow only moderators and managers to move discussions to the Promotions area.
  - o Enable/Disable Jobs tab.
    - » Allow/Disallow only moderators and managers to move discussions to the Jobs area.
  - o Automatically remove content flagged by group members. You can set the number of flags a Discussion needs to receive before it is removed.

- **Display the Subgroups tab (or not).**

- **Permissions**: choose one of these options. Members of this Group

  o Are free to post (discussions, promotions, jobs and comments).

  o Are free to post promotions, jobs, comments, and submit everything else (for approval).

  o Are free to post jobs, comments only, and submit everything else.

  o Are free to post comments only and submit everything else.

  o Submit everything for approval.

- **Restrictions:**

  o Require/Not require moderation for new Groups members.

    » Number of days that a person remains "new" to the group (your choice).

  o Require/Not require moderation for new people on LinkedIn.

    » Number of days that a person remains "new" to LinkedIn (your choice).

  o Require/Not require moderation for people with few or no connections. Since people with zero connections are possible fake Profiles created for SPAMMING, you may want to require moderation for them.

- **Membership**: choose between

  o Auto-Join: Any member of LinkedIn may join this group without approval from a manager.

    » Remark: Users with few or no connections will ALWAYS require approval from a manager to join the group.

    » Display (or not) this group in the Groups Directory.

    » Allow/Disallow members to display the logo on their profiles.

    » Allow/Disallow members to invite others to join this group.

  o Request to Join: Users must request to join the group and be approved by a manager.

As you can see there are many ways you can control the settings of your Group. Use these options to make the Group function in the best way for its members.

Which Actions to Take

Once you have set up the Group Rules and Group Settings, there are several actions you need to take, depending on how strict the settings are.

The stricter the settings the more you will need to use the Submission Queue and the Moderation Queue.

In the Submission Queue you have the following options:

- Discussions: Approve, Move to Promotions, Move to Jobs, Delete
- Promotions: Approve, Move to Jobs, Delete
- Jobs: Approve, Move to Promotions, Delete

In the Moderation Queue you need to decide whether you want to move flagged Discussions to Promotions or Jobs or delete them.

What can you do with someone who keeps spamming?

1. Look them up via "Participants" and then search for their name in the "Members" tab.
2. Decide which action to take:
   a. **"Remove"** takes the member out of the group, but does not delete the member's past contributions. They can request to join the group again.
   b. **"Block"** takes the member out of the group and places them on the Blocked tab, which prevents them from requesting to join again. It does not delete the member's past contributions.
   c. **"Block & Delete"** takes the member out of the group and places them on the Blocked tab, which prevents them from requesting to join again. It also deletes all past contributions.
   d. Or you can be mild and change their permission to "**Requires Moderation**".

If you click Unblock & Remove from the Blocked tab, it takes the member out of the group without deleting the member's past contributions and they can request to join the group again.

Conclusion of this Chapter

In this chapter you learned the benefits and challenges of being a Group Manager.

You also learned that the 1-9-90 rule is crucial for success with LinkedIn Groups as is knowing what you want with your Group and deciding who belongs to the target audience.

Finally, you received tips about the three challenges to a Group Manager:

1. How to get more members for your LinkedIn Group.
2. How to stimulate interaction among Group members.
3. How to deal with Group spammers and other unwanted actions.

Chapter 13: Keep Control: Home Page & Settings

Some people complain that they get too many emails from LinkedIn (most of the time they mean they get daily digests of all the Groups they joined), that they get too much information on their Home Page, or that too many Invitations arrive from people they don't know.

Even if you are content with how LinkedIn works for you right now, read the part about "Settings" to become aware of the possibilities. At the end of the chapter there is a list with the most important settings to consider.

Home Page

You can customize your Home Page so you will only see the information that interests you.

Left column:

- Status Update Box: not customizable.

- LinkedIn Today: you can delete this box. Click on the delete cross that appears on the right side when you hover over it.

- Updates: you can filter the results via the options in this menu or via your "Settings" (see next subchapter). You can also search the updates; a useful feature is that you can use search criteria that you have saved (this belongs to the "Signal" part of LinkedIn, see "Chapter 18: How LinkedIn Provides Us with More Insights: News & Labs").

- Just joined LinkedIn: not customizable.

Right column:

- People You May Know, Ads, Who's Viewed your Profile, Your LinkedIn Network, Jobs You May Be Interested In and Groups You May Like: not customizable.

- Applications: drag them to change their order or you can delete them. If you delete them from your Home Page, they still will appear in your Profile. If you want to remove an Application completely, do so via "More/My Applications" (top menu).

Settings

LinkedIn offers a whole range of settings to refine your experience (click on your name on top of the page and then select "Settings"). The disadvantage is that there are so many different options that many people don't always understand what they do and what the consequences of changing those settings are. So let's take a look at them.

Let's call the top of the page the overview.

Note: before actually going to the Settings page, you have to log in again. This is a security measure to avoid others changing your settings while you are away (e.g., gone to a meeting) or without your knowing.

Overview

Primary Email

Click on "Change" to:

- Change your primary email address
- Add all your other email addresses. It is recommended that you do this in order to:
    - o Avoid creating multiple LinkedIn accounts without knowing.
    - o Always being able to login to LinkedIn, even if you changed jobs or forgot your password or if your primary email address is temporarily or permanently unavailable.

Password

To change your password, you need your old one!

Account Type

Your current account type is listed here.

You can explore premium (paid) features, compare account types, and upgrade your account.

The account types for Job Seekers & Recruiters can NOT be found here. You need to go via "Jobs/Job Seeker Premium" or "Jobs/Hiring Solutions".

InMails (paid option)

InMails are messages you can send to anyone on LinkedIn.

They come with a guaranteed response: InMail credits are returned if you don't get a reply within 7 days.

There is also InMail Feedback: when someone sends you an InMail you see "New" or 0 to 5 stars next to their name. This is a rating system.

- New: The sender has received InMail Feedback less than 5 times.
- If the sender's last 10 InMails received:
  - At least 9 positive responses: 5 stars
  - At least 8 positive responses: 4 stars
  - At least 7 positive responses: 3 stars
  - At least 6 positive responses: 2 stars
  - At least 5 positive responses: 1 star
  - Less than 5 positive responses: 0 stars

Introductions

You can see how many Introductions you have available (5 with a free account, more if you upgrade) and how many are outstanding. "Outstanding" means that you have sent a request to get introduced to someone, but that it hasn't reached the final recipient yet or this recipient hasn't taken any action (yet).

OpenLink (Paid option)

If you have an upgraded account you can join the OpenLink network. This means that non-first-degree contacts who have upgraded their account can send you a message without having to use a (paid) InMail.

Premium Badge (Paid option)

With an upgraded account, you can show this badge on your Profile. It might give the impression that you take LinkedIn more seriously because you pay for the extra feature and thus may be more professional. However, perception depends on the individual; follow your intuition whether or not you should display this the badge.

Profile Settings

LinkedIn offers different settings regarding your Profile.

Turn on/off your activity broadcasts

You can enable (default) or disable notifications to people when you change your profile, make recommendations, or follow companies.

When would you want to turn this off?

- When you are making lots of changes to your Profile in one day (every time you save a change, this appears in your first-degree contacts' Network Updates). Remember to turn it back on later so people are notified when you gradually add more applications or change positions or companies.
- When you are looking for a new job and don't want your current employer to see that you're updating your profile. Of course they still will see those changes when they look at your Profile, but at least they are not notified.

Select who can see your activity feed

Your activity feed displays actions you've performed on LinkedIn. This is what people see in their Network Updates on their Home Page and weekly emails.

Your options are:

- Everyone
- Your network (first three degrees)
- Your connections (first-degree contacts)
- Only you

Select what others see after you've viewed their profile

Your options are:

- Your name and headline.
- Anonymous profile characteristics such as industry and title.
- Total anonymity.

Note: Selecting option 2 or 3 will disable Profile Statistics.

Select option 2 or 3 when you don't want people to know who you are. Sometimes people looking for new customers, new employees, or a new job do this. However, if they notice that you have visited their Profile and are able to see who you are, they might want to start the conversation with you. And that's more comfortable than your having to approach them.

Select who can see your connections

Select who can see your connections: your first-degree connections or only you.

People will always be able to see shared connections and you will still appear as a mutual contact in search results.

Sometimes, people are not willing to show their network. We always ask: "What do you expect from the other people on LinkedIn? Do you expect them to open their network for you, but you don't want to reciprocate?" If you don't allow your network to see your connections, but also don't expect them to share their connections with yours, that is fair.

Some people don't want others to browse through their connections because they don't want their competitors to see their customers. If you fear that someone might "steal" your customers because they see connections on LinkedIn, you need to strengthen your relationship with your customers. Contented customers don't switch, even neutral ones do not switch necessarily, because change brings uncertainty. In most cases, people prefer to remain with the same provider, especially when they already obtain a quality product/service for a reasonable price, and enjoy a good relationship.

Change your profile photo & visibility

In addition to users you contact, you need to choose to whom your profile photo is visible:

- My Connections
- My Network
- Everyone (default)

For us there is no reason to hide our photo. On the contrary, having a nice, up-to-date photo on a Profile helps to build the Know, Like, and Trust factor.

Manage Twitter Settings

There are several options:

- Add another Twitter account.
- Account visibility: display your Twitter account on your LinkedIn profile: yes/ no. Choose "yes" if you want people to know you are on Twitter and want to encourage them to follow you.
- Sharing Tweets: share only tweets that contain #in or #li in your LinkedIn status: yes/no. Choose "yes" to avoid the risk of your more personal and private messages arriving on LinkedIn.
- Tweet Display: show rich link display where possible (photo, page title, and short description): yes/no. Choose "yes" to increase its appeal.

Email Preferences

LinkedIn offers many ways to limit the amount of emails you receive and to choose the type of emails and messages.

Select the types of messages you're willing to receive

Messages:

- Introductions, InMail, and OpenLink messages (Default if you have an upgraded account)
- Introductions and InMail only (Default if you have a basic account)
- Introductions only

Some people choose "Introductions only" when they don't want to receive sales pitches or job offers from people who use InMail for that purpose. This is the reason why you might not be able to reach some people even if you pay for InMails.

Opportunities:

- Career opportunities
- Expertise requests
- Consulting offers

- Business deals
- New ventures
- Personal reference requests
- Job inquiries
- Requests to reconnect

You can choose which opportunities are acceptable. This gives other people an idea when to contact you, or not.

Also keep this in mind when you contact other people. However, most people have never really looked into this option, and the data in their Profile might not be accurate. Take the cautious approach if they didn't list the reason why you are contacting them. Writing something like, "I see in your Profile that you are not open for a career change, but I would like to know if that is up to date or not." Still, we don't recommend taking the cold approach; use a Magic Mail instead.

Advice to people who contact you

Explain what you are open for, or not. Select how you want people to contact you: via LinkedIn, via email, via the telephone, etc.

Set the frequency of emails

LinkedIn offers many different kinds of messages that can be sent. Some will be more important to you than others.

You can set the frequency of each type to:

- Individual Email
- Weekly Digest Email
- No email (you read it on LinkedIn. However, this is a dangerous option because you might forget to look at it and miss opportunities)

You can customize your settings: for example, to receive an individual email when someone sends you an Invitation or a direct message. For Network Activity (Network Updates) you may prefer a weekly email.

Select who can send you invitations

Options:

- Anyone on LinkedIn (default)
- Only people who know your email address or appear in your "Imported Contacts" list
- Only people who appear in your "Imported Contacts" list

If you get too many unwanted Invitations, you may want to change these settings. However, you risk missing Invitations from interesting people who don't know your email address or who are not in your "Imported Contacts" list.

Set the frequency of group digest emails

Review this option when you feel you receive too many emails from LinkedIn.

For each Group you've joined you can choose to receive:

- A daily digest email of Group activity
- A weekly digest email of Group activity
- No email (you go to LinkedIn and follow the actions yourself)

Today, LinkedIn monitors your involvement in the Groups and moves you from "Daily Digest" to "Weekly Digest" if you are not active (and notifies you by email). This might already deal with some of the email overload, but you probably might want to control this yourself by adjusting the settings.

If you get annoyed by emails from Groups, it usually means that you find the value insufficient. Evaluate your Group memberships from time to time and leave the Groups that are no longer of interest.

LinkedIn Communications

From time to time LinkedIn sends emails on behalf of the company or its partners. You can indicate whether you want to receive those or not.

Turn on/off LinkedIn announcements

Choose whether or not you would like to get announcements, tips, and insights into new products and features. Default = yes.

Turn on/off invitations to participate in research

LinkedIn periodically invites users to participate in market research studies. Users are identified based on non-personal information such as title, company size or region. Participation is completely voluntary and personal information is not revealed.

Choose whether or not you would like to receive invitations to participate in online research studies. Default = yes.

Turn on/off partner InMail

LinkedIn Partner InMails are messages from its partners with informational or promotional content that is part of a marketing or hiring campaign. These Partner InMails are sent to LinkedIn users based on non-personal information, such as the title of your current position, your primary industry, or your region, and are not from individual recruiters using LinkedIn. Your name and email address will not be disclosed to LinkedIn's marketing partners.

- Choose whether or not LinkedIn's marketing partners may send you informational and promotional messages. Default = yes.
- Choose whether or not LinkedIn's hiring campaign partners may send you informational and promotional messages. Default = yes.

Groups, Companies & Applications

You can change these settings related to Groups, Companies & Applications

Groups

Select your group display order

There are two options:

- Set the order of the Groups you have joined, with the most-valued Groups first.

- Choose how many Groups you want to see in the navigation menu (= when you hover over Groups in the top menu). Default = 3, you can have as many as 10.

Set the frequency of group digest emails

This is the same option as already discussed: you have the option to receive a daily digest email, a weekly digest email, or no email. You can change the setting per Group.

Turn on/off group invitations

Choose whether or not to accept invitations to join a Group.

Default = yes.

Applications

View your Applications

LinkedIn Applications

Listed here are applications you have either installed or granted access to while you were using LinkedIn. Removing them here will remove them from your home page, profile page, and prevent any further access to your LinkedIn data. To remove them from your home page only, visit the home page and click the X on the application title bar. To remove them from your profile page only, visit the Edit My Profile page and click the Remove link next to the title of the application.

If you want to remove an application temporarily, you can select More/ Get More Applications in the navigation menu and select the application. At the bottom right of that application page you can uncheck both boxes (display on my profile, display on LinkedIn homepage).

External Websites

Listed here are external partner websites to which you have granted access to your LinkedIn profile and network data. If you remove access here, your LinkedIn data will no longer be accessible to these sites. To re-enable them in the future, visit the website and grant access again.

Websites here include HootSuite (http://bit.ly/li-book9) or tools from the LinkedIn Labs like InMaps or Year-In-Review (see "Chapter 18: How LinkedIn Provides Us with More Insights: News & Labs").

Turn on/off data sharing with third-party applications

You can choose whether or not to share data with third-party applications.

Default = yes.

Since you need this turned on to be able to use HootSuite (http://bit.ly/li-book9) or tools from the LinkedIn Labs, it makes sense to leave the default setting.

Account

Privacy Controls

Manage Social Advertising

LinkedIn may sometimes pair an advertiser's message with social content from LinkedIn's network in order to increase the relevance of an ad. When LinkedIn members recommend people and services, follow companies, or take other actions, their name/photo may show up in related ads shown to you. Conversely, when you take these actions on LinkedIn, your name/photo may appear in related ads shown to LinkedIn members. By providing social context, LinkedIn makes it easy for their members to learn about products and services that interest their LinkedIn network.

Choose whether or not LinkedIn is allowed to use your name and photo in social advertising. Default = yes.

Turn on/off enhanced advertising

LinkedIn works with partner websites to show enhanced advertisements on their sites to LinkedIn members. This collection of partner sites is called the LinkedIn Audience Network. Advertisements shown to you on the LinkedIn Audience Network are selected based on non-personally identifiable information from your LinkedIn profile

Advertisers may target only segments of the LinkedIn membership, based on categories such as Industry, Job Function, and Seniority. For example, advertisers may choose to target advertisements to LinkedIn members who work in the Textiles industry. If you work in the Textiles industry and visit a site on the LinkedIn Audience Network, you may be shown a relevant advertisement rather than one unrelated to your field.

LinkedIn will not share personally identifiable information to enable these services.

Choose whether or not the LinkedIn Audience Network may show you enhanced advertising.

Default = yes.

Settings

Show/hide Profile photos of other members

Select if you would like to see photos of:

- Everyone
- Your network (first three degrees)
- Your connections (first-degree contacts)
- No one

In some parts of the world recruiters are not allowed to see photos of candidates until a certain stage in the process because of anti-discrimination laws. That would be a reason to make access to other people's photo temporarily unavailable.

Customize the updates you see on your home page

The first tab page (Update Type) is the place to customize the Network Activity or Network Updates you see on your Home Page.

First, choose how many updates you want on your Home Page: between 10 and 25.

Then choose the type of updates you want. By default you will receive everything, but you probably want to change this according to your own situation and interests. This is the list:

- General
  - New connections in your network
  - Updates from your extended network
  - Status updates from your connections
  - Posts from your connections
- Profile & Recommendations
  - When connections change profile information
  - When connections change profile photos
  - When connections receive recommendations
  - When connections upgrade to a premium account
- Questions & Answers
  - Questions from your connections
  - Answers from your connections
- Jobs
  - Jobs you may be interested in

- Events
  - o Events your connections are interested in or attending
- Polls
  - o Polls from your connections
- Groups
  - o Groups your connections have joined or created
  - o Discussions from your groups
- Applications
  - o Application updates from your connections
- Company Pages
  - o When connections modify or add a Company Page
- News
  - o When connections follow news

The second tab page (hidden) shows the list of people whose updates you don't want to see anymore on your Home Page. The reason you have done that might be: too many updates, not the right content (too much personal information via Twitter) or perhaps you no longer have a good relationship with this person.

You can undo this action by clicking the "Show updates" button.

Select your language

You can change the language of your user interface to another one of the supported languages.

Click on the link to see the supported languages.

Get LinkedIn content in an RSS feed

RSS is a technology that gives you access to LinkedIn content through your favorite RSS feed reader (like Google Reader (http://bit.ly/li-book14), Newsgator (http://bit.ly/li-book15) or Netvibes (http://bit.ly/li-book16)). LinkedIn offers two types of feeds, public and personal. Public feeds offer the same content to all LinkedIn members. Personal feeds contain private information from your LinkedIn network.

The Network Updates feed publishes your personal Network Updates in RSS format.

This is disabled by default.

As already mentioned: each LinkedIn Answers category has its own RSS feed. You can find the whole list on this page.

Conclusion of this Chapter

LinkedIn offers many ways to refine your experience.

The most important settings are:

- Select what others see when you've viewed their profile
- Manage Twitter Settings
- Select the types of messages you're willing to receive
- Set the frequency of emails
- Set the frequency of group digest emails
- Select your group display order
- Customize the updates you see on your home page

You might want to change other settings as well depending on your situation and preferences.

> If you want to watch a small video about the most important settings, go to the "Video & Tools Library" at www.how-to-really-use-linkedin.com.

Chapter 14: How to REALLY Use LinkedIn to Find New Customers

This chapter is for sales managers, sales reps, business development managers, freelancers, members of referral clubs and everybody else who needs new customers.

The same tips apply for non-profits looking for sponsors and advertisers.

Since we discuss the strategies throughout the book, this chapter serves as a quick reference guide; many of our trainees like to have an overview of the different steps. As well, we offer a few tips for members of referral clubs.

Overview

Passive Strategy

	Ingredients	Where to find pointers
1	**Create an attractive LinkedIn Profile**	Chapter 4: How To Craft an Attractive Profile
2	**Use Applications to build the Know, Like, Trust factor further**	Chapter 9: Lead Generation Tools & Visibility Boosters: Applications
3	**Use Applications as a lead generation tool for new customers**	Chapter 9: Lead Generation Tools & Visibility Boosters: Applications
4	**Join Groups where your current customers and prospects are members**	Chapter 6: The Heart of LinkedIn: Groups
5	**Join Groups where your (potential) referrers** are members	Chapter 6: The Heart of LinkedIn: Groups
6	**Create an attractive Company Profile** or ask the responsible person to do this	Chapter 17: How Organizations Can Benefit from LinkedIn (versus Individuals)

Active Strategy

	Ingredients	Where to find pointers
1	**Post Status Updates and Like, Share or Comment on other people's Status Updates**	Chapter 10: Personal Branding, Raising Your Visibility and Credibility on LinkedIn
2	**Ask for Recommendations**	Chapter 10: Personal Branding, Raising Your Visibility and Credibility on LinkedIn
3	**Share information via the Sharing Bookmarklet**	Chapter 10: Personal Branding, Raising Your Visibility and Credibility on LinkedIn
4	**Contribute to Groups**: start Discussions yourself and comment on other people's Discussions	Chapter 6: The Heart of LinkedIn: Groups
5	**Contribute to Answers**	Chapter 10: Personal Branding, Raising Your Visibility and Credibility on LinkedIn
6	**Confirm your attendance via LinkedIn Events** when available	Chapter 11: The Power of Combining Online and Offline Networking: Events
7	**Start your own Group** Make sure you think through this commitment!	Chapter 12: The Heroes of LinkedIn: Group Managers

Proactive Strategy

	Ingredients	Where to find pointers
1	**Use the 5 step basic strategy to find new customers**	Chapter 3: How To REALLY Use LinkedIn: a 5 Step Basic Strategy
2	**Use the 10 strategies to find the people who can help you reach your goals**: new customers or people who have access to them	Chapter 7: 10 Strategies to Find People Using LinkedIn
3	**Attend offline events**, whether or not supported by LinkedIn Events and Groups	Chapter 11: The Power of Combining Online and Offline Networking: Events

Extra Tips for Members of Referral Clubs

If you are in sales or have your own company and you are already a member of BNI, BRE, LeTip, BOB, Flevum, Red Peppers or any other referral club—well done, you are on your way to success!

LinkedIn can help you to get more out of your membership. The tips in this part are very similar to the ones for finding a new customer, but adjusted to guide the people in your referral group so you can help them to help you better.

Tip 1: Make a Good Profile and Connect with Every Member of Your Referral Group

This might seem obvious, but many times we lack a good Profile and we aren't connected to all the other members from our own group. As a consequence we miss many opportunities to exchange help.

When making a Profile on LinkedIn your function should make clear what you do to everybody and especially the members of your referral group.

Connect with all the other members so you can see to whom they are connected (and who might be a good prospect for you.) With this action you give them the opportunity to see whom you can refer them to as well.

Some people from your referral group won't have a Profile on LinkedIn yet. Offer to assist with their Profile to get them started. Better still; organize a session for a few people to help at the same time.

Also, add extra value to newcomers by inviting them to LinkedIn. If a new member gets 20 invitations to connect on LinkedIn after the first meeting, he might already experience the potential power of this group (and the network behind this group). This will encourage him to return and become and active member.

Tip 2: Make a Definition of Your Customer/Prospect

This is a crucial, but too often overlooked step. Failing to define and update a good definition of a prospect stops the flow of referrals. If you lack a clear definition, the members of your referral group don't know how to help you. Or they send you useless referrals—a waste of time and a frustration for all involved.

Maybe you already have the name of a person or a company from your prospect list. Use this information to help members of your referral group to find the right people for you.

Tip 3: Look in the Network of Other Members to Find Prospects

Many times your fellow members could give you a good referral, but they don't realize it. They could be connected to people who might be good prospects, but they never think of them when viewing your products or services.

By looking for prospects you might discover that someone from your referral group knows one of them. The power of LinkedIn makes these connections visible.

The first strategy to receive more introductions to prospects known to your referral group colleagues is browsing their network. Chances are that they are connected with potential customers.

Of course, use the strategies regarding "Advanced Search" and creating the alerts via "Saved Search" as well.

Tip 4: Create a Group on LinkedIn

If you are responsible for the local chapter of your referral organization, you might consider starting a Group on LinkedIn. We recommend this if your chapter has no other online forum.

This Group can facilitate the exchange of advice and tips among members. This may increase your value at face-to-face meetings.

See also "Chapter 12: The Heroes of LinkedIn: Group Managers".

Tip 5: Answer Questions in the Discussions of Your Group

If your referral group has a Group on LinkedIn (or on another website), this is an excellent place to introduce yourself to the other members.

Don't promote yourself (unless this is explicitly encouraged by the Group Manager), but look for ways you can help your fellow members.

By answering the questions they pose and providing good advice you increase your visibility and credibility. Also share the positive comments you hear from contacts following any introductions you make for a referral group member. Honest public praise is ideal. It works even better online because it is written instead of spoken (and keeps being recycled). Also invite your contact to write a Recommendation on LinkedIn for your referral group colleague.

As a consequence of your being active in the LinkedIn Group, your Know, Like and Trust factor will increase and your referral group colleagues will hold you in higher esteem and give you more referrals.

Tip 6: Attend Every Meeting of Your Referral Group to Reinforce Your LinkedIn Efforts

By now you already understand how LinkedIn can expand the results you get from your referral group membership.

It also works the other way around: by attending the meetings of your referral group, you will have more actions to take on LinkedIn.

The benefits of attending meetings:

- When attending meetings you should **give examples** of projects you did for customers. This will help your colleagues think of extra contacts they may have for you on LinkedIn and other networks. Even an excellent Profile has little room for examples or stories. You may add some, but be sure to keep your Profile succinct and easy to read.

- After discovering that a fellow referral group member is in contact with a prospect, you can **talk before or after a meeting about how well they know each other, give more background information about a request, and suggest the best way to refer to you**. This will help him give you a better referral—and a better result.

- It is **easier for people to get to know, like, and trust each other when they meet face-to-face**. They experience how the other person interacts with them and the other members.

As you see, membership in a referral organization combined with a proactive presence on LinkedIn is an ideal way to get referrals.

> *Tip: if you want even more tips on building an effective referral strategy, look at our Everlasting Referrals Home Study Course: www.networking-coach.com*

Conclusion of this Chapter

LinkedIn offers a variety of ways to find new customers. This chapter gave you an overview of three different steps:

- Passive Strategy
- Active Strategy
- Proactive Strategy

If you are a member of a referral club, these 6 LinkedIn tips can help you get more out of your membership:

1. Create a good profile and connect with every member of your referral club
2. Define your customer/prospect
3. Look into the network of other members to find customers/prospects
4. Start a Group
5. Answer questions in Discussions of your Group
6. Attend every meeting of your referral club to reinforce your LinkedIn efforts

> **Tip:** for people who want more support in finding new customers via LinkedIn including a step-by-step plan, webinar access, extra tools, video tips and email support, we offer special packages. Look at www.how-to-really-use-linkedin.com for the details.

Chapter 15: How to REALLY Use LinkedIn to Find a New Job

This is a chapter for people who are looking for either a new job or an internship.

Looking for a new job is a job in itself. Take the challenge seriously and spend enough time on it. More than 50% of open jobs is not advertised therefore it is crucial to be proactive to find the job of your dreams.

LinkedIn is a great tool to help you reach your goal. Since you can find most of the strategies throughout the book, this chapter is first and foremost a quick reference guide, but you will also get some extra tips to find a new job or internship.

Overview

Passive Strategy

	Ingredients	Where to find pointers
1	**Create an attractive LinkedIn Profile**	Chapter 4: How To Craft an Attractive Profile
2	**Use Applications to build the Know, Like, Trust factor further**	Chapter 9: Lead Generation Tools & Visibility Boosters: Applications
3	**Use Applications to show your expertise**	Chapter 9: Lead Generation Tools & Visibility Boosters: Applications
4	**Be a member of Groups that recruiters have joined**	Chapter 6: The Heart of LinkedIn: Groups
5	**Be a member of Groups that your future colleagues are member of**	Chapter 6: The Heart of LinkedIn: Groups
6	**Upgrade your account (Paid)**	See below

Active Strategy

	Ingredients	Where to find pointers
1	**Post Status Updates and Like, Share or Comment on other people's Status Updates**	Chapter 10: Personal Branding, Raising Your Visibility and Credibility on LinkedIn
2	**Ask for Recommendations**	Chapter 10: Personal Branding, Raising Your Visibility and Credibility on LinkedIn

	Ingredients	Where to find pointers
3	**Share information via the Sharing Bookmarklet**	Chapter 10: Personal Branding, Raising Your Visibility and Credibility on LinkedIn
4	**Contribute to Groups**: start Discussions yourself and comment on other people's Discussions	Chapter 6: The Heart of LinkedIn: Groups
5	**Contribute to Answers**	Chapter 10: Personal Branding, Raising Your Visibility and Credibility on LinkedIn
6	**Confirm your attendance via LinkedIn Events** when available	Chapter 11: The Power of Combining Online and Offline Networking: Events
7	**Start your own Group** Make sure you think through this commitment!	Chapter 12: The Heroes of LinkedIn: Group Managers

Proactive Strategy

	Ingredients	Where to find pointers
1	**Use the 5 step basic strategy to find a new job**	Chapter 3: How To REALLY Use LinkedIn: a 5 Step Basic Strategy
2	**Use the 10 strategies to find the people who can help you reach your goals**: new employers or people connected to them	Chapter 7: 10 Strategies to Find People Using LinkedIn
3	**Attend offline events**, whether or not supported by LinkedIn Events and Groups	Chapter 11: The Power of Combining Online and Offline Networking: Events
4	Use the **Find Jobs** opportunities LinkedIn offers	See below
5	Contact recruiters and Hiring Managers directly via **InMail (Paid)**, but remember that a Magic Mail via a mutual contact may work much better	See below

Extra Tips to Find a New Job via LinkedIn

LinkedIn offers tools geared toward job postings. Use them to your advantage! However, remember that only a small percentage of job offers are posted on LinkedIn. Use the other strategies from this book as well!

Find Jobs

Go to "Jobs/Find Jobs" (top menu).

There are 4 tab pages:

- Jobs Home
- Saved Jobs
- Saved Searches
- Advanced Search

Let's look at these 4 pages first and then go into the details of a Job page.

Jobs Home

Here you find:

- Search box (with a link to Advanced Search)
- Jobs You May Be Interested In: LinkedIn matches jobs with your Profile.
- Email Alerts: select when you want to receive emails about Jobs You May Be Interested In:
  - o Daily
  - o Weekly (default)
  - o No email alerts
- "See more" takes you to a page with more "Jobs You May Be Interested In". If the list is too long, refine the results. When you hover over a job posting, you can save/unsave it and find similar jobs.

Advanced Search

Parameters for a focused search:

- Keywords
- Job Title
- Company
- Location: country, postal code, and radius
- Functions

- Experience
- Industries
- Date Posted
- Salary (when available)

You can sort the results by:

- Relevance
- Relationship
- Date Posted (most recent)
- Date Posted (earliest)

Refine the results list with the same parameters.

Actions:

- **Create alerts** by saving your searches (press the "Save" link next to the number of results).
  - o You can choose daily, weekly or monthly alerts. Or none (then you have to go to LinkedIn and look for the results yourself).
  - o You can save up to 10 searches.
- **Find similar jobs**. When you hover over a job posting, you can save/unsave it and find similar jobs.
- At the bottom of the last page of the results list, click on the link **"See more jobs from Simply Hired that fit these criteria".** You will be presented with extra jobs from listings outside LinkedIn. Within LinkedIn you already have the option "See who you know at *name company*". When you click on the posting itself, you will leave LinkedIn. Make sure you have the JobInsider toolbar (see below) installed to give you extra insights into how you may be connected to this company, even when you are not on LinkedIn anymore.

Saved Jobs

This is the place where you can find all the jobs you have saved.

Since the "find similar jobs" option is not available here, remember to use it when you search for jobs or when you find one while looking at Jobs You May Be Interested In.

Job postings that have expired will appear in gray and you will not be able to view the posting. If a job you've applied for doesn't appear on the Saved Jobs tab, you may have accidentally removed it.

Saved Searches

Up to 10 alerts may be stored here.

You can look at the results, adjust the email settings, and delete an alert.

Job Posting Page

When you have found a Job posting via a search result or via Jobs You May Be Interested In, you will be presented with the content of that Job posting, and some extra useful information.

Before you take further action, look at this information:

- **Posted By**. In most cases, the LinkedIn Profile of the recruiter or hiring manager is shown. When you have mutual contacts, they are automatically presented. This useful information helps you find some background details about the job and to be introduced via a Magic Mail (or ask for an introduction via LinkedIn—but remember that the perception is different!). If you have upgraded your account, you can also contact this person directly via an InMail. (You can also send an Invitation to connect with you, but not everybody will accept it before they know you).

- **Your connections at *name company***. LinkedIn shows you your first- and second- degree contacts at this company. Again this might give the opportunity to get some background information and have an introduction to the right people via a Magic Mail.

Actions you can take:

- **Apply**:
  - o Mandatory:
    - » Your Profile will be included, so be sure it is up to date.
    - » Choose the email address you want for the application.
    - » Add a telephone number.
  - o Optional:
    - » Add a cover letter.
    - » Add a resume. If you use your LinkedIn Profile as (basis of) your resume, consider using the Resume Builder application. See "Chapter 18: How LinkedIn Provides Us With More Insights: News & Labs".
    - » If you have an upgraded account, you can choose to be included in the Featured Applicants section at the top of the applicant list.
- **Save the job posting**
- **Share the job posting** via LinkedIn, Facebook, or Twitter (if it's not the job you want, but there are some people in your network who may be interested)
- **Follow the company** (so you will get updates about the company including job postings)

Extra information that could point you to another job posting you may be interested in:

- Similar jobs
- People who viewed this job also viewed (other jobs)
- See more jobs

☞ **Assignment**: search for a job and save the search.

Upgrade Your Account

LinkedIn offers 3 account types directed toward job seekers:

- Job Seeker Basic
- Job Seeker
- Job Seeker Plus

You can find them (and current pricing) via "Jobs/Job Seeker Premium" (top menu).

This is an overview of the features of these account types (August 2011):

	Job Seeker Basic	Job Seeker	Job Seeker Plus
Get noticed by recruiters and hiring managers with a Job Seeker Badge [1]	On your profile	On your profile	On your profile
Select only $100K plus jobs with detailed salary information [2]	Included	Included	Included
Move to the top of the list as a Featured Applicant [3]	Included	Included	Included
Contact anyone directly with InMail	0 InMails per month	5 InMails per month	10 InMails per month
Who's Viewed My Profile: Get the full list (but still only anonymous if this is the visitor's setting)	Yes	Yes	Yes
Get introduced to the companies you're targeting	10 outstanding	15 outstanding	25 outstanding
Let recruiters reach you for free with OpenLink	Yes	Yes	Yes

(1) You can choose whether or not to show the Job Seeker Badge (the symbol is a briefcase) to indicate that you are actively looking for a new job. By default it is NOT shown.

(2) Salary information is provided by PayScale and is available for most jobs posted in the United States, Canada, United Kingdom, and Australia. Salaries are based on job-specific attributes, including industry, title, location, and other factors. The companies that post jobs on LinkedIn do not necessarily provide salary information, and actual compensation may vary.

(3) Every time you apply for a job on LinkedIn, your profile will be featured at the top of the list of applicants.

Extra Tips & Tools

LinkedIn offers extra tools and insights to find the right job for you and to guide you toward that job.

LinkedIn Jobs Twitter account

You can follow @LinkedIn_Jobs on Twitter. Every Job posting on LinkedIn is automatically tweeted by this account.

LinkedIn JobsInsider

JobsInsider is a tool that comes with the LinkedIn Browser Toolbar for either Internet Explorer or Firefox. It automatically appears as a browser pane when you search for a job on a website outside LinkedIn. The LinkedIn JobsInsider increases your chances of being hired by:

- Identifying people in your network or Groups who work at the company posting the job.

- Offering the option to request Introductions to hiring managers and send your resume to the right person.

JobsInsider currently works with Monster, CareerBuilder, HotJobs, Craigslist, Dice, Vault, and more.

To download one of the toolbars listed above, click on "Tools" at the bottom of any LinkedIn page. The JobsInsider preferences can be set to show when browsing a known job site and/or to appear upon browser startup.

It might not always work, but if it does it may give you extra information and increase your chances of being hired.

LinkedIn Career Explorer

LinkedIn Career Explorer is a tool for students.

The Career Explorer is currently in beta testing with a few chosen universities and a small number of select members and groups. Although LinkedIn is not accepting volunteers during the beta release, you can see some features in LinkedIn's blog article titled "LinkedIn Career Explorer: Helping College Graduates Find Their Career Path" (http://bit.ly/li-book17).

LinkedIn Career Explorer will include:

- Path Builder—Build your career path.

- Recent Career Tracks.

- Jobs for You.

- Industry Statistics.

- Featured discussions.

- Books read by people on this track (Amazon reading list).

- Top profiles of your school.

- Expand my network (People You May Know).

Connect with other Job Seekers

If you are in a program with other people who are looking for a new job, connect with each other on LinkedIn. This way your network expands and you could find new opportunities.

If you are a student you may believe you have a limited network. But when you start linking with the following list of people, you already have a good basis: fellow students, parents, family members, neighbors, people from the sport or hobby club, professors, guest lecturers, representatives of companies at Job Days, company visits or conferences, internship contacts, coordinator of the career program, and people you know from other social networking websites such as Facebook or MySpace.

Also clarify what kind of job you are seeking, when meeting others personally or via email. You can share the role of mutual ambassadors.

Connect with the Career Coordinator at Your College or University

Mary Roll, career coordinator for the international MBA program at Vlerick Leuven Gent Management School, mentioned that career coordinators help alumni as well as current students. Career coordinators are a valuable resource since they are continuously in touch with different companies and organizations.

Conclusion of this Chapter

When looking for a job follow these three strategies:

- Passive Strategy
- Active Strategy
- Proactive Strategy

You have also received some extra useful tips for your job hunt:

- Go to Jobs/Find Jobs with Jobs Home, Advanced Search, Saved Jobs and Saved Searches
- Job Posting Page
- Upgrade Your Account
- Follow @LinkedIn_Jobs
- LinkedIn JobsInsider
- LinkedIn Career Explorer
- Connect with Other Job Seekers
- Connect with the Career Coordinator of Your College or University

Tip: for people who want more support in finding a new job via LinkedIn including a step-by-step plan, webinar access, extra tools, video tips and email support, we offer special packages. Look at www.how-to-really-use-linkedin. com for the details.

Chapter 16: How to REALLY Use LinkedIn to Find New Employees

This is a chapter for recruiters, hiring managers or other people who need to find new employees, interns or volunteers.

Since you can find most of the strategies throughout the book, this chapter is first and foremost a quick reference guide.

But there are some extra tips to find more candidates in this chapter as well.

Overview

Passive Strategy

	Ingredients	Where to find pointers
1	**Create an attractive LinkedIn Profile**	Chapter 4: How To Craft an Attractive Profile
2	**Use Applications to build the Know, Like, Trust factor further**	Chapter 9: Lead Generation Tools & Visibility Boosters: Applications
3	**Use Applications as a lead generation tool to attract new employees**	Chapter 9: Lead Generation Tools & Visibility Boosters: Applications
4	**Be a member of Groups that your potential candidates** are member of	Chapter 6: The Heart of LinkedIn: Groups
5	**Be a member of Groups that your (potential) referrers** are member of	Chapter 6: The Heart of LinkedIn: Groups
6	**Create an attractive Company Profile** or ask the person who is responsible to do this	Chapter 17: How Organizations Can Benefit from LinkedIn (versus Individuals)
7	**Create a Career Page on Company Profile (Paid)**	Chapter 17: How Organizations Can Benefit from LinkedIn (versus Individuals)
8	**Upgrade your account (Paid)**	See below

Active Strategy

	Ingredients	Where to find pointers
1	**Post Status Updates and Like, Share or Comment on other people's Status Updates**	Chapter 10: Personal Branding, Raising Your Visibility and Credibility on LinkedIn
2	**Ask for Recommendations**	Chapter 10: Personal Branding, Raising Your Visibility and Credibility on LinkedIn
3	**Share information via the Sharing Bookmarklet**	Chapter 10: Personal Branding, Raising Your Visibility and Credibility on LinkedIn
4	**Contribute to Groups**: start Discussions yourself and comment on other people's Discussions	Chapter 6: The Heart of LinkedIn: Groups
5	**Post jobs in the relevant Groups**	Chapter 6: The Heart of LinkedIn: Groups
6	**Contribute to Answers**	Chapter 10: Personal Branding, Raising Your Visibility and Credibility on LinkedIn
7	**Confirm your attendance via LinkedIn Events** when available	Chapter 11: The Power of Combining Online and Offline Networking: Events
8	**Start your own Group** Make sure you think through this commitment!	Chapter 12: The Heroes of LinkedIn: Group Managers
9	**Post Jobs (Paid)**	See Below
10	**Do a Reference search (Paid)**	See Below

Proactive Strategy

	Ingredients	Where to find pointers
1	**Use the 5 step basic strategy to find new customers**	Chapter 3: How To REALLY Use LinkedIn: a 5 Step Basic Strategy
2	**Use the 10 strategies to find the people who can help you reach your goals**: new employees or people connected to them	Chapter 7: 10 Strategies to Find People Using LinkedIn

	Ingredients	Where to find pointers
3	**Attend offline events**, whether or not supported by LinkedIn Events and Groups	Chapter 11: The Power of Combining Online and Offline Networking: Events
4	**Give co-workers and especially future colleagues the tools** to help you find candidates. Assist them to create a good Profile	Chapter 17: How Organizations Can Benefit from LinkedIn (versus Individuals)
5	**Contact people directly via InMail (Paid)**, but remember that a Magic Mail via a mutual contact usually works better	See below

Extra Tips to Find New Employees via LinkedIn

Post a Job on LinkedIn

The simplest way to have someone know you have a job opportunity is to post a job via "Jobs" (top menu) and then "Post a Job". This is a paid option; discounts are available if you buy packs.

Interesting characteristics of job posts on LinkedIn:

- You can **choose whether or not to post your Profile on the job listing** and if you do there are several options:
  - Hiring Manager
  - Company Employee
  - Company HR
  - Recruiting/Staffing firm
  - The first two options might be more effective in finding candidates than the latter two, especially if their personal LinkedIn Profile is an attractive one. Becoming part of that person's team feels different from having a meeting with a recruiter before being able to talk to the people from the team itself.

- You can choose whether to:
  - Collect applications on LinkedIn and be notified by email.
  - Direct candidates to an external site to apply.

- When you post a job,
  - You immediately get an **overview of up to 24 of the LinkedIn Profiles** of the best possible candidates. However, these are anonymous profiles. If you want to see who they are and receive 10 InMails to contact them directly, you need to pay $95 extra.

- o It is **automatically posted on Twitter** via @LinkedIn_Jobs, giving it extra attention.
- o It is **automatically added to the Careers page** on your Company Profile.
- o People can:
  - » Take action
    - Apply
    - Save it for future reference
    - Share it on LinkedIn, Facebook and Twitter
    - Follow your Company
  - » See if and how they are connected to you
  - » See if and how they are connected to your company (their first- and second-degree contacts in your company are shown)
- Extra benefits:
  - o Since LinkedIn has a high Page Ranking in Google (meaning it is a popular website), job posts might also appear high in Google's search results.

After the Job is posted, you can forward it to your first-degree contacts. Ask your colleagues to do the same (especially the future co-workers of the candidate).

Upgrade Your Account

LinkedIn offers 3 account types directed toward individual recruiters:

- Talent Basic
- Talent Finder
- Talent Pro

You find them via "Jobs/Hiring Solutions" (top menu) and then click on the "Compare accounts" link.

Features of these account types (August 2011):

	Talent Basic	Talent Finder	Talent Pro
Contact anyone on LinkedIn with InMail	10 InMails per month	25 InMails per month	50 InMails per month
See expanded profiles of everyone on LinkedIn, even candidates outside your network.	Yes	Yes	Yes
Number of people in search result list	500	700	1000
Search for top talent within your groups		Up to 50 Groups	Up to 50 Groups
Save and manage your candidate pipeline in Profile Organizer	25 folders	50 folders	75 folders
Open to active candidates—allow people outside your network to contact you free with OpenLink	Yes	Yes	Yes
See names of your third-degree and Group connections	First Name	Full Name Visibility	Full Name Visibility
Who's Viewed My Profile: Get the full list (but still anonymous if visitor chose that setting)	Yes	Yes	Yes
Get alerts when new candidates meet your criteria	7 per week	10 per day	15 per day
Reference Search	Yes	Yes	Yes
Advanced search filters (see table below)	Premium Filters	Premium + Talent Filters	Premium + Talent Filters

Premium (4 filters)	Premium + Talent (8 filters)	Recruiter Exclusives (5 filters)
Seniority	Seniority	Years at Company
Company Size	Company Size	Years in Position
Interests	Function	Any Groups
Fortune 1000	Interests	Company Type

Premium (4 filters)	Premium + Talent (8 filters)	Recruiter Exclusives (5 filters)
	Years of Experience	Recommendations
	Fortune 1000	
	Your Groups	
	New to LinkedIn	

If you are working with a team, you might want to consider the Recruiting Solutions (and have access to the "Recruiter Exclusive Filters"). Read a short overview of the options in "Chapter 17: How Organizations Can Benefit from LinkedIn (versus Individuals)" or go to http://talent.linkedin.com

Remark: log in to LinkedIn to see the current pricing.

Extra tips

Use the Company Profile

Extra tips for recruiters regarding the Company Profile.

1. **Look at the people who are following your Company**. Chances are they are more interested in working for your company than others.

2. **If you do campus recruitment, use "Insightful statistics" to discover what top universities your current employees attended**. Since many people retain ties with their former university or college your current employees might be your ambassadors, even if it's just with a telephone call, a post in an alumni LinkedIn Group, or making a connection for you. They may even agree to join you at a campus event where you could speak to the students.

Be Present on SimplyHired

If you are unsure whether or not to post a Job on LinkedIn, at least post a job on SimplyHired (www.simplyhired.com). When someone is searching for a job via LinkedIn and there are no results, LinkedIn looks at SimplyHired for extra results.

Avoid the experience of one of our clients who neither had a Job posting on LinkedIn nor SimplyHired. When someone searched for a job at their company, the Simply-Hired results appeared from a staffing agency that had worked for them. On a positive note: the job posting was found by a potential candidate, but this route was more expensive than if they had posted it themselves.

On the last page of the search result list on LinkedIn, there is always the link "See more jobs from Simply Hired that fit these criteria". Jobs from job listings outside LinkedIn will be shown here to give job seekers extra opportunities.

Another reason to have a presence on SimplyHired is that other websites use the jobs posted on SimplyHired to show jobs on their website.

> **Remark:** SimplyHired listings do not appear on the Careers page of your Company Profile.

> If you want to watch a small video about how SimplyHired and LinkedIn work together, go to the "Video & Tools Library" at www.how-to-really-use-linkedin.com.

Conclusion of this Chapter

LinkedIn provides recruiters with a number of ways to find new employees:

- Passive Strategy
- Active Strategy
- Proactive Strategy

In addition to these strategies you also learned a couple of extra tips:

- Post a Job on LinkedIn
- Upgrade Your Account
- Use Your Company Profile
- Be Present on SimplyHired.com

> **Tip:** for people who want more support in finding new employees via LinkedIn including a step-by-step plan, webinar access, extra tools, video tips and email support, we offer special packages. Look at www.how-to-really-use-linkedin.com for the details.

Chapter 17: How Organizations Can Benefit from LinkedIn (versus Individuals)

Most tips in this book describe how LinkedIn can benefit you as an individual.

Since we have seen a change in requests during our presentations and workshops from individuals and teams to "What can we do with LinkedIn as a whole company" this chapter will examine that question.

Many organizations (both profit and not-for-profit) have realized that LinkedIn is here to stay and now wonder how they can use it strategically.

As we explained in the prologue, we see a shift on the Rogers Adoption Curve. We have seen individual and team USE of LinkedIn (not mere presence) move inside the "Early Majority" part of the curve (although remaining at the beginning). Organizations who have integrated LinkedIn *companywide* are leading in the Innovators/Early Adopters stage.

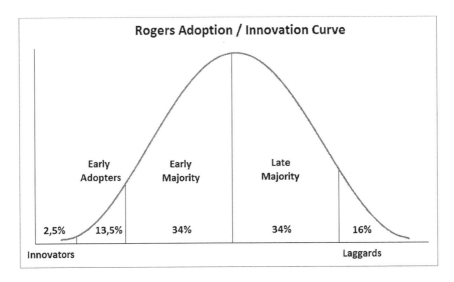

Strategies to Tap the Power of LinkedIn as an Organization

Before we share some practical tips, it is important to look at a few essential elements for an organization to be successful with social media in general, and LinkedIn in particular.

The Changing Roles of Marketing and Recruiting

We already explained in the first chapter that the real power of the network is in the second degree. We assume you can understand this as an individual.

The second degree also plays an important role in an organizational strategy. The larger the organization the fewer direct contacts its management has with its customers, suppliers, partners, potential new employees, etc.

To reach those stakeholders, the management needs begin with the co-workers. In other words: the co-workers form the first-degree network and the external stakeholders (customers, suppliers, partners, media, government, etc.) are the second-degree network of the management.

In the past, few people were in contact with the external stakeholders of an organization. But this has changed now since so many people have a LinkedIn Profile. All those LinkedIn Profiles serve as ambassadors for the organization, 24 hours a day, 7 days a week.

For example: let's assume an organization consists of 100 employees, including 5 sales representatives and 1 recruiter. Instead of having 5 people with personal contact with potential customers and 1 person with some potential new employees, instead you have 95 extra (passive) sales people and 99 extra (passive) recruiters.

As a consequence, the management team—including marketing and recruiting—will need to SUPPORT ALL co-workers in searching for new customers and employees, instead of developing a SEPARATE marketing or recruitment strategy, carried out by a small team.

Thus, the roles of marketing and recruiting teams will change. They will reach the people they want to attract via co-workers and will communicate with external stakeholders via the Profiles and actions of all employees.

As a further consequence, managers will be forced to abandon the traditional approach of "brute force". Instead they will need to INVITE their co-workers to cooperate for a bigger goal. They will need to develop materials to support their co-workers to be the organization's ambassadors and give them insights why this is important for all co-workers in the entire organization.

Trust Becomes Even More Important

Connecting via other people requires giving up control—most companies are afraid to do so. This is something new, few management teams have ever done this before. Many worry what their employees might do. And isn't it interesting that this discussion always centers around the harm that can be done, never the good? But times are changing. Let's look at an article from Jan's blog (feel free to comment at http://bit.ly/li-book18):

"Being successful with social media starts with creating a supportive working environment in which people are empowered and trusted. Only then will organizations really benefit from the tremendous power of LinkedIn and other social media.

Employees have always been the ambassadors of an organization. In the past, interaction occurred at parties with friends, in the gym, and in the pub. Now it is visible also on the Internet. This shift makes organizations that tend to be hierarchical or "dictatorial" nervous. They fear they are losing control over their "slaves".

LinkedIn and other social media invite organizations to look internally and develop human relationships first. Organizations are challenged to rethink why these people are working together and how the talents of each individual can be recognized and developed for the greater good of the organization.

In other words, the "new" media invite us to connect with each other as the wonderful, talented, and inspired human beings we are and to encourage each other to live up to our potential.

And isn't that what it has always been and always will be about?"

Trust also plays another role. When someone reads a message, status update, or document from a peer in another company, they will trust information from those sources more than an advertisement for a product or job posting by a recruiter.

In the past, this was difficult to accomplish, but with social media in general and LinkedIn within professional environments it becomes easier.

Before You Start Your Organizational LinkedIn Strategy

Remember that you can't force anyone on LinkedIn to do anything for the organization. Someone's LinkedIn Profile is his or her own "property" and does not belong to the organization. Rather, you need to invite them and support them.

Create materials to help your co-workers and facilitate opportunities for them to be authentic ambassadors for the organization via their Profiles and actions on LinkedIn.

In this chapter we will focus on two kinds of goals: attracting more customers and finding new employees—the two critical issues for most organizations.

☞ **Assignment**: connect with your colleagues on LinkedIn.

LinkedIn Strategy Matrix© for Organizations

This is a summary of the strategies on LinkedIn that can be applied by an organization (details follow).

	Passive	Active	Proactive
Organizational level	• Company Profile	• Advertising Solutions • Recruiting Solutions	
Level of a major representative of an organization (CEO, spokesperson, etc.)	• Personal Profile • Use Applications in Personal Profile	• Status Updates	
Employee level	• Personal Profile • Use Applications in Personal Profile	• Group Managers of internal and alumni Groups or external Groups • Active member of internal and external Groups • Contribute to Answers • Status Updates • Share information • Attend events and use LinkedIn Events	• Project Managers: find project members • Sales: find new customers • Recruiting: find new employees • Everybody: find internal and external expertise

In this multidimensional model, some actions can be taken on an organizational level, some by "major representatives" like the CEO or spokesperson, and most by the co-workers. The largest benefit will come from the proactive behavior of employees. It is the responsibility of the top management to organize support for all employees. We will explain how to do that below. Since many tips have been discussed in other chapters (and you will find a reference to them) only new information will be shared here.

Strategy 1: Your Company Profile

Let's start with a tool that is still "comfortable" for most marketers and recruiters: the LinkedIn Company Profile. The comfort arises from the degree of control over it.

We advise you to pay close attention to the Company Profile pages. They might become very important in the future. Nowadays, few people are visiting these pages because most don't know of their existence yet. But in a few years these pages may well attract many more people and could rank higher in search engines—attracting even more people.

Company Profile: Overview Page

Overview is the page on the Company Profile over which you have the least control. Most of the content on this page, and its sub pages, comes from the LinkedIn Profiles of the people who are current or former workers in your organization.

You DO have control over (via "Admin Tools"):

- **Company Description.** Make it interesting and appealing without turning it into a sales pitch. Your co-workers link to this description with their personal LinkedIn Profiles. Make sure they feel comfortable to share this information with their contacts.

- **Company Specialties.** A few key words will help people find your Company Profile when they search using these words.

- **Twitter ID.** The Tweets from your organization's Twitter account (or the one you have linked) will be shown.

- **Blog posts.** Your company's blog posts will automatically be displayed each time a new blog post appears.

- **News about your company.** This can be turned on or off. Its value depends on the name of your organization, regardless of the content. For our company, Networking Coach, this was not useful since news was displayed about any networking coach in the world.

- **Practical details** like Company Type, Company Size, URL, Main Company Industry, Company Operating Status, Year Founded and Company Locations (maximum 5 different ones).

A major concern of many companies was that others could change these details if they share the same email extension as the person who created the Company Page. Now it is possible to assign dedicated users with the authority to change the Company Profile. There needs to exist a first-degree connection with the people you want to assign as the administrators, but the individuals don't need to work for the same company. This could be useful if you work with a virtual assistant.

Company Profile: Careers Page

This page can only be "activated" when you post a job on LinkedIn or you buy a "Premium Careers Page".

Possibilities with a "Premium Careers Page" (information from the LinkedIn website):

- Deliver a custom experience:
  - o Your content adapts to viewers, based on their LinkedIn profiles.
  - o Job seekers see jobs tailored to their backgrounds.
  - o You control and update content.
- Differentiate your brand through rich, engaging content:
  - o Employee spotlights showcase employee stories.
  - o Video clips and custom modules bring your culture to life.
  - o Recruiter Profiles connect candidates directly with your company.
  - o Detailed analytics show you who are engaging with your brand.

> To experience what a Premium Career Page might look like, go to LinkedIn's own Careers Page: http://linkd.in/li-book19.

Company Profile: Products & Services

LinkedIn offers you the opportunity to showcase your products & services—for free!

First, you create an overview page and then add a separate page for each product and service.

Overview page

- **Title, Description and Picture**:
  - o Title: free text
  - o Description: free text as well
  - o Photo: will be automatically copied from the "main" Overview Page
- **Banners**: you can add up to 3 banners to showcase a product or service.
- **Feature Specific Products or Services**: you can promote up to 5 products and services.
- **YouTube**: provide a title and a YouTube URL and the video will be shown on the overview page. This is easier than the work-around on your personal LinkedIn Profile. We strongly suggest that you add a video with tips or other information to build the Know, Like, and Trust factor (instead of a commercial).
- **Disclaimer**: you can add a disclaimer.

If you are expecting different groups of people on your Company Page it can be adapted to suit the profile of the visitor. You can create multiple versions of this page so a marketing assistant from New York will see different products and services from ones offered to a HR manager from South Africa. You do this Via "Admin Tools" within Products & Services.

Product or Service page

Fields for every product or service:

- Category
- Name
- Picture
- Description
- List of Key Features
- Disclaimer
- URL for this product or service
- Contact (you can add only people from your first-degree network)
- Promotion (title, URL, description): we suggest that you add a video with tips or other information to build the Know, Like, Trust factor instead of a commercial!
- YouTube (title, YouTube URL): the same tip applies, but you can also add product demonstrations, testimonials or other content. Just avoid too blatant sales pitches.

We like these additional "Products" features because people can write recommendations about products or services from a company on these pages, which is different from recommendations for an individual (the latter are shown on your personal LinkedIn Profile). A product or service is a joint effort from everybody working for the same organization. Also, you also do not have to be connected in the first degree to write a recommendation about a product or service, while that is necessary when you recommend a person.

For example: our company, Networking Coach, benefits from this feature because we give a lot of presentations for large groups of people with whom we do not have a personal connection (yet). Through the company profile page they are able to share their experiences. These recommendations also benefit us as a company since their network is notified via Network Updates. So if you like this book, please leave a recommendation at: http://linkd.in/li-book22.

You can ask via LinkedIn for products/services recommendations. However, just as with a personal recommendation, a more personal approach is more significant. Read "Chapter 10: Personal Branding, Raising Your Visibility and Credibility on LinkedIn".

To watch a small video about the Products & Service page of the Company Profile, go to the "Video & Tools Library" at www.how-to-really-use-linkedin.com.

Company Profile: Analytics Page

On this page you can find analytics about the people who have visited one or more of the Company Profile pages.

You see following data:

- **Page Views**: All page views, Overview, Careers, Products & Services
- **Unique Visitors**: All page views, Overview, Careers, Products & Services
- **Clicks Products & Services:** Contact Employees, Promotional Banners, Special Promotional Links
- Evolution of **members following your Company**
- **Member visits**: Industry, Function, Company (especially this last one might be interesting although you don't receive any other information)

The Analytics tab is visible only to Company Page administrators. When no administrator is assigned, the tab is visible to employees with a confirmed company email address and a current position at your company listed on their Profile.

Challenge for International Companies

International companies face a challenge with LinkedIn Company Profiles: "Do we have one Company Profile for all countries or a separate one per country?"

The advantage of having one Company Profile worldwide is that is the identity of the company is clear. This simplifies communication with co-workers, customers, suppliers, partners, potential new employees, etc. As a co-worker it is easy to find a colleague whose expertise you need or people for your project team.

The disadvantage is that the larger the company, the harder it becomes to appeal to the Company Profile visitors: someone who wants to work for the German branch of an American company might not find appropriate Job Posts. Not all products and services are equal in every country. And which product to feature and which to set aside?

One solution is to create two Company Profiles: one for the international parent company and one for the local organization.

When you want to use LinkedIn's Recruiting Solutions (see next subchapter) it is especially important that all employees are linked to the same Company Profile(s). Most recruiting is done country-by-country and not worldwide, hence our advice is to work with two Company Profiles.

☞ **Assignment**: update the Company Page (if you have the rights to do so).

Strategy 2: Attract More Customers or Employees via Individual LinkedIn Profiles

To reap the benefits of all co-workers' ambassadorship through LinkedIn, excellent input for their LinkedIn Profiles is required. Again, forcing this won't work, but many people are pleased to accept suggestions for their LinkedIn Profiles. In our training courses many participants don't even know where to start and are relieved to be offered help from the marketing or recruiting department!

Websites

We advise using the websites on the Profile of the employees in the following way:

1. **Website 1: link to the home page of the website of the organization** (for example: www.company-abc.com) using the same description for all co-workers. Remember to use the "Other" function to add the description.

2. **Website 2: link to the job website** or the job page on the website of the organization, using the same description for all co-workers. Again, use the "Other" function.

3. **Website 3: "free" link.** This can be used to link to a blog, a personal website, or a specific page on the website of the organization that relates to the individual's job. For example: www.company-abc.com/products/copiers.html for an account executive in the department for copiers.

Summary and Specialties

Remember the difference between Summary and Specialties. In Specialties you find jargon, abbreviations, and "tech talk". Use Summary to explain what you do in words that everybody can understand, whatever their background.

Remember our advice for the three blocks for the Summary:

1. **Block 1**: one paragraph about the organization that is the same for all co-workers. This elevates company branding.

2. **Block 2**: one or two paragraphs about the professional expertise of the individual. This helps their personal branding.

3. **Block 3**: one paragraph describing some personal interests. Show visitors to your Profile more than just your resume! When potential new employees see that your organization adopts this more personal approach, they may feel more welcome and more attracted to your organization.

If you want to have a consistent image as an organization, prepare the first block well. Also, provide everybody with examples for the 2 other blocks. Many people suffer writer's block when staring at a blank page.

Applications

As you could read in "Chapter 9: Lead Generation Tools & Visibility Boosters: Applications", Applications are amazing tools for lead generation. If you are working for a large organization, think about what they could do for your company!

First, make sure you (or your marketing or recruitment team) assemble the information for your co-workers. Remember we focus on building the Know, Like, Trust factor via Applications, not on direct sales or immediate recruitment.

The reasons for using documents that build the Know, Like, Trust factor:

- People who read your information will stay longer on the page. If you created interest and value, then they have a reason to go to your own website to learn more and get in touch with you (whether by leaving their email address, chatting with a representative, or anything else).

- Your co-workers will be more likely to add interesting content to their LinkedIn Profile than a marketing brochure.

For example:

- Have them link your company blog to their LinkedIn Profile
- PowerPoint slides with tips (for the SlideShare Application)
- PowerPoint slides with job openings (for SlideShare)
- A movie clip with tips (for Google Presentation)
- A movie clip (for Google Presentation) with (objective) testimonials from co-workers
- PDFs, Word documents, or MindMaps, with tips or job openings (for Box.net)

To achieve the most success, create an overview with tips, a Profile template, and a list of co-workers who have already modified their Profile. Present this information to the rest of the organization. The easier you make it for them the better and faster they will cooperate.

☞ **Assignment**: make your colleagues aware of interesting documents to use in Applications.

Remember if you want to get more leads, it is crucial to guide people to a website where they need to sign up for more free information.

These are some helpful resources:

- If you don't have a website yet, look at **Godaddy** (http://x.co/Ycxt). They offer domain names, hosting, and servers at a low price.
- To build your database and send them automated emails (this is called autoresponders), take a look at **Kickstartcart** (http://bit.ly/li-book27) and look

beyond the first outdated page. It's a very useful tool. Or use **Aweber** (http://bit.ly/li-book24). These websites also offer integrated payment solutions.

- If you only want to sell something on your website, use **PayPal** (http://bit.ly/li-book28).

- If you need help to make documents, slideshows, video or other ways of content, use **Elance** (http://bit.ly/li-book43). It is a market place for freelancers.

- To take it a step further and host a webinar to share tips like we do in our free LinkedIn Fundamentals webinar and our (paid) LinkedIn Steps to Success webinar series, use a tool like **GoToWebinar** (www.gotowebinar.com)

- If you want to record tips to share on your computer screen (like we do in the "Video & Tools Library"), use **Camtasia** for Windows or Mac (http://bit.ly/li-book32) or **IShowU** for Mac (http://bit.ly/li-book39).

- Take it a few steps further and self-publish a booklet or even a book or CD, look at **CreateSpace** (http://bit.ly/li-book39), it is part of Amazon.

Strategy 3: Improve your Organization's Visibility and Attract More Customers or Employees via Actions on LinkedIn

When you have created a Company Profile and all co-workers (or at least the ones who WANT to be your organization's ambassador) have an attractive Profile you have completed the first step—the passive phase.

Now go to the next level and ask them to become active as well.

Again we recommend preparing for this.

When you want the world to know something, like a new job opening or a new blog post with great tips, create the copy for the "Status Update" and ask (a selection of) your co-workers to post this Status Update and use it as a Tweet as well.

Tip: provide a link to your website, using a URL shortener like http://tinyurl.com. In this way you track the traffic, and if the link points to a website with nice graphics, those graphics are shown on someone's Profile as well. This makes it more appealing to read.

When you are a recruiter and want help from your colleagues, help them to help you. After providing them with a link to the job website, slides with job openings, and Status Updates/Tweets to post, also look up Groups wherein potential employees may be a member. Tell your colleagues about the Groups and ask them to post the job description in the Job Page.
Why have someone else do this instead of the recruiters themselves? Because recruiters are not in the "natural" network of the profiles they are looking for. For example, when recruiters are looking for a quality manager and they put a job description in the Group this will be perceived totally differently from one a quality manager does.

Do not be afraid of asking for help from future colleagues of the profile you are viewing. If you are going to help them reduce their workload by hiring someone for their team they will be more than willing to help you.

The Leverage Factor for an Organization of Applications and Actions

Applications have a leverage factor. For example a blog might help your organization be more visible on the web and on LinkedIn, using strategy 2 (Applications on Profiles) and strategy 3 (actions on LinkedIn). Let's look at some numbers to see what this leverage factor might be.

The larger the organization is, the greater the number of people who could contribute occasionally. If you have 50 people writing 1 blog post a year, you already have enough content for a whole year.

In reality you will learn that there is a small group of people who are already busy writing and would love to contribute on a very regular basis. Just ask who is interested.

When you link your blog to your personal LinkedIn profile and your Company Profile, those are automatically updated when a new article is posted on the blog.

If you are the only person working in your organization, the "leverage factor" is small: 1 blog post is shown on 1 LinkedIn Profile and on 1 Company Profile. Let's assume a person has on average 50 connections on LinkedIn and a small business has 30 followers via their Company Profile. Then the potential readership via LinkedIn is 80.

But if you are working for an organization with 1,000 colleagues who have linked the blog in their Profile (remember they have to do this only once) the "leverage factor" reaches 30,500:

- 1,000 colleagues times 30 connections = 30,000
- 500 people following the Company Profile = 500

Of course, this is theoretical. Not everyone reads the blog posts on their connections' profiles.

But you can increase the likelihood:

- Ask everybody to mention the blog post in a Status Update.
- Ask people who have a Twitter account to mention it there as well.
- Ask (a select group of) people to post it as a Discussion in the Groups.

Remark: *people will only take these proactive steps if the blog posts are interesting and helpful. For example: free tips outweigh sales pitches by far.*

In this way the potential readership can be increased even more.

Let's assume that:

- 100 people share the post via a LinkedIn Status Update times 30 connections: 3,000 extra potential views.
- 50 people share it via their Twitter account times 30 followers: 1,500 extra potential views.
- 50 people share it via a post in a LinkedIn Discussion with a membership of 1,000 people per Group: 50,000 extra potential views.

Result: in total we have 85,000 potential views.

Even if only 1% of the potential readers actually reads it, your blog post still has 850 readers.

An extra benefit is that this blog post will rank higher in Google. Why? Google registers traffic to a webpage. As a result, even more people will discover this blog post when making a general search on the web.

What excellent exposure for 30 minutes work per year (assuming that you have a pool of contributors who write one blog post per year)!

The Leverage factor might also apply to solo entrepreneurs

If you are a solo entrepreneur, you may feel this doesn't work for you.

Remember that the power of networking is in the second degree and you can utilize this by blogging in a business environment.

These are the steps to take

- Define your target group.
- Research other suppliers to this target group.
- Invite them to start a blog TOGETHER.
- Make a list of topics and who's going to write about which topic.
- Make a timeline and make sure the team has a blog post at least every week.

Advantages:

- You don't have to write much yourself. For example: if there are 5 contributors, each of you has to write only 10 blog posts a year!
- You benefit from each other's network: their network will read the post and you will be noticed. The same happens with your network and fellow bloggers when you post your tips and insights.

In other words: in this way you can have some of the same advantages as larger companies when using Twitter, LinkedIn Status Updates and posts in LinkedIn Group Discussions.

Strategy 4: Having an Attractive LinkedIn Profile for CEOs, C-level Executives, Spokespeople and Managers

From an organizational point of view some need an attractive LinkedIn Profile more than others.

In first instance one would think of sales people and recruiters since they are the most proactive ones.

But there are other roles that also need a high quality personal LinkedIn Profile to support the organization's needs.

Why an Attractive Profile is Necessary for CEOs, C-Level Executives and Spokespeople

Having an attractive LinkedIn Profile for CEO's, C-level executives and spokespeople is essential for marketing and PR reasons!

Today, when CEOs, General Managers, other chief executives and board members are mentioned in the press, often a link to their LinkedIn Profile is used in the interview or in the quote.

If people click on that link and see an incomplete, boring Profile they might assume that the organization represented is also boring.

Many recruiting and lead generation opportunities are missed in this way.

What can CEOs add to the already-mentioned tips from a marketing or PR point of view?

- A SlideShare presentation with tips showing their organization's expertise.
- The books they are reading via the Amazon Reading List (this adds a personal flavor to the Profile).
- A SlideShare presentation with their personal point of view or strategy that can be shared with the outside world.
- Box.net files application: share their notes, articles or interviews.
- A movie clip with tips, insights, an empowering message, or an interview.

It is important to avoid praising your own organization too much, but instead share information that can help others. Remember networking is based on building the Know, Like, and Trust factor.

Why an Attractive Profile is Necessary for All Managers

We assume you now understand why CEO's have to have an attractive LinkedIn Profile. But what about other managers? Let's look at a request from one of our customers.

A telecom company asked us to present a LinkedIn workshop for their managers only for the purpose of creating an attractive personal LinkedIn Profile.

But what was different, is that they didn't want to learn how to attract new customers, new employees, new partners, new investors or help some of them find a new job in an outplacement program (these are the questions we normally get). They only wanted to learn to create an attractive LinkedIn Profile.

When asked why they didn't want the usual topics, and why it was so important to have good LinkedIn Profiles, the answer was: "These are managers from our IT department who don't have to find new customers, suppliers, partners or investors and who are not in an outplacement program. The reason why they need to have an excellent LinkedIn Profile, is that **potential employees check our managers' LinkedIn Profiles before even considering applying for a job with us.**"

What we learned that day, is that is necessary to have an engaging LinkedIn Profile as a manager for **recruitment purposes**.

For managers, important features in their LinkedIn Profile to interest potential new employees include:

- Create an attractive **Summary** of your job description and interesting details about your current job. People like to work in an interesting environment with an inspired manager.

- Share a **specific function you held in the past**. This might be the actual job the other person is seeking.

- List all the jobs you did in the **past**. This shows your career path that other people might be interested to follow.

- **Link to the job site** of your company in the "Websites" field of your LinkedIn Profile.

- Use SlideShare, Google Presentation, Box.net and other applications to upload **presentations** you have given. Revealing the topics you are engaged in might appeal to potential employees.

- Use SlideShare, Google Presentation, Box.net and other applications to upload **job openings** in your team.

- Use SlideShare, Google Presentation, Box.net and other applications to **showcase** the activities of your team or department. (Note: this might also be beneficial for your visibility WITHIN your own organization)

- **Ask your team members as well to apply all these tips** They may set an even better example for the potential new employee.

These actions create a "passive" strategy. If you urgently need new team members we advise working jointly with your recruiters to develop a "proactive" strategy as well. When you **combine the experience of recruiters with the networks of managers in the business units, you will achieve additional recruitment power!**

How CEOs and Other Top Managers Can Have an Attractive LinkedIn Profile without Being Stalked

Although most organizations recognize the value of having an attractive LinkedIn Profile for a manager, many CEOs still lack a Profile on LinkedIn.

Reasons include fear of the unknown, not understanding the value of LinkedIn, and wanting to avoid stalking by annoying sales people.

Fortunately, LinkedIn has many ways to protect privacy and to limit the number of invitation requests, messages, and emails.

You can find these options in "Settings" (on top of each page on LinkedIn, click on the small arrow next to your name and it will pop up).

For CEOs it might come in handy to use these settings (under "Email Preferences"):

- Select the types of messages you're willing to receive -> I'll only accept Intro-ductions.

- Who may send you invitations -> only people who appear in your "Imported Contacts" list.

Of course, this approach severely restricts networking options, but it might help to persuade top management to have a LinkedIn Profile. No pesky sales person can stalk them while the organization enjoys the marketing, PR, and recruitment benefits of having a LinkedIn Profile.

☞ **Assignment**: inform your CEO, spokesperson, other C-level executives and managers of the importance of having an attractive LinkedIn Profile.

Strategy 5: Alumni Groups

Groups form the heart of LinkedIn. As we have seen in previous chapters, being both a member and a Group manager can benefit both the individual and the organization they represent.

An alumni Group can benefit organizations tremendously, but is often overlooked as a platform to bring together current and former co-workers.

Former employees can be valuable ambassadors of an organization, for both new customers and new employees. Many times this lever is overlooked because they don't have a clue how they could help their former employer.

The Group is a means to inform them of job openings. When aware of them, alumni might notify their network or even return to the organization themselves.

Another benefit of an alumni Group is access to specific knowledge or best practices. Often, knowledge departs with the employee. But if the current co-workers still have access to the now-external knowledge, the drain can be partially prevented.

Tips about running Groups can be found in "Chapter 12: The Heroes of LinkedIn: Group Managers".

If you want to combine Groups with live events (which we strongly recommend), read the tips in "Chapter 11: The Power of Combining Online and Offline Networking: Events".

☞ **Assignment**: join your organization's Alumni Group on LinkedIn.

Strategy 6: Advertising with LinkedIn

Some companies investigate the (paid) advertising opportunities LinkedIn offers.

For small to large companies there are the LinkedIn Ads that resemble Google ads; you see them on the right side of many of LinkedIn's pages.

For larger companies (those with a larger budget) there are other opportunities as well.

LinkedIn Ads

LinkedIn Ads are Google-like ads. You find them at the bottom of each page of LinkedIn under "Advertising".

Let's look at the steps you need to follow when you want to use these LinkedIn Ads.

1. **Create a campaign**
   a. Name Campaign
   b. Create up to 15 ad variations, including
      i. Name
      ii. Text
      iii. Landing page (a website or a LinkedIn page, for example, your Company Profile page)
      iv. Note: from xxx is automatically filled in whether with your name or that of your company (the latter is used when you access LinkedIn Ads from within your Company Profile to promote a product)

2. **Choose the target Audience**
   a. Geography
   b. Companies: by name or by category
   c. Job Title: by name or by category
   d. Group

e. Gender

f. Age: 18-24, 25-34, 35-54, 55+

g. Also reach LinkedIn members on other websites through the LinkedIn Audience Network (collection of partner websites that display targeted LinkedIn Ads on their sites): yes/no.

3. **Financial Options:**

a. Pay per Click or Pay per 1000 Impressions.

b. Daily Budget.

c. Show my Campaign: continuously or until a specific date.

LinkedIn Marketing Solutions

If you want to go a step further than LinkedIn Ads, you can look at the Marketing Solutions.

Via http://marketing.linkedin.com you can find an up-to-date overview of the solutions, more insights in the LinkedIn audience, success stories, and contact details.

Company Pages

As already mentioned, alongside the free Overview, Products & Services and Analytics page, there is also the Careers tab.

A job you post on LinkedIn automatically appears in the Careers tab.

You can also purchase a Premium Careers Page to appeal more to job seekers by creating interesting content, even directed toward the visitor's profile.

While you can grow the Recommendations for your products and services by asking yourself for Recommendations, LinkedIn also offers Recommendation Ads. These are network-aware ads that showcase your existing endorsements and seek more of them.

Custom Groups

For many organizations "Custom Groups" might help to create Groups of current and potential customers, and stakeholders.

You will get a more visually attractive and interactive Group (video, polls, Twitter, etc.), and LinkedIn also helps you find potential members for your Group. So your Group could grow very fast!

No ads (except your own) are shown in your Group. Thus, there is no potential danger from a competitor's ads.

However, the remarks regarding starting and maintaining successful Groups remain. See "Chapter 12: The Heroes of LinkedIn: Group Managers".

Display Ads

LinkedIn provides a variety of ads:

- Standard Ad Units and Text Links
- Homepage Takeover
- Content Ads
- Recommendation Ads

For details, see http://marketing.linkedin.com

Sponsorships

Companies can sponsor some of the content pages of LinkedIn. Sponsorships are available for:

- Answers
- Polls
- Applications
- Events

White Paper Distribution

Benefits:

- Deliver highly relevant white papers to specific audiences on LinkedIn.
- Pre-filled profile data in the registration form makes it easy for members to provide contact information and receive your white paper.

Partner Messages

Benefits:

- Deliver targeted messages to specific audience segments using LinkedIn's InMail messaging platform.
- Partner Messages allow for extensive marketing copy on a co-branded landing page, an ad unit, and a call-to-action element.

As you can see there are many ways LinkedIn helps organizations in their marketing. To receive more detailed information and read customer stories, contact LinkedIn directly at http://marketing.linkedin.com.

Strategy 7: Find New Customers Proactively

LinkedIn is a marvelous tool to find new customers.

Read the tips from "Chapter 14: How to REALLY Use LinkedIn to Find New Customers" and apply them with the whole sales team.

Strategy 8: LinkedIn Recruiting Solutions

To go a step further with your recruiting efforts, look into LinkedIn's Recruiting Solutions (paid tools).

The difference between LinkedIn and other job boards is that many people are not joining LinkedIn to find a job, but may be open for one.

LinkedIn Recruiting Solutions offer several ways to find new potential employees and increase employer branding.

You find Recruiting Solutions at the bottom of each page or go to http://talent.linkedin.com

The information in the rest of this subchapter is from the Recruiting Solutions pages.

Sourcing & Pipelining

Recruiter

Recruiter is LinkedIn's main tool for proactively seeking matching profiles. A major benefit is that it allows collaboration, which is not possible with a "normal" LinkedIn account, even with upgrades.

Benefits of Recruiter:

- Access to all LinkedIn Profiles, independent from the recruiter's own network.
- Up to 50 saved searches.
- The team shares 50 InMails per month/seat, which rollover if unused.
- InMail templates save time and allow sharing best practices with the whole team.
- Keeps the whole team on the same page with shared searches, profiles, notes on candidates, and InMails.
- Advanced project management tools allow organizing the workflow and keeping track of interactions with candidates.
- Set profile reminders to follow up with candidates in a timely manner.
- Post jobs directly from Recruiter to the LinkedIn Jobs network, helping find and target both passive and active candidates on LinkedIn.

There is also a special version for recruiting agencies and staffing firms, called Recruiter Professional Services.

Talent Direct

Talent Direct is a highly-targeted InMail Campaign.

Features:

- Your subject line appears on the candidate's LinkedIn home page for maximum visibility.

- Your message remains in the candidate's inbox until they act on it (click or clear).

- InMail links to a landing page matching your message to the candidate's profile.

- Landing page includes banner ad options and a prominent call-to-action button for easy response.

Jobs & Referral Hiring

Jobs Network

When you post a Job on LinkedIn, you tap the power of the Jobs Network.

Advantages:

- Members discover when job openings are a good fit for them or their connections.

- Referrals are simplified, with packaged messages that can be sent with a single click.

- The job poster can automatically broadcast openings to their connections.

- Jobs automatically get indexed by search engines and job aggregators.

- LinkedIn's matching algorithm generates a list of up to 50 strong candidates, most likely passive, for each position.

- Accurate and well-qualified member profile data targets jobs to the appropriate professionals.

- Candidates see how they are connected to the poster and your company.

- Quick links to company profiles or LinkedIn Custom Company Profiles provide relevant insights.

- Professionals interested in your company find your jobs on your LinkedIn company profile and in LinkedIn's Job Search engine.

Referral Engine

LinkedIn looks at the connections between candidates and your employees.

Features:

- Identify your employees' most qualified contacts — not just the active candidates.
- LinkedIn combines powerful matching algorithms with profile data to suggest the most appropriate candidates.
- Automatically deliver referral suggestions directly to employee email inboxes.
- Employees connect you with the best matches in just a few clicks.
- Engage employees with regular referral suggestions automatically.

Jobs for You - Web Ads

LinkedIn works together with other websites—the LinkedIn Audience Network.

The advantage is that if someone with a matching profile visits a website of the LinkedIn Audience Network, he or she will be shown an ad that fits their profile.

Recruitment Branding

Next to the recruitment tools, LinkedIn also has some offerings for branding. Let's look at the different options.

Career Pages

See above.

Recruitment Ads

Targeted ads, using several parameters such as profession, seniority, industry, company size, and more, are shown on the right side in the middle of the page.

Recruitment Insights

Recruitment Insights reveals which elements of your employment brand matter most to your target audience, allowing you to maximize the impact of your messages to attract top talent. It also helps to benchmark other companies and measure campaign effectiveness and return on investment (ROI).

Work with Us

Work with Us Ads give you exclusive ownership of the ad units on every one of your employees' LinkedIn profiles. Every time someone visits one of your employees' Profiles, they will see this ad.

As you can see there are many ways LinkedIn helps organizations find new employees. To receive more detailed information, case studies and white papers, contact LinkedIn directly at http://talent.linkedin.com.

Strategy 9: Attract New Employees Proactively

LinkedIn is a great tool to find new potential employees.

Read the tips from "Chapter 16: How to REALLY Use LinkedIn to Find New Employees" and apply them with the recruitment team.

Strategy 10: Find the Right Project Team Members

Many organizations today work with a matrix structure: people work together in one project and then continue on to the next.

In large, multinational organizations this structure has challenges: is the right knowledge available in-house and if so, will this person fit in the team?

Consequently, organizations have developed internal databases to capture at least an overview of the skills and knowledge of the current employees.

We have seen many problems with this approach:

- Not everybody keeps their data up-to-date since it doesn't always serve their own needs (many think it is bureaucratic hassle to be avoided).

- In the databases only the skills and knowledge related to the projects within the organization are stored, usually. Hence, valuable achievements at former employers might not be known inside a later organization.

- Most databases are created on a national level. As a result it is very difficult to do staffing for cross-border projects.

- Even if a project manager finds someone with the right skills, it is unknown whether this person will fit in the manager's personality and the rest of the team.

LinkedIn may help to overcome these issues:

- Many people don't update their profile in internal databases, but they do on LinkedIn. Showing their peers in other companies, their colleagues and friends about their professional career is a higher priority.

- On LinkedIn most people list their current skills and knowledge, and also courses they took in the past, and other possibly relevant information.

- LinkedIn knows no borders. Thus, it's very easy to find colleagues all around the world. Of course, this works only when everybody links his or her personal Profile to the same international parent company (as well as the national one where they work most of the time).

- Project managers can see how they are connected to the potential team members. The next step is to call the mutual contact and check internal references.

To find potential project team members, use the strategies from "Chapter 7: 10 Strategies to Find People Using LinkedIn".

Does LinkedIn solve all issues? No, but it can be a productive extra tool. Our advice is to use BOTH internal databases and LinkedIn to find the people who will be the best project team members.

Strategy 11: Find Internal and External Expertise

LinkedIn is a great tool to find new customers, new employees and project team members, and also to find experts inside and outside of your organization.

The larger the organization, the more difficult it is to know whether some expertise is already in-house or not. As a consequence, the same investigations are repeated many times inside the same organization.

LinkedIn can help to minimize this risk:

- Use "Advanced Search" to look for the expertise you need. Use the 5 step strategy from "Chapter 3: How To REALLY use LinkedIn: a 5 Step Basic Strategy".
- Use internal Groups and your organization's alumni Groups.
- Use external Groups of peers or other people who can help you find the solution.

For more tips, read "Chapter 14: How to REALLY use LinkedIn to Find New Customers" and replace the word "customer" with "expert".

☞ **Assignment**: find internal experts and other people who can help you getting your job done faster.

Conclusion of this Chapter

LinkedIn changes the process for marketing and recruiting managers. Instead of finding new customers and employees themselves their role will shift toward supporting their colleagues being ambassadors to open the door to new customers, suppliers, partners, employees, investors and other relevant people. Moreover, social media, including LinkedIn, invite us to explore how we work together and how much we trust ambassadors of our organization.

Organizations can use one or more of the following strategies to raise their visibility, (employer) branding, attract more customers and potential employees:

1. Use your Company Profile

2. Tap the power of individual LinkedIn Profiles

3. Make use of actions by employees on LinkedIn

4. Make an attractive Profile for CEO's, C-level Executives, Spokespeople and Managers

5. Benefit from alumni Groups

6. Advertise on LinkedIn

7. Use a proactive sales strategy

8. Use LinkedIn's Recruiting Solutions

9. Use a proactive recruitment strategy

10. Find the right project team members

11. Find the experts inside or outside your organization

Remark: we observe that more and more organizations start to realize that the benefit of networking is in the combination of online AND offline networking. As a result, we have experienced a shift from requests for individual training courses to integrated ones. For example: in the past we got requests for a LinkedIn workshop for recruiters or a training course about "Networking at Events" for sales people. Now we get more requests to have an introductory session for the WHOLE organization (passive strategy) first and then (proactive) integrated LinkedIn, "networking at events" and referral workshops for smaller teams from the sales and recruitment departments. With this trend in mind we invite you to re-evaluate your organization's network strategy. It is one of the most powerful and cheapest resources available. Use it!

Chapter 18: More Insights: News & Labs

LinkedIn is more and more focused on bringing together the right people and the right information in the professional world. That's why they have added the "News" and "Labs" sections. Let's look at what they are about.

News

In the top menu you find the "News" menu. At the time of writing there were 3 sub-menus: LinkedIn Today, Saved Articles, and Signal.

LinkedIn Today

LinkedIn Today gives an overview of business-related news.

LinkedIn is proud of the fact that the top articles are those shared on LinkedIn or tweeted on Twitter, not picked by an editor.

You can also see who shared the article. You can even filter on Company Name, Industry, and Location.

A nice feature is that you can personalize your Front Page, using the "Browse All" link in the LinkedIn Today menu.

You can select (by choosing "follow" and "unfollow"):
- Categories like Automotive, Banking, IT, Staffing and Recruiting, and Non-Profit.
- Sources like Cable News Network TV (CNN), Harvard Business Review, and the Wall Street Journal, and also SlideShare.

You can save an article you like. Later on you can find it via "News/Saved Articles" (top menu) or via the "Saved" link in the LinkedIn Today menu.

You can also search any topic via the "search box". You will end up in LinkedIn Signal (see below).

If you never visit this page, you will get an email with news from your preferred categories. By default you will receive a weekly digest email, but you can change this to daily or no email via the "Settings" menu, "Email preferences -> Set the frequency of emails" and then "Top articles news digest". Or you can use the Email Settings in the LinkedIn Today menu (small arrow on the right hand side).

You can also read LinkedIn Today on your Smartphone and save articles for later.

LinkedIn Signal

Signal lets you see and filter updates and tweets from LinkedIn professionals who choose to make their updates visible to anyone.

It is similar to Twitter, but with many more filters.

Filter the Signal stream by:

- Network
  - o Your own status updates and tweets
  - o First-degree status updates and tweets
  - o Second-degree status updates and tweets
  - o Third-degree + anyone status updates and tweets
  - o Combination of above options
- Company
- Location
- Industry
- Time
  - o Last Minute
  - o Last Hour
  - o Last Day
  - o Last Week
  - o Last 2 Weeks
- School
- Group
- Topics (selection via Twitter hashtags)
- Update Type
  - o Shares
  - o Groups
  - o Profiles
  - o Answers
- View Updates per Category
  - o Status Updates
  - o Profile Updates
  - o Company Updates
  - o Questions and Answers
- View Updates per Connection

Depending on the magnitude of your network and your filter options, you might receive an avalanche of information or a smaller stream of relevant content.

You can save your parameters using the "save this search" option on top of the page. It then becomes available as a link on the top left side under the search box.

How to apply this in practice? For example you can save a search to find which of your first-degree contacts has changed anything in their Profile in the last day, week, or two weeks. This will help you to stay current if your contact person at a customer changes position, or to congratulate someone from your network if they are promoted.

☞ **Assignment**: explore LinkedIn Today and Signal.

Watch a small video about using Signal to keep up-to-date with your network, go to the "Video & Tools Library" at www.how-to-really-use-linkedin.com.

LinkedIn Labs

There is no direct link between the LinkedIn and the Labs websites (http://labs. linkedin.com), making them unknown to most people. As you may have never heard of LinkedIn Labs, we will discuss the introduction and different applications.

LinkedIn Labs Introduction

LinkedIn Labs share projects and experimental features built by LinkedIn employees. These employees are encouraged to work on ideas that inspire, and some are worth sharing.

Experiments are products and innovations that LinkedIn is testing; they are intended to be low-maintenance and may have some kinks needing work. Over time some experiments may become full production features, while others may eventually disappear from Labs. Check back regularly as LinkedIn employees are always creating something new!

LinkedIn Labs Experiments

Some LinkedIn Labs experiments might provide more insights into your LinkedIn network or help get more results.

InMaps

Visualize your professional network, clustered in real-time based on their inter-relationships.

This might give you more insights in who is related to whom.

However, when you have a large network, this application isn't of much use because the visuals become blurred.

Link: http://bit.ly/li-book62

Infinity

Visualize your professional network with a wall of profile photos. You can easily scroll through all of your connections. When clicking on a contact's photo, you see the Professional Headline, Status Update, and Summary.

Link: http://bit.ly/li-book63

Connection Timeline

View your connections across the timeline of your career.

In a small movie your own photo goes along a timeline. Your LinkedIn first- degree contacts appear in the first year you have in common with them (this information comes from both your and their Profiles). It doesn't mean you got to know each other that year. For example: you may have met a colleague in 2008, and you both went to the same university in 1990.

When you click on someone's photo you arrive at his or her LinkedIn Profile.

Link: http://bit.ly/li-book64

Year in Review

This is a visual representation of everyone in your network who changed jobs in a given year (starting from 2009).

You might be a little bit familiar with this application since you probably received an email from LinkedIn in January with an overview of people who changed jobs, due to "Year in Review".

You see an overview of photos of first-degree contacts who that changed jobs in a given year. When you click on their photo arrive at their LinkedIn Profile.

Link: http://bit.ly/li-book67

Resume Builder

To use your LinkedIn Profile to make a resume, this tool might help.

Options:

- Choose between several templates
- Outline: rearrange content and choose what is visible and what not
- Share via email, LinkedIn, Twitter, Facebook
- Privacy: select who can see your resume: anyone on the web, only someone who already is linked, or only you.
- PDF/Print: makes a PDF file of your resume. This is the best way to print it.

If you have updated your LinkedIn Profile, you need to do a manual refresh with the "Resume Builder" to reflect the changes.

Link: http://bit.ly/li-book65

Other LinkedIn Lab experiments

There are other LinkedIn Lab experiments, but they might not be as interesting to you as the ones mentioned above.

- **NewIn**: This application shows new members joining LinkedIn from around the world (requires Google Earth). Fun to watch, but not useful.
  Link: http://bit.ly/li-book66
- **Swarm:** A visualization of popular company search queries on LinkedIn. Again, nice to watch, but not of much use. Link: http://bit.ly/li-book67

Go for an updated list to http://labs.linkedin.com

Conclusion of this Chapter

LinkedIn provides you with several tools to stay up-to-date with what's going on within your network and with professional news.

You might want to refine LinkedIn Today to your own preferences and create some "saved searches" on Signal.

To get more insights in your network, you might want to try out some of the experiments from the LinkedIn Labs like:

- InMaps
- Infinity
- Connection TimeLine
- Year In Review
- Resume Builder

Chapter 19: Answers to Hot Discussion Topics and Burning Questions

Due to the great numbers of questions we receive about following or not following certain strategies, we have listed some topics that always lead to discussions, and also answers to frequently asked questions.

Sometimes we provide direct advice; other times we will show you both sides of a discussion.

Not Everybody is on LinkedIn so it Doesn't Work.

A comment we hear often is: "Not every person or every function is on LinkedIn. I can't always find the right person. LinkedIn doesn't work for me." It is true that not everybody is a member of LinkedIn. But the network is growing VERY fast. **Every second a new member joins LinkedIn!** So maybe the person you were looking for signed up today.

A few years ago, when LinkedIn didn't exist, it was almost impossible to find paths between people. Or it cost a lot of time. Now LinkedIn makes it a much easier. If you don't find the person you are looking for, then do it "the old way".

We repeat: despite the fact that not every person is on LinkedIn, it is a website for business networking. The majority of organizations is represented on LinkedIn (In the USA, all Fortune 500 companies have an executive-level presence). Maybe you won't find the Marketing Manager of a company, but you might find the IT Manager. The Marketing Manager is only one step away from him. This solution is still much easier than before LinkedIn existed.

No-one Has Contacted Me Yet, So LinkedIn is a Useless Business Tool.

On the contrary! LinkedIn is a super tool, to help you find people who are in the best position to help you reach your goals.

However, many people think that if they make just a Profile other people will contact them. When we ask the people who complain about this if they ever contacted someone, almost all remain silent.

If you apply the strategies explained in this book to use LinkedIn proactively, it can quickly bring you new customers, a new job, new employees, suppliers, partners, sponsors, volunteers, expertise, and more.

Remember that if you want to see results, you have to take action. And LinkedIn is a great tool to support you.

I am Happy with My Current Professional Situation, Why Should I Build a Network on LinkedIn (or Elsewhere)?

All the tips in this book are suggestions and tips derived from our experience having given hundreds of training courses and presentations about online/offline networking and referrals. Also, we share what we have experienced from using LinkedIn ourselves.

Almost everybody needs some expert advice once in a while, or could use new connections inside or outside a company. LinkedIn helps you to find these experts and the people who can introduce you to them.

The second—and maybe even more important reason—is that we see too many people only start building their network when it is too late. People who were unexpectedly fired and needed to find a new job suddenly realized a network could help them. Then they join LinkedIn and start building their network, which takes time. In many cases, this is time they don't have.

The same applies to entrepreneurs. We meet many people who have a great idea, leave their job, start a company, invest a lot of money and after a few months realize they also need customers; many customers, and fast, because expensive monthly costs and investments are accumulating. Only then they realize they should have started building their network months ago.

In these two examples they start building the network when they NEED it URGENTLY. This creates a sense of desperation. People sense this and it turns them off. So start building your network before you actually need it. You can then interact normally with the networking attitude of sharing without expecting anything immediately in return.

Why Would I Use LinkedIn if I Can Use Google to Find Information?

Google is an excellent resource to find information. So use it when you look for **information**.

LinkedIn is a collection of people and the relationships between them. Use LinkedIn when you are looking for a **person**.

People with Thousands of Connections.

Some members of LinkedIn have tens of thousands of contacts. Most of the time they call themselves LIONS, which is an abbreviation of LinkedIn Open Networkers. They are open to anyone who wants to connect with them and they also actively connect with as many people as possible.

Since LinkedIn shows the amount of people you have in your network only up to 500, many of them will list in their description how many connections they actually have. Examples are [+7500] or [+21K].

Many times we hear in our presentations and training courses: "These people are focused only on collecting people (like stamps), they are not looking for real connections". Some of the participants then say they want to connect only with people they know very well and whom they are willing to recommend.

The LIONS themselves defend their number of connections by claiming that they can connect with many people to reach their goals, and that they are also able to help people from their network better because they have so many connections.

Our own approach lies in between those points of view, and relates to the quality-diversity topic we addressed in the first chapter.

Personally, we connect with people:

- When we have met them personally in real life and had a conversation of at least 10 minutes.

- Or when they start by sending us a personal message with a good reason why they want to connect with us, and our relationship has developed as a result.

- Or when they fit into (one of our) networking goal(s) and we have taken action to start building the relationship.

So does that mean we connect with everybody? No, neither of us is a LION. We acknowledge there is value in having a large network, but for us there still has to be a personal contact moment. Only when we've had a personal experience with contacts will we write a Recommendation for them.

Which approach should you take? It's up to you. We shared the two different perspectives so you can make an educated choice.

Block Access to LinkedIn for Employees?

Some organizations block websites like LinkedIn because they fear that their employees will get job offers from other companies. Others block LinkedIn and other websites because their employees spend too much time there.

Blocking the websites is not a good idea in our opinion.

For organizations that fear their employees might leave because someone contacts them, we have the same remark as for people who fear their competitors might "steal" their customers because they have connections. If people are content, they won't leave a company. So make sure they feel happy and respected. Then you have nothing to fear. If they are unhappy and you block LinkedIn at work, they will use it at home on their own time.

For organizations that fear that their employees are wasting their time on LinkedIn instead of being productive we have the following advice: instead of blocking websites, teach people how to use them to save time and get better results faster. Blocking websites like LinkedIn doesn't make much sense in today's world where almost everybody and everything is connected. Social networks are the tools of the younger generations who will continue to use them. There is no stopping them from doing that in their spare time. Instead of resisting these technologies, use them to your advantage.

Hide or Show My Connections?

On the "Settings" page under "Profile" and after following the link "Select who can see your connections" you can turn off the option allowing other people to browse through your network from your Profile.

Sometimes people claim reasons to be unwilling to show their network. We always ask the question: "What do you expect from other people on LinkedIn? Do you expect them to open their network to you, but you don't want to reciprocate?" This doesn't seem fair to us.

If you don't allow your network to see your connections but have no expectations for them to share their connections with yours—that is fair.

Some people don't want others to browse through their connections because they don't want their competitors to see their customers. If you fear that someone might "steal" your customers because they see the connections on LinkedIn, then you better improve your relationship with your customer. Satisfied customers don't switch, even neutral ones do not switch necessarily. Because change brings uncertainty, people generally like to stay where they are and especially when they get a product/service of a good quality for a reasonable price.

Remarks:

- If you use the search function and find someone who is in the network of a contact who has turned off the "Connections Browse", both will still appear in the list.
- You will also always see shared connections with the people who don't allow you to browse their network.
- In other words, hiding connections is not 100% effective.

When Should I Start Building My Network?

The answer is: now! Many people only start building or maintaining their network when they need a job, new customers or something else. And most of the time they start when they urgently need a network. As a consequence, they are under such time pressure that they want to bypass the fundamental principles of networking. People react negatively toward this rushed, self-serving behavior, which makes the jobless or people looking for new customers even more desperate to bypass the principles, thus sinking into a downward spiral.

So start building your network now when you are not under time pressure. Apply the fundamental principles and enjoy the process.

How Much Time Do I Have to Spend on LinkedIn?

We all are different people, with different personalities and different goals.

Some people love to be as connected as possible via telephone, email, online networking, and instant messaging. Others like to work alone or enjoy a quiet time in the evenings and weekends.

There are also times in your life where you want or need more interaction than at other times.

So which approach to take?

We advise you to invest time in applying the basic strategy, write down the G.A.I.N. exercise© for one goal (see the '"Video & Tools Library" at www.how-to-really-use-linkedin.com) and then use the strategy that best fits your situation to experience the value of LinkedIn.

Afterward, it is your own choice how much time you allocate to LinkedIn.

We suggest as a minimum time allocation when you are not actively working on a goal (maintenance) one hour a week to look at the Discussions of the Groups you have joined, and contribute to them. Also, look at the Network Updates from your network and see if you could connect some people or respond to a question in Answers.

As well as a daily or weekly update of your Groups' exchanges, we also suggest to have personal messages delivered immediately so you can seize an opportunity. When people are looking for someone or something they nowadays don't have much time to wait for a reply.

Can I Only Connect with People I Know Very Well? If I Connect with Others I Can't Recommend Them.

It is important to keep in mind the difference between an introduction and a recommendation. You can honestly recommend only people you know by experience. But you can make plenty of introductions. You can always introduce two people to each other without knowing either well. However, the words you use when you make the introduction are important.

If you have met someone only for 5 minutes, but think that he might be of help to one of your business contacts, use a phrase like: "Hi Marie, I want to introduce you to John Smith. I met John at the Safety conference last week. In the few minutes we were able to chat he told me he just finished doing a safety project at a large chemical plant. Maybe he can help you, too, with your projects."

When you use words like "met last week, a few minutes, and maybe" Marie will know that you don't have any personal experience with John and that you are not in a position to recommend him. But she will be pleased about your thought to help her.

When is a Relationship Good Enough to Send Someone an Invitation? And How to Do That?

No number of meetings or number of hours you talked with someone can be an indicator. Sometimes you can send an invitation after one conversation; other times you will never send one.

For us the indicator is how the conversation went. Did you share something in common? Was there some rapport? Bringing up LinkedIn in a conversation also helps facilitate the process. You can then learn whether this person uses LinkedIn or not, and how he feels about receiving invitations. (If they say, "LinkedIn is a waste of my time and useless like Facebook or Netlog", it is better to NOT send an Invitation because it could impair your reputation with them.)

The best way to mention LinkedIn is after you have focused in the conversation on what you could do for the other person or whom you could connect him to. Then it is easy to say: "May I send you an invitation on LinkedIn so you will be immediately connected via me with the person we were discussing?"

Always find a way to help someone else: often this opportunity is via your network.

I Have Many Contacts from Years Ago, May I Still Contact Them?

Yes, you may always reconnect with them. Don't feel concerned that your last contact dates from such a long time ago. They didn't take action either and probably share the same hesitation.

When you reconnect with them, always make your message personal. Refer to the time you have spent together, the projects you have worked on or the time in college. In your invitation message use the name you were known by at that time. This applies especially to people who now use the name of their partner.

What to Do with an Invitation from Someone I Don't Know Very Well?

Of course, it depends on your own strategy with LinkedIn and the nature of the invitation. But let's assume you don't want to be connected. There are four choices:

1. **Do nothing**. Don't accept, don't push on "Ignore" or "Report Spam" and don't reply.

2. **Use the "Ignore" button.** Clicking this button will move the invitation to your "Archived" folder without accepting it. The other person won't be notified that you've ignored their invitation, so they may try to connect with you again. After you have clicked on the "Ignore" button you can choose "I don't know *name*", "Report as Spam", or do nothing. When you choose "I don't know *name*", this is registered with LinkedIn. They won't be able to send you any more Invitations. If someone gets too many "I don't know *name*" registrations, their account will be restricted. This limits their Invitations to only those whose email address they know. The same applies to "Report as Spam", but this is even more strict. Be aware that this could happen to you if you invite people who don't know you.

3. **Use the "Reply" button** (small arrow of the "Accept" button) to explain that you connect only with people you know well. We used to ignore impersonal messages, but were glad to switch to the "reply, don't accept" option. We learned that many people don't know how to work with LinkedIn properly (yet). In several cases we were glad we used the "reply" button because we could have missed important customers who tried to get in touch with an impersonal "Hi, I'd like to add you to my network" message.

4. **Accept the invitation**. Then later use "Remove Connections" (top right side under "Contacts/My Connections"). This person won't be notified of the removal.

How to Deal with Invitations from People I Don't Know at All (or Believe I Don't Know)?

A great number of people don't know they can personalize the invitation message, and some don't even see a good reason why they should.

We hope you understand by now that LinkedIn is a tool to build relationships. It is hard building relationships with impersonal messages. Next to that, an invitation is another contact moment you have with a particular person. So make your messages personal!

However, few people send a personalized invitation. Personally we receive a lot of impersonal messages. Because we meet many people sometimes we don't know if we have already met them or not. From these experiences we have developed the policy to always reply, even if it's just with a semi-personal message.

These are two messages Jan uses:

Message 1:

Hi, xxx,

Thank you for your invitation to connect!

Unfortunately, I meet so many people I can't always connect the name and face.

Please help by reminding me where we met?

Thanks and have a great networking day!

Jan

Message 2:

Dear xxx,

Thanks for your message! However I meet a lot of people and I receive many requests to connect.

I have written a blog article about sending and accepting LinkedIn Invitations: http://tinyurl.com/2vlxxpa

Let me know your response!

Jan

It depends on the answer whether we accept the invitation or not. If we never hear from them again, then we take no further action. If they are indeed able to refresh our memory or give us a good, personal reason to connect with us, we accept the invitation.

How to Deal with Requests for Recommendations from People I Don't Really Know

People commonly fear that an invitation to connect with people they don't know personally may lead to a request to recommend them. Understandably, they don't want to give a recommendation if they have no personal experience with them.

Guidance for what do when you are connected to someone you don't really know and they ask you for a recommendation can be found in "Chapter 10: Personal Branding, Raising Your Visibility and Credibility on LinkedIn".

Should I Include All My Previous Employers in My Profile?

It depends on your situation.

If you are looking for a new job, you might want to do it for a complete resume. Since recruiters always compare your LinkedIn Profile with your resume, you had better be sure they have the same information.

If you own your own company, it makes sense to mention only the experience that is relevant for your current position and what you desire in the future.

Also remember that LinkedIn uses the "current and previous employers" fields to match you with current and former colleagues. If you don't put some previous employers in your Profile, LinkedIn will be unable to present you and your former colleagues with each other as potential connections.

Do I Need to Upgrade My Account?

Most people are content with a basic (free) account. However, if you are a heavy LinkedIn user who wants more than 5 introductions en route at the same time, who wants to contact people directly via InMail, who wants to have more than 3 "Saved Searches", who wants to use "Profile Organizer" or who wants to be able to do reference searches, then you should upgrade.

LinkedIn offers three kinds of upgraded memberships for individual users:

- Job Seekers: see "Chapter 15: How to REALLY Use LinkedIn to Find A New Job"

- Talent Finder (for recruiters and hiring managers): see "Chapter 16: How to REALLY Use LinkedIn to Find New Employees". There are also Recruitment Solutions for teams.

- LinkedIn Premium Accounts: see table below.

Below is an overview of the most interesting features of LinkedIn Premium Accounts:

Feature / Account Type	Free (Basic)	Business Plus	Executive	Pro	Our remarks and opinion
Send Requests for Introductions	5 per month	25 outstanding	35 outstanding	50 outstanding	Although this might be an appealing function, it is always better to have someone else send a Magic Mail or send a normal message to you and the person you want to reach, because the action comes from someone they know instead of from a stranger.
Send InMails	No	10 per month	25 per month	50 per month	An InMail is a direct message to someone who is not in your network and who is not a member of the OpenLink network (see below). This is a way to directly reach people, but everybody can turn off the option to be contacted through InMail. An introduction via a mutual (trusted) contact always works better. However, when you need to get in touch immediately, this could be a useful option.
Receive OpenLink Messages	No	Unlimited	Unlimited	Unlimited	Everybody with an upgraded account can choose whether or not anyone can send them a direct message, even if they are not first-degree contacts. This can be an interesting feature for account managers who want to make it easy for potential customers to get in touch with them.
Reference Searches	No	Yes	Yes	Yes	This is a valuable option to check with some colleagues or to find someone you want to hire or have as business partner.

Feature / Account Type	Free (Basic)	Business Plus	Executive	Pro	Our remarks and opinion
Search Results	100	500	700	1000	In our opinion more than 100 search results makes sense only for sales people using LinkedIn to make a list of prospects and for recruiters. Even then, it makes sense to add extra search criteria to diminish the results.
Saved Searches	Maximum 3, weekly alerts	Maximum 5, weekly alerts	Maximum 10, daily alerts	Maximum 15, daily alerts	Saved Searches which run automatically (alerts) are interesting: when someone joins with a Profile of interest, or changes jobs, you are notified automatically. This is a very useful feature.
Expanded LinkedIn Network Profiles	No	Yes	Yes	Yes	When you have an upgraded account you can see expanded Profiles of everybody. Otherwise, you can see only the expanded Profile of the people in your first-, second- and third- degree networks, and your fellow Group members.
Who's Viewed My Profile: Get the full list	No	Yes	Yes	Yes	Although you can see the entire list of people who have visited your Profile, their settings define their visibility. If they have chosen to be anonymous, you will never find out who they are.
Save important profiles and notes using Profile Organizer	No	25 folders	50 folders	75 folders	With Profile Organizer, you can: • Save important profiles for 1-click access • Create multiple folders to organize your profiles • Add detailed notes to each profile This might be useful if you want to keep interesting profiles at hand.

Feature / Account Type	Free (Basic)	Business Plus	Executive	Pro	Our remarks and opinion
Premium Search Filters	No	Premium Filters	Premium + Talent Filters	Premium + Talent Filters	These search filters give you extra options. See table below.

Premium (4 filters)	Premium + Talent (8 filters)
Seniority	Seniority
Company Size	Company Size
Interests	Function
Fortune 1000	Interests
	Years of Experience
	Fortune 1000
	Your Groups
	New to LinkedIn

Our conclusion: at the time of writing most people do not need to upgrade their account.

You can find an overview of actual features and fees on the "Settings" page. On the left side you will find the link "Compare account types".

If Only a Few People Pay for Their Membership, Where Does LinkedIn Get Its Money?

In addition to venture capitalists who invested in the company and the stock market, these are LinkedIn's revenue channels:

- Recruitment Solutions
- Advertising: LinkedIn Direct Ads and special projects for larger customers
- Upgraded accounts

Remark: in the Help Center pages LinkedIn says, "Joining LinkedIn is and will remain free."

What is the Number of Connections I Need to Make LinkedIn Work for Me?

Of course it depends on the situation. Many contacts with people from the Telecom sector in Australia will not help if you want to find a job in the Health sector in Budapest.

If you have followed the strategies in this book, we can agree with Jason Alba who stated in "I'm on LinkedIn, Now What?" (http://amzn.to/li-book20) that 60 connections and their networks should be enough to reach one's goals.

Should I Add My Email Address to My Name?

Many LIONs and others who want to receive many invitations apply this tactic. You can do this, but be warned that it is against the LinkedIn User Agreement. As far as we know, they haven't banned anyone yet, but they have the right to do so.

What is the Value of Recommendations?

Many people get Recommendations from friends and befriended co-workers who are not very objective or give vague Recommendations. Only a specific Recommendation is of value.

A few remarks:

- It is better to have a few Recommendations than none.
- People who really value Recommendations will read them. If the Recommendations lack details, they will be ignored.
- That's why it is important to ask for a modification if you are not happy with a Recommendation. Ask the other person to be more specific.
- People value Recommendations from people they know (their first- degree network) more than from strangers. Then there is the possibility to check these Recommendations. If they do that and the person who gave the Recommendation can't add any details, the Recommendation will be considered useless.

My Profile is Not 100% Complete. How Will People React to This?

Relax. Nobody else can see your percentage. This percentage is only to help *you* to develop your Profile.

I Want to Reach the Help Desk, but I Can't Find the Contact Form.

During the last couple of years LinkedIn has been changing the location of the Help Center and we hope the current location is permanent.

At the bottom left of each page you will notice the "Help Center" link. Click on it and search in the database. After you have done that the second tab on top titled "Contact Us" becomes available. Post your question here. LinkedIn is a multinational company and has employees working in the Help Center who speak different languages. (For all official LinkedIn languages there are native- speaking Help Center employees, and sometimes also for languages that are not officially supported). So ask your question in your mother tongue. If they don't understand, they will let you know.

How Do I Put Video on My Profile?

Normally, you can't put video on your Profile, unless you use Google Presentation (or SlideShare, but we don't recommend that) together with a YouTube movie.

See "Chapter 10: Personal Branding, Raising Your Visibility and Credibility on Linked-In" for the steps to accomplish this.

How Do I Save My Searches and Where Can I Find the Ones I Have Already Saved?

After you have performed a search, next to the number of results you find the option: Save this search. Depending on your account type you may have 3 (basic account=free) to 10 saved searches.

To find your "Saved Searches" go to your Home Page, click on "Advanced (Search)" and then you will see that "Saved Searches" is tab four at the top of the page.

When to Send and Accept Invitations?

Let us share Jan's personal policy about accepting LinkedIn Invitations, which he has posted on his blog. This also indicates when sending an Invitation might be a good idea and when not. Feel free to comment on the blog (http://bit.ly/li-book21).

Jan's personal policy regarding accepting LinkedIn Invitations

I give a lot of presentations to large audiences about networking, referrals, and LinkedIn.

Mostly, I include a moment to talk about the Know, Like, Trust factor in the session.

If people come up to me afterward, and we have a nice 10 minute chat in which they explain what they do, my Know and Like factor towards them might have increased enough to accept a LinkedIn invitation to continue building the relationship online and offline. This doesn't mean that I already trust them (or even know and like them enough) to introduce them to other people, but it is a start toward building a relationship.

What happens a lot is that people who were in the audience and didn't come up and talk to me, send me the impersonal "Hi I'd like to add you to my network" message afterwards and then are disappointed when I don't accept their invitation.

At least, I require some background information where we have met and why you want to connect with me (even if it's for your own benefit, not mine, clarity is still important). Make some effort to create a personal invitation to show me that you care to build a relationship. Keep the Know, Like, Trust factor in mind: what do you expect from me (or from someone else) when we have never met and never have talked with each other. How would you react if a total stranger does the same thing to you?

Adding to the previous statement from my personal experience: I meet approximately 1500 people EACH year face-to-face and tens of thousands of people EACH year attend a seminar, conference, workshop, or web seminar where I am one of the speakers or the only speaker. My profession is different from that of most people with its pros and cons. Pro: I meet a lot of very interesting people. Con: typically I don't have enough time to spend even with the people I want to spend time with. Some people meet only tens of people of year due to the nature of their job, so for them it might be easier to be more personal.

Whether it's me you want to invite to connect with on LinkedIn or someone else, it's always a good idea to follow these 3 steps:

1) Ask yourself: "Why do I want this connection?"

2) Keep the Know, Like, Trust factor in mind.

3) Customize your invitation to initiate a real connection and to show the other person that you are willing to make an effort to start or continue building the relationship.

How Can I Download the Contact Details of My LinkedIn Connections?

A frequent question during our networking and LinkedIn courses is: "How do I get my contact details out of LinkedIn and into the contacts folder in my email program?"

If you want to download **only one person's contact details**, follow these steps:

1) Go to their Profile

2) At the bottom of the "short overview" box under your name and picture you see a few action items and a few icons (the first icon is named "Share")

3) Click on the fourth icon, vCard.

4) Import it to your email program (in some email programs this is automatically done when you press "save")

If you want to download the **contact details of all of your connections**, follow these steps:

1) Choose from the top menu "Contacts" and then "My Connections"
2) Scroll down to the bottom of the page
3) Under the table, above the menu at the bottom, click on "Export connections"
4) On the next page, choose your email program or type of export
5) Save the file
6) Import the file in your email program

Important: this only works for your first-degree contacts!

> If you want to watch a small video about downloading the contact details of your first-degree network, go to the "Video & Tools Library" at www.how-to-really-use-linkedin.com.

Why Does LinkedIn Tell Me There is a Website in My Invitation When There is none?

When you send out an invitation, you sometimes receive the notification: "You can't use websites (URL's)".

When you then look at your message, you see no website.

This response is caused by a missing space after a period. For example, "Hello Dan, nice to see you on this **website.Do** you remember the time when ..."

There is no space between "website" and "Do" and hence LinkedIn thinks it is a website. Normal punctuation will avoid this.

How Can I Change the Order of My Current Positions?

Many people are on boards of organizations, or volunteer, or have a job on the side and want to share that information on their Profile.

The problem is that the most important position is not always the first that is shown.

To change the ranking of a position you have to cheat a little bit. Since LinkedIn ranks the most recent first, you need to change the dates so the most important position is the most recent one.

The Person I Want to Connect with on LinkedIn Has Only a Few Connections. Now What?

A common misunderstanding about a professional networking website is that such websites don't work when the people you are looking for are not very active.

Remember that a major benefit of LinkedIn is that it reveals who is connected to whom.

Thus we see who can introduce us to the customer, partner, employer, employee, investor, expert or other person whom we want to meet.

So it doesn't matter much whether they are active or not.

To get in contact with the people you want to meet, always consider these three steps:

1. Use a professional networking website as a research database to see who is connected to whom.

2. Pick up the telephone and call the person you both know.

3. Ask to be introduced via a Magic Mail.

Conclusion of this Chapter

In this chapter you received answers to the many frequently asked questions in our training courses, presentations, and webinars.

Recall the advice in this chapter when using LinkedIn. Also return to this chapter when you have a question yourself.

If you haven't found an answer to your question, you might also consult the "Answers" section on LinkedIn (subcategory Using LinkedIn). If you still haven't found an answer yet, you can always contact the LinkedIn Help Center (at the bottom of every page).

You could also post your question in the Global Networking Group (http://linkd.in/li-book11). Our Networking Coach team and lots of other people are willing to look at your question, too.

Chapter 20: Little Known, But Interesting Features and Behavior of LinkedIn

LinkedIn has many small and big features, which are generally unknown. Or at least not enough people understand how they really work.

This chapter will provide more insights into those sometimes hidden gems, and sometimes seemingly obvious options.

LinkedIn is a Three-Degree Network

It is important to know that LinkedIn considers only your first three degrees as your network. Connections of the fourth degree or higher will appear as "out of your network". This restriction makes sense because the more degrees in between, the less personal the connections and the harder to reach them.

If you still want to reach people who are not in your network, become a member of a Group they have joined. Then you can contact them directly (if they didn't change the standard Group settings; what most people don't).

Hidden Connections Can Still be Found

You can turn off the option allowing others to browse your network from your Profile. On the "Settings" page under "Profile" choose "Select who can see your connections"

However, mutual connections are always visible.

If this person who is not allowed to see your first-degree connections uses the search function and finds someone who is one of your connections, they will still see that you are the (wo)man in the middle.

Direct Contact Still Possible Despite Invitation-Filtering

On the "Settings" page under "Email preferences/Select who can send you Invitations" you can choose who may contact you:

1. Anyone on LinkedIn (default).

2. Only people who know your email address or appear in your "Imported Contacts" list.

3. Only people who appear in your "Imported Contacts" list.

Some people choose option 2 or 3 to limit invitations and messages to only people they know.

However, they still can receive messages from people they don't know, such as the members of the Groups they joined.

There is an option to refuse messages from other members, but the default is "on". You need to change that for every Group you joined.

Go to one of your Groups and then click on "More/My Settings". Then check the box "Allow members of this group to send me messages via LinkedIn." You have to do this manually for each Group.

Please examine why you want to restrict people from contacting you since LinkedIn serves to build your network and stay in touch with your contacts.

You Have Lots of Controls over the Emails You Receive through LinkedIn and over Your Overall User Experience

LinkedIn offers many options including whether to receive invitations from people or not, to receive daily or weekly emails, or to personalize your Home Page.

The majority of these settings are found at:

* Home Page and Settings page: see "Chapter 13: Keep Control over LinkedIn: Home Page & Settings".

* Settings page of a Group: Select a Group and then the tab "Settings".

Send Invitations from Outlook

Most people use the LinkedIn website to send invitations to other people. This is also possible within Outlook if you download the free Outlook Toolbar. This can be found at the bottom of every page under "Tools".

Once you have installed the Outlook Toolbar, in every email you see a small "Info" icon on the right side.

When you move your mouse over the icon, you have the possibility to "invite" the person (if he is not in your network on LinkedIn yet) or "keep in touch" (you get a re-minder if you haven't emailed with this person in 60 days).

> **Remark:** if you are switching to a Mac, but still want to use your Windows software, use Parallels (http://bit.ly/li-book60). In that way you can install Windows next to your Mac environment on the same computer!

Everybody in the Chain Can Read Every Message of an Introduction

When you send an introduction request to someone via "Get introduced through a connection", you always have to write two messages: one for the final recipient and one for your first-degree contact.

Be aware that everybody who is part of the sequence can read all messages. In practice this means that your first-degree contact can read your message to them and the final recipient, that the second-degree contact can read your two messages and the message from your first-degree contact to them and that the final recipient can read your two messages, the message from your first-degree contact to your second-degree contact and from the second-degree contact to them.

Conclusion? Take care to be professional in any message you send whether it is an introduction request from yourself or whether you forward a message from someone else.

Warren Buffet warned, "It takes a lifetime to build a reputation, but only a few seconds to destroy it."

Name is Automatically Included When Sending Invitations to Imported Contacts

When you have imported contacts from Outlook, Webmail, or another email program, you can select people to send an invitation with a request to connect with you.

As we already mentioned before, make sure this message is (semi-) personal. A good way to make a message personal is to use the other person's name. The good news is that LinkedIn does that for you. The bad news is that you can't see it (there is no preview for this message) and you can't change what LinkedIn puts there.

LinkedIn inserts only the first name, not "Hi, John" or "John Smith" but "John".

Use this information wisely!

Groups Can Help You Raise Your Visibility

In the first chapter we explained the Golden Triangle of networking: sharing/giving, asking, and thanking. By taking actions on those three levels you will strengthen your relationships with your network.

Groups are an excellent place to build relationships and increase your visibility and credibility at the same time.

- **Giving/Sharing**: answer questions in the Discussion forums and post REL-EVANT articles in the News section.

- **Asking**: ask for help and information. Always make sure you have given thought to your question. Then people will gladly help you and take the opportunity to build a relationship with you and other members.

- **Thanking**: thank someone in public, in a current Discussion or open a new one. Be specific and generous.

Amount of Groups You Can Join is Limited

Few people know that the number of Groups they can join is limited to 50. In the beginning there was no limit, so some people had to leave some Groups when LinkedIn imposed this limit.

Although annoying for some, most of us will join only a few Groups. In our opinion it is better to be an active member in some of the Groups, than a passive member of many, or wanting to join hundreds of Groups.

Groups Have an Initial Limit of 1000 Members

If you are joining a Group, but are not immediately accepted it could be that the Group has reached the limit of 1000 members. This is not a real problem, if Group Manager asks LinkedIn management to increase the number. This can take a day or two. So if your membership is not approved, check the number of members and if it is 1000—be patient.

Abusing Answers Might Block You from Being Able to Ask Questions Ever Again

If you abuse Answers to promote your services or to post job offers, you might be blocked from using Answers ever again. Members can flag undesirable submissions.

How to Become an "Expert"

The first step to MAYBE earn "expert points" is answering questions in the Answers section. The person who asked the question can then award the best answer with an "expert point". So it is not because you have merely answered a question that you are awarded "expert points". Only one person—the one with the best answer—gets a point.

Remark: you can't earn expert points when you answer a question in a private message or in a Discussion, only via Answers.

How to Remove a Connection

There are occasions when you want to remove a contact. The reasons might be that something happened between you and another person, that you are changing jobs, or that you are reorienting yourself and don't want to be associated with a certain industry anymore. For us only the first reason would be reason enough to remove a connection. In the other cases you might never know whom they know or who can help you in your new situation.

Before we show you how to remove a connection, let's start with a question that many people have: "I don't want to be connected anymore to that person, but I don't want him to know that because I don't want to offend or hurt him. Will they know if I disconnect from them?"

Rest assured, the person you remove as a connection won't be notified.

These are the steps to remove someone:

1. In the top menu, click "Contacts/My Connections".

2. In the new page you will see at the top right side: "Remove Connections".

3. Choose the connection you want removed and click the button "Remove connections".

The connections will be added to your list of "Imported Contacts" in case you want to re-invite them later.

> If you want to watch a small video about how to remove a connection, go to the "Video & Tools Library" at www.how-to-really-use-linkedin.com.

The Consequences of Choosing "Report as Spam" or "Ignore" and Then "I Don't Know This Person" When Receiving an Invitation

When someone has received 5 times the response "Report as Spam" or "I Don't Know This Person" (after "Ignore") their possibilities to link with other people will be limited to inviting only people whose email address they know.

This is LinkedIn's way to limit spamming.

What to Do When Your Account is Restricted

Your account could be restricted because people whom you invited either:

- Clicked "Ignore" and then "I don't know name".
- Reported your Invitation as spam.

If this has happened to you once, you can un-restrict yourself via this link: http://www.linkedin.com/unrestrict?display

If you get restricted again, you need to go via the Help Center, but LinkedIn can deny your request or delete your Profile. So be careful whom you invite.

Why You Can't See the Name of the People in "Who Viewed My Profile" in Many Occasions

Some people would like to know who visited their Profile. Mostly, they see only descriptions and not names. Some of them then pay for an upgraded account to be able to see the names. However, paying won't get you this information.

You always have the choice to limit the information someone sees about you when you visit their Profile, whatever account they have. This is part of the privacy policy of LinkedIn.

These are the steps to change what people see when you have visited their Profile:

- Go to "Settings"
- Under "Profile" click "Select what others see when you've viewed their Profile"
- Then there are three options under "What will be shown to other LinkedIn users when you view their profiles?"
  - o Your name and headline
  - o Anonymous Profile characteristics, such as industry and title
  - o You will totally be anonymous

The second option was the default for a long time and not everybody changes the default settings, thus often you won't see the name of the person who visited your Profile.

The Reason Why You Have Two (or More) Accounts on LinkedIn

Sometimes people find themselves with two or more accounts without understanding how this happened. Most of the times it results from one of these two scenarios:

1. At one time they got an invitation from someone on their home email address, responded to it, and made a Profile. Then they forgot about it. Then after a year their colleagues were discussing LinkedIn and they decided to make a Profile using their work email address.

2. They made a Profile on LinkedIn using their work address and got some connections. After a few weeks someone sent them an invitation via their home email address. They accept without realizing that this creates a new Profile.

Multiple accounts thus arise from different email accounts; email addresses are used as the unique identifier.

To prevent this, list all your email addresses in one Profile.

What to Do When You Have Multiple Accounts

A frequent question is: "I have two (or more) accounts, what do I need to do to keep just one?"

The short answer is: you have to keep one and close the other one(s). Unfortunately, they can't be merged so you need to re-invite all the people you are linked to in the account you are going to delete.

See the tip about exporting your connections so you create a list of people to re-invite.

If you can't access your LinkedIn Profile because you forgot your password, go to www.linkedin.com, click on "Sign in", and then "Forgot password?" Then put in the email address you used to create your LinkedIn Profile.

If the email is not delivered, check your SPAM folder. If it's not there, the email address you have entered is not on record with LinkedIn. Sign in with a different email address that may be listed on your account.

If you have only one email address linked to your LinkedIn account and you can't access that email address any longer (for example because you changed companies and they deleted your old email address), the sole option is to start all over again.

This is what LinkedIn says: *We're sorry, but we can't access your account on your behalf, reset your password for you, or change any of your account information. This policy helps us protect all of our members' privacy.*

To avoid problems we strongly suggest to add more than email address to your LinkedIn account, preferably one you can access at all times like Gmail, Yahoo, or Hotmail.

The Reasons Why You Should Add All Your Email Addresses to Your LinkedIn Account

The first reason is to avoid creating more than one LinkedIn account. The two previous tips should have made it clear that this creates a situation you want to avoid.

The second reason is to always have access to your LinkedIn account. When you forgot your password and your primary email address is temporarily or permanently unavailable, you still have one ore more other email addresses to receive the password.

What Happens with My Contacts When I Import Them? Can Everybody See Them?

Only you can see your contacts.

LinkedIn is also a licensee of the TRUSTe Privacy Program. In its Privacy Policy, LinkedIn declares adherence to the following privacy principles:

- LinkedIn will never rent or sell your personally identifiable information to third parties for marketing purposes.

- LinkedIn will never share your contact information with another user without your consent.

- Any sensitive information you provide will be secured with all industry standard protocols and technology.

How to Change Who Can Contact You

Some people choose to only receive invitations from people they know or introductions via their network. LinkedIn helps you to decide from whom you want to get invitations and messages.

How to change these settings?

- Go to "Settings" (top of the page under your name)
- Then go to "Email Preferences"
  - o Click on "Select the types of message you are willing to receive"
    - » What type of messages will you accept?
      - **Introductions and InMail** (default): InMail allows people who have an upgraded account to contact you even if you don't know them.
      - **Introductions only**: people you don't know can only reach you via your first-degree contacts.
    - » The settings on the rest of the page are to give people more information about what you are interested in. It doesn't influence who can contact you.

o Click on "Select who can send you Invitations"

» **Anyone on LinkedIn (Recommended):** Default.

» **Only people who know your email address or appear in your "Imported Contacts" list**: if you get too many unwanted invitations you can choose this option. However, if your email address is easy to construct, some people might use it.

» **Only people who appear in your "Imported Contacts" list**: if you choose this option, make sure you have imported all the people from your email program.

Playing with the combination of these settings will help you to receive the invitations and introductions you want and filter out the rest.

How to Create a Twitter List from Your LinkedIn Connections

If you use both LinkedIn and Twitter, you can easily create a list on Twitter of people you are connected with on LinkedIn.

1) Add the Tweets Application to your LinkedIn Profile (via More/Get More Applications).

2) The Tweets Application now also appears under "More". Click on it.

3) Click on "Connections" (second tab on top of this new page).

4) Choose "Save as Twitter List".

In our opinion, it makes more sense to create your own lists on Twitter depending on your relationship with each Twitter user you are following, or depending on the topic. But this is yet another way LinkedIn helps with a free tool to keep up-to-date with your network.

The Reason Why You Still Can't Reach Some People Despite Upgrading Your Account

We already explained that it is much easier to have yourself introduced by a mutual contact (preferably using a Magic Mail) than to send messages to strangers.

However, some people still want to have direct contact and since you can send direct messages only to people from your first-degree network, they will pay and upgrade their account so they can send InMails (= direct messages to people who are not first-degree contacts).

However, some people still can't be reached because everybody can choose whether or not to accept InMails!

This can be done under Settings/Email Preferences/Select the messages you're willing to receive. There are two options:

• I'll accept Introductions and InMails (default)

• I'll accept only Introductions.

Therefore, if people change the default setting to the limited one, you still can't reach them, even if you upgraded your account.

If you really want to send a direct message to someone, look in his/her Profile to see which Groups she or he has joined and become a member as well. The default settings allow people to accept direct messages from other Group members whether they are in their first-degree network or not! This option can be turned off as well, but most people leave it active.

How to Ask a Question to Many People at Once

Option 1: Use Answers

You can use "Answers" to ask a public question and/or 200 people from your first-degree network. "Public" means that it will be posted in "Answers". Everybody can react on it. However, you can also choose to send it only to (up to 200 of) your contacts.

Here is how to do it:

- Click on "More/Answers" in the top menu.
- Type your question in the "Ask a Question" box and click "Next".
- If there are similar questions posted by someone else, they will pop up. Maybe you will already find the answer there.
- Below the question text field, you can select the "only share this question with connections I select". Use this only if you do not want your question posted publicly.
- Complete the provided form.
- Click on the "Ask Question" button at the bottom of the "Ask a Question" page.
- If you did not select the "share this question with connections" your answer will be posted publicly. You then have the option to select up to 200 connections you wish to send the question to and click on "Finished". If you DID select the "share this question with connections" you immediately have the option to choose up to 200 connections (and your question won't be posted publicly).
- Compose your email to your connections and click "Send".

Option 2: Compose a Message

You can also send a message to people from your network. Per message you send you can add up to 50 people.

How do you do that?

- **Option 1: start from your message.**
  o Click "Inbox" in the top menu.
  o Click "Compose Message" (left hand side).
  o To choose the recipients you have two options:

1) Start typing the first or last name of one of your first-degree contacts and LinkedIn will present you with everybody whose name starts with the letters you have typed.

2) Click the "In" icon. Your Contacts list appears. Pick the contacts to whom you want to send the message.

o Click "Send Message".

• **Option 2: start from your contacts.**

o Click "Contacts/My Connections" in the top menu.

o To choose recipients you have two options:

1) Select the people you want from the list.

2) Use one or more of the categories on the left side. You can choose be-tween Tags, Last Name, Companies, Locations, Industries and Recent Activity. These are categories that LinkedIn made but you can create your own lists as well by tagging people.

o Click "Send Message" (on top in the third column).

o Compose your message and click "Send Message".

o Remember you can select up to only 50 people. If your list has too many people, delete a few so you will have a list of maximum 50 people. Do this by clicking "all" in the second column. They will appear in the third column where you will be able to delete a few of them. They are deleted out of your selection only for this message, not from the tag or your contact list!

How to Tag One of Your Contacts or Remove a Tag

You can tag people via "Contacts/My Connections".

Tags can be very handy if you want to use LinkedIn to send messages to a group of people. LinkedIn automatically tags people for you.

• Tags: these are generated from the relationship that was mentioned in the Invitation message. You can also create up to 200 tags of your own here!

• Companies, Locations, Industries: people are automatically tagged with their company name, location, and industry.

You can tag one or more contacts or remove their tags by selecting them in the sec-ond column and then clicking "edit tags" in the third column.

Why Does LinkedIn Work with a (Confusing) Area Designation instead of My Company's Location?

We often receive this question particularly from residents of Belgium. This is a small, but complex country, which is divided in a Dutch- and a French-speaking part (and a small German speaking part, too). Through the postal (zip) code system of LinkedIn some companies who are situated in the Dutch-speaking part now seem to be located in the French-speaking part (and vice versa). This can be very confusing, especially when potential customers who look by area code for a supplier in the area of their same language.

However confusing this is, LinkedIn is probably not going to change their system because they use the postal code for safety and privacy reasons.

Tip: if you are not happy with the area designation, change the location to another city. However, don't choose one too far away from your current location, because it might influence your search results if you use the location parameter in your advanced searches.

How to Get Blog Link to Work

The Blog Link Application works differently from WordPress.

In order to get the Blog Link Application working, one of the websites in your Profile needs to be your blog. Blog Link uses that input.

What to Do When You Have Two Blogs

Use the WordPress application for one blog and Blog Link for the second one.

How to Quickly Post a Message in Several Groups

A frequent question is: "How do I post my message in several LinkedIn Groups without having to copy/paste it?"

It is not very intuitive, but rather simple.

These are the steps:

1. Post your message in one LinkedIn Group.

2. In that same Group, click "Search" and find your message.

3. Below your message you will see the option "share" (caution: this only works in the standard view, which equals "All Discussions" on the left side).

4. Click "share" and choose the other Groups you have joined in which you want to post the message. Be sure that the Groups where you are posting appreciate your doing this by checking the Group rules and the behavior in the Group first.

Remark: an alternative is to use the Sharing Bookmarklet. See "Chapter 21: Tools to Save You Time When Working with LinkedIn".

How to Remove and Block Someone Who is Spamming the Group Discussions

As a Group manager you can do this following these steps:

- Go to Group/Manage/Participants and then the second tab "Members".
- Search for their name.
- At the top: click the grey button: "Block & Delete". As a result their contributions will be deleted and they will be removed from the Group. If you want only to remove them from the Group (leaving them with the possibility to request to re-join) but keep their contributions, choose "Remove". When you want to keep the contributions, but remove them from the Group with no option to re-join choose "Block".

Conclusion of this Chapter

In this chapter you received insights and advice regarding the functions of LinkedIn.

If you haven't found an answer to a question, look in the Help Center (at the bottom of each page). You also might consult the "Answers" section on LinkedIn (subcategory Using LinkedIn). If you haven't found an answer yet, you can always contact the LinkedIn Help Center.

The latest updates can be found on the LinkedIn blog: http://blog.linkedin.com

Chapter 21: Tools to Save You Time When Working with LinkedIn

Many people don't want to work with LinkedIn or another online network because they lack time.

We hope that you understand by now the spectacular value of LinkedIn. And also that it does not really take much time. Of course, there are the initial steps to build your network, but you reap the rewards by finding the right people very fast.

However, when you receive many messages and are building a huge network, extra tools that help you do more in less time are most desirable.

In this chapter we will show you some tools that LinkedIn offers and also other tools to make your online networking life much easier. Some tools mentioned in this chapter are free; others require a small fee.

LinkedIn Tools

LinkedIn Mobile

LinkedIn developed several apps for Smartphones (iPhone, BlackBerry, Android & Palm). There is also a special mobile website http://m.linkedin.com. You can easily find and connect with other LinkedIn members. As well, you can also get the latest News Headlines and Status Updates, or share your own.

Since mobile Internet is growing very fast and LinkedIn is investing in their mobile apps, it is worthwhile to download and use them.

LinkedIn Outlook Toolbar

Download the free Outlook Toolbar, which can be found at the bottom of every page under "Tools".

Once you have installed the Outlook Toolbar, extra features appear in Outlook:

- **Dashboard Button**: overview of actions.
- **Grab Button**: when you select the email signature of someone and then click the "Grab" button a new contact card is automatically created with the details of the signature automatically filled in. Some aspects of this function are:
  - Street, town, state and country data are not always retrieved. For the other contact details this works almost always perfectly!
  - Can be used within the preview pane and within an opened email.
  - To change the folder where the new contact cards are saved: click "Dashboard", "Preferences" and then "General".
- **Search bar**: search in LinkedIn within Outlook. The LinkedIn website will then show results in Outlook.
- **"Info" icon in emails**: when you move your mouse over the icon, you have the possibility to "invite" the person (if he is not in your network on LinkedIn

yet) or "keep in touch" (you get a reminder if you haven't emailed with this person in 60 days).

LinkedIn Browser Toolbar

Download the free Internet Explorer or Firefox Toolbar, which can be found at the bottom of every page under "Tools".

After installing the Toolbar these tools are available in the browser:

- **Search bar**: search in LinkedIn from the toolbar (so you don't have to go to the website).
- **Bookmarks**: after you have bookmarked some Profiles on LinkedIn, you can manage them from here.
- **JobsInsider**: opens up a new pane in your browser. When looking at job postings in your normal browser window you can use this extra pane to observe how you are connected to people from the organization of interest.

LinkedIn Sharing Bookmarklet

The Sharing Bookmarklet is a tool LinkedIn developed to help you share interesting content on LinkedIn. You can find it under "Tools" (at the bottom of each page).

After you have installed it in your browser you have these options:

- **Post to Updates**: you share your current web page with a personal note, as a Status Update on LinkedIn.
- **Post to Groups**: post this web page (together with a note) to one or more LinkedIn Groups you joined.
- **Send to Individuals**: send this web page via a (personalized) LinkedIn message to your first-degree contacts. You can also add email addresses from other people.

This Sharing Bookmarklet helps you post interesting information in a minimum amount of time.

However, keep in mind that not all Groups apply the same criteria for allowed content in their Discussions. Always make a considerate choice where you want to post.

If you use this way only to contribute to Groups and never answer a question, people might perceive you as a spammer. Then the negative Know, Like, Trust factor starts; instead of recommending you members may warn people to NOT contact you.

LinkedIn Mac Search Widget

This widget appears on your Mac Dashboard. You can search on LinkedIn for people, jobs, answers, groups, and within your inbox. The widget automatically opens a new tab in your preferred browser to show the results. You can find this widget under "Tools" at bottom of every page.

Google Toolbar Assistant

After you have installed the Google Toolbar, LinkedIn lets you optimize it by installing the LinkedIn search button. This works only for Internet Explorer and Firefox browsers. You can find the Google Toolbar Assistant under "Tools" at bottom of every page.

LinkedIn Plugins

LinkedIn Plugins are small applications that other organizations can use on their website or blog. They can be found at the bottom of every page under "Developers". At the time of writing there were already a few plugins, but it seems that LinkedIn wants to offer more in the future. These are the currently available plugins:

Company Insider

Description from the LinkedIn website: *"Let your users discover how they are connected to companies on your site. You pass a company name and we'll show how many people the user knows and a few sample names. This plugin works great for news sites and blogs, letting readers connect to people at companies you mention. It also works well on jobs sites where job seekers can see who they know at hiring companies. Use it anywhere to inject professional networking into your site."*

An example for how to use it: share some up-to-date information about the people inside your company. You could include New Hires, Promotions & Changes. When the visitor is logged in to LinkedIn they will see whom they know inside your company and be inspired to apply for a job.

Share on LinkedIn

Description from the LinkedIn website: *"Add a Share on LinkedIn link to your website or blog allowing your users to share your content with their LinkedIn connections or networks. This gives your content legs: one user visits your site and can notify literally tens, hundreds, or thousands of others. This sharing works well for news sites, blogs, and other content–rich sites.*

For visibility, it could perform well. If you put this plugin on your blog or your own website and your LinkedIn connections use it, you could get some extra exposure.

Member Profile

Description from the LinkedIn website: *"Bring LinkedIn member profiles to your site to help users discover common professional connections."*

You have 3 options:

1. Embed Profile summary card directly on your webpage
2. Embed LinkedIn logo with full name revealing Profile summary card on click or hover
3. Embed LinkedIn logo only revealing Profile summary card on click or hover

This interesting plugin can be integrated in your website or blog, and users see your LinkedIn Profile summary card before actually going to your full profile.

How could you use this? Have a popup with a LinkedIn Profile for your staff members on your own company page. When the visitor is logged in to LinkedIn they see mutual connections.

Full Member Profile

Description from the LinkedIn website: *"Make your site content richer by showing the summary, work experience and educational background for people featured on your site. Also, enable users to easily discover who they know in common, send a message, or establish a connection."*

This is an expansion of the "Member Profile" plugin.

Company Profile

Description from the LinkedIn website: *"Make your site content richer by showing the summary, location, logo, and number of employees for companies featured on your site. Also, help users discover who they know at a company and enable them to track news and insights by using the follow button."*

How could you use this? Show your Company Profile overview from LinkedIn. When the visitor is logged in to LinkedIn they will see whom they may know inside your company.

Recommend with LinkedIn

Description from the LinkedIn website: *"Enable users to recommend your products and services to LinkedIn's professional audience, and drive traffic back to your site."*

How could you use this? Add it to your website to get more Recommendations for your Products & Services page.

Sign In with LinkedIn

Description from the LinkedIn website: *"Make it easier for people to sign in or register with your site by using their LinkedIn identity. With LinkedIn's new APIs, it's easy to let your users bring their LinkedIn professional identity and network to interactions on your site. Customize functionality based on a user's geography, work experience and network. With minimal work, you can grow your site registrations and build a rich, personalized experience."*

How could you use this? Have your participants register with their LinkedIn Profile for your events.

LinkedIn APIs

LinkedIn lets you easily enhance your professional identity and insights on your site or business application through APIs. Since this part is setup for developers specifically, we will limit this section to a current overview of the different APIs:

- **People and Connections**. Add a professional identity to your site with the LinkedIn member profile and connection data. Search across over 120 million profiles in the professional graph by company, education, industry, relationship, and more.

- **Groups**. Access LinkedIn Groups and enable your users to engage with professionals. One can integrate the ability to retrieve discussions, post new discussions, comment, like, follow posts, interact with group members and join the group. Also, retrieve a user's current and suggested groups.

- **Companies**. Display a detailed overview of company information in combination with LinkedIn data. Search across company profiles by industry, location, size, and more. Enable your users to follow a company and see suggested companies to follow.

- **Jobs.** Search LinkedIn's jobs by company, industry and more, to display relevant jobs to your users. Post and retrieve LinkedIn jobs for a company, and enable people to save jobs to their LinkedIn accounts and retrieve job suggestions.

- **Social Stream**. Access the update stream for LinkedIn members and their network, and drive traffic to your app by posting to your user's stream. Let users share, comment, and like content in the LinkedIn ecosystem direct from your application.

- **Communications.** Use LinkedIn's Inbox to make your application a social communications hub. Let your customers send invitations to connect on LinkedIn and messages to existing connections.

Tools to Make Life on LinkedIn Easier

In addition to the tools LinkedIn itself offers, there are also other tools that can help you save time or increase your results.

URL Shorteners

Posting the URL (web address) of a website where people can find interesting information (for example, in Discussions, Answers or Status Updates on LinkedIn or on your own website or any other place) can be tiresome when URL is a very long.

The link can break and most of the times it negatively affects the readability of a posting.

A URL shortener is an online application that allows the user to enter a full URL for any specific web page. Automatically it reduces a long wordy URL to a short domain name using a generated or a custom code (of your choice). When users click that short link they are redirected to the original URLs just as if they had entered the entire text.

On the website TinyURL (http://tinyurl.com/) you can transform a long URL into a short one and choose a custom keyword. TinyURL is a free service.

TinyURL is one of the most frequently used URL Shorteners. There are literally hundreds of others, like bit.ly, ow.ly, goo.gl, is.gd, su.pr and even LinkedIn has its own: lnkd.in.

Texter

This is a small tool that allows you to replace chunks of text with a "hotstring" (= a shortcut). What does this mean in practice?

Do you remember the tip about responding invitations from people you don't know? This was the text that we use ourselves:

> *Hi xxx,*
>
> *Thank you for your invitation to connect!*
>
> *Unfortunately I meet so many people I can't always connect the name and face.*
>
> *Can you help me by reminding me where we met?*
>
> *Thanks and ... have a great networking day!*
>
> *Jan*

We dislike repetition as much as we like to save time. So we used Texter to create a "hotstring" called link-inv. When we type "link-inv" and then hit "enter" the text above appears. The only thing we still need to do is replace xxx with the actual name of the person who invited you.

Of course you can also use these hotstrings for many other chunks of text you use frequently in your daily job. They work in almost every program: Word, Excel, Power-Point, emails, websites, blogs, Twitter,…

You can download Texter (Windows only) for free from the Lifehacker website: http://tinyurl.com/texter

> *Tip: when you have installed Texter, go to the Texter directory (most often this looks like C:\Program Files\Texter). Create a shortcut (right-click) of the texter. exe file and drag it into your StartUp folder under Programs. By doing this, Texter will launch (every time) as soon as you start up your computer. If you don't do this, you will have to launch Texter manually.*

For Mac users we recommend a similar tool: Text Expander. After a free trial, you will have to pay ($ 50), but you will receive more advanced (compared to Texter) features, such as nested snippets, snippets with formatted text and pictures, sync snippets via DropBox and application specific snippets.

You can download Text Expander from the Smile Software website: http://tinyurl.com/textexp

> If you want to watch a small video on how to use Texter, go to the "Video & Tools Library" at www.how-to-really-use-linkedin.com.

Google Alerts

Google Alerts give you updates on specific topics or people whenever something on the web is published about them.

Setup of this free tool is very easy:

- Go to www.google.com/alerts
- Then set the parameters:
  - o Search term: topic or person about whom you want information.
  - o Type: where you want Google Alerts to search for you (Blogs, Videos, Web, etc).
  - o Frequency: as-it-happens, once a day or once a week.
  - o Email address: you receive alerts via email.

Use this to follow the news on a prospect or a company you want to work for. Or for updates on an expert, information for your project, or for trends in the marketplace, or yourself.

Google Keyword Tool

LinkedIn is a great tool to enhance visibility and build the brand of the organization where you work, or your personal brand.

To increase your chances of being found on LinkedIn, and also on the web, you use the right words. Many times we are unaware of the jargon we use in our own company or industry. Someone who is looking for our expertise might never use those words.

The Google Keyword Tool is primarily used to find synonyms and alternatives for ads on Google, but you can use it to find the right words for your Profile.

This free tool can be found at: http://bit.ly/li-book12 (or search on "Google Keyword Tool").

Be selective with keywords; people still need to be able to read your Profile.

Simple Image Editors

We already pointed out the importance of having a good photo on your LinkedIn Profile. Some people have a great photo, but not in the right format, dimensions, or even with others.

Use these tools to help you.

1. DrPic

    DrPic.com is probably the easiest free online picture editor. You can re-size, crop (cut out a part of the image), rotate, insert text, etc. You can save it in JPG, GIF, PNG or BMP. See http://bit.ly/li-book33

2. Pixlr

    Pixlr.com is a more advanced free online image editor. You can even work with layers and be almost as creative as with Adobe Photoshop. See http://bit.ly/li-book34

RSS Reader

RSS (originally RDF Site Summary, often dubbed Really Simple Syndication) is a family of web feed formats used to publish frequently updated works—such as blog entries, news headlines, audio, and video—in a standardized format. LinkedIn uses RSS. If you want to receive LinkedIn content in an RSS feed, you can use your favorite RSS feed reader (like Google Reader (http://bit.ly/li-book14), Newsgator (http://bit.ly/li-book15) or Netvibes (http://bit.ly/li-book16)). LinkedIn offers two types of feeds, public and personal. Public feeds offer the same content to all LinkedIn members. Personal feeds contain private information from your LinkedIn network.

RSS feeds on LinkedIn are available in different places on LinkedIn. The Network Updates feed publishes your personal Network Updates in RSS format. Each LinkedIn Answers category has its own RSS feed. As a Group Manager you can create a newsfeed of websites and blogs in your Group.

Tools That Make Your Virtual Networking Life Easier

Much of our virtual networking life goes via email. Here are a few tools that can help you spend less time and be more effective.

Plaxo Toolbar

Plaxo is nowadays more known for its online networking platform Plaxo Pulse. However we find the Plaxo Toolbar far more interesting. It gives you extra tools in your email program (Outlook, Outlook Express, Mac, Mozilla Thunderbird). We want to share the most interesting ones with you:

- **Automatic fill of contact details in a contact card**: when you open a new contact card and fill in only the email address, Plaxo will search whether or not this person is also a Plaxo member. If so, the contact details of this person from his Plaxo profile are automatically inserted on the contact card. So you no longer have to type in all the contact details from people. This is useful when you have downloaded someone's contact details from LinkedIn, or you want to extract details from business cards.

- **Automatic updates of changes**: if someone changes his contact details on Plaxo, this is automatically updated in all the address books that are connected to this person. In other words, if your contact changes their details in Plaxo, it is automatically updated in your email program (if you use Plaxo).

- **Build Address Book**: find all the people with whom you have exchanged emails, but who are not in your contact folder yet. This tool will search emails for such email addresses. You can then make contact cards for these people. If they are also Plaxo members their contact details are automatically filled in.

- **Ask for updates**: you can ask the people in your address book to check whether the information about them you have in your address book is up-to-date. You can also use this in the last step of the "Build Address Book" process. Remember to change the standard message to a (semi) personal one!

You can download the free Plaxo toolbar from http://bit.ly/li-book35.

Xobni

Another tool that can boost your efficiency in communicating with people is Xobni. This free tool is available only for Outlook and Blackberry at the moment of writing. Versions for Gmail, Android and iPhone are on the way too.

Xobni (the reverse of Inbox) puts another "layer" on emails. Outlook is email centric, while Xobni is people-centric.

After installing Xobni you get an extra toolbar next to your emails. In this toolbar you will find information about the sender of the email:

- **Contact details**: derived from signatures in emails and from LinkedIn if this person has a Profile on LinkedIn.

- **Network**: the people who were in "to" or "cc" fields of the emails you have exchanged. Although it is not certain if they actually know each other, there is a chance they do.

- **Conversations**: emails you have exchanged with each other independent of the folder where you stored them.

- **Files Exchanged**: files in attachment of the emails you have exchanged independent of the folder where you stored them. The most recent is always at the top.

- **Emails exchanged**: you see a visual chart of the occasions when you sent emails to this person and when he sent you emails. You can use this information to find a good time to call someone (=most emails are sent when someone is at his desk).

- **Schedule time with**: when you click this link, Xobni looks in your Outlook calendar when you have free time in a determined period and assembles them together in an email you can send to the other person.

It is clear that this tool gives you another view on your emails and makes it easier to contact someone, and to quickly retrieve your exchanged emails and files.

Also check out their Gadget Store to be even more productive. Gadgets are small tools that plugin in to Xobni. Xobni launches new tools regularly. Here is an overview of their current gadgets: LinkedIn, Facebook, Twitter, Huddle, YouTube, Flickr, Evernote, Salesforce.com, Yammer, DropBox, Webex, Chatter, JIRA, Hoover's, EchoSign,

Klout, Nimbb, GoldMail, Google Translate, Xing, Yelp, Microsoft SharePoint, Active Directory, Oracle and SAP.

Social Media Dashboard

If you use the "Status Update" feature on LinkedIn, and also on other platforms like Plaxo, Facebook, Twitter and MySpace, you can save time by using a tool, which updates all these platforms simultaneously.

A website offering this free service, is Ping.fm (http://ping.fm).

Making an update on Ping.fm pushes the update to a number of different social websites at once. When using multiple social networks it allows you to update your status only once, without having to update it in all your social media individually. Ping.fm group's services fall into three categories—status updates, blogs, and micro-blogs—updates can be sent to each group separately.

Ping.fm is already a great tool, but you probably want to go a step further by using a social media dashboard.

Probably the best Social Media Dashboard is HootSuite (http://bit.ly/li-book9). HootSuite helps you distribute your Status Update to several Social Media platforms and to launch marketing campaigns, identify and grow an audience, and distribute targeted messages across multiple channels.

An additional advantage is that HootSuite allows teams to schedule updates collaboratively. It also integrates with Ping.fm, so you can spread your Status Update to even more online platforms.

An alternative to HootSuite is Tweetdeck (http://bit.ly/li-book10).

FourSquare

Foursquare (http://4sq.com/li-book36) is a web and mobile application that allows registered users to connect with friends and update their location. Users "check-in" at venues using a mobile website, text messaging, or an app by running the application and selecting from a list of nearby venues located by the application.

Among other things, you can use this platform to let your network know where you are, to see who is at the same location, to inform them which places you recommend, to connect with others, to earn badges, to explore new venues, and to share tips.

Another similar platform is Gowalla (http://bit.ly/li-book37).

Conclusion of this Chapter

There are many great tools that can help you save time when working with LinkedIn. LinkedIn also offers ways to integrate its tools in other websites via Plugins and APIs.

This is a small overview of the tools that were featured in this chapter:

- LinkedIn Tools: LinkedIn Mobile, LinkedIn Outlook Toolbar, LinkedIn Browser Toolbar, LinkedIn Sharing Bookmarklet, LinkedIn Mac Search Widget, Google Toolbar Assistant

- Tools to Make Life on LinkedIn Easier: URL Shorteners, Texter, Google Alerts, Google Keyword Tool, Simple Image Editors, RSS Reader

- Tools That Make Your Virtual Networking Life Easier: Plaxo Toolbar, Xobni, Social Media Dashboard, FourSquare

More tools to help you to be more effective in your networking and referral strategy can be found on our Networking Coach website: www.networking-coach.com. We add interesting tools on a regular basis so please visit or follow the updates on our blogs (www.janvermeiren.com and http://blog.bertverdonck.com)

Also explore these websites and blogs for more tools to make your (networking) life easier:

- www.lifehacker.com
- www.lifehacking.nl
- www.martijnaslander.nl

Epilogue

Now you know why you are (or should be) on LinkedIn, what it is (and what it is not) and how to use it to reach your goals faster than ever before.

However, knowledge alone is not enough. It's up to you to take action.

Remember that most people start to build their network only when it is too late: they start building it when they need it. Other people sense this urgency, and perhaps desperation, even online. Such a need repels rather than attracts them.

So start building your network now. If you follow the 5 fundamental principles of networking using the strategy in this book, results are guaranteed!

LinkedIn is not the only website. There are other online business networks. Many more. We selected a handful of them, which might be useful for you to use alongside LinkedIn. Despite the fact that the features might be different, the fundamental principles and the "start with your goal in mind" apply to all of them. You find them in the appendix.

As we already mentioned: a book about a website can be outdated the minute it is published. But for us it is important you get the most value out of this book and out of LinkedIn. That's why we will publish updates and extra tips whenever something changes or whenever we glean new insights.

To get these updates and extra tips for free, together with Profile Self Assessment, go to the "Video & Tools Library" at www.how-to-really-use-linkedin.com. You will also gain free access to video tips wherein we show a number of tips you have been reading in this book, and share some other notable resources to help you leverage the power of your network to achieve your goals.

To help you get even more value out of this book and achieve more success, we have started the "Global Networking Group" on LinkedIn (http://linkd.in/li-book11). It is open to anyone who wants to abide by the rules of this Group. So come and join us and experience the power of networking via LinkedIn!

To your success!

Jan & Bert

PS: when you have closed your 100 million-dollar deal by applying the tips in this book or found your dream job, don't send us a check. Just write a Recommendation on LinkedIn (http://linkd.in/li-book22) with how the tips worked for you. Reading about other people's successes is the most gratifying moment in our day!

Appendix A: Other Online Business Networks

Of course, LinkedIn is not the only online business network. However, at the time of writing it had the largest number of members. And LinkedIn has also the lowest entry threshold to become a member. As a result, many people all over the world, from different industries and with different functions, are now on LinkedIn.

However, there are many more online business and social networks. LinkedIn has its origins in the USA like many others, but there are very popular online business networks also in Europe and Asia.

Because the online world changes so quickly the numbers of users will already have changed when you read this. Also some websites might have added some extra functions, which would cause a different review on our part.

Viadeo

URL	www.viadeo.com
Description	Viadeo is primarily a business network. Members can also list personal interests.
	The forums where members can give and receive help to each other on the website are most important for a satisfactory user experience.
	In many regions, the added value of membership resides in the network meetings and events the local representatives organize. Members appreciate this combination between online and offline networking a lot.
Number of users	35 Million
Target Audience	Any professional
Regional focus	World
Type of memberships	Free basic membership
	Premium membership (monthly fee)
Country of origin	France
Remarks	• Multilingual user interface lowers the threshold to participate in this network for people who don't speak English well. However, participation is limited in discussions on forums where the user doesn't speak the native language of the founder of that club.
	• The combination of online and offline networking is a big plus!
	• Half the members are located in China.

Xing

URL	www.xing.com
Description	Xing is primarily a business network. Members may also list personal interests.
	The forums where members can give and receive help to each other are the most significant for the user experience on the website.
	In many regions, the added value of membership is in the network meetings and events the local representatives organize. Members report that this combination between online and offline networking is of value for them.
Number of users	10 Million
Target Audience	Any professional
Regional focus	World
Type of memberships	Free basic membership
	Premium membership (monthly fee)
Country of origin	Germany
Remarks	• Multilingual user interface lowers the threshold to participate in this network for people who don't speak English well. For some the discussions on forums are limited to those who speak the native language of the founder of that club.
	• The combination of online and offline networking is a big plus!

Ecademy

URL	www.ecademy.com
Description	Ecademy is a social BUSINESS community; emphasis is on the business part. However, there is also room for the more personal side so members can meet each other as "whole persons". It is the most social business network presently. The public and private clubs on the website are where members can give and receive help to each other. In many regions the added value of membership is in the network meetings and events the local representatives organize. Members report that this combination between online and offline networking increase the worth for them.
Number of users	500,000
Target Audience	Especially small business owners and freelancers.
Regional focus	World
Type of memberships	Free basic membership PowerNetworker (monthly fee) Blackstar (life membership or monthly fee)
Country of origin	United Kingdom
Remarks	• Feature rich, which makes long-term members happy, but is sometimes overwhelming for new users. • The combination of online and offline networking is a big plus!

Facebook

URL	www.facebook.com
Description	Facebook is a SOCIAL (business) network. Started as a platform for college students to share personal interests, Facebook has grown exponentially. More and more professionals have an account on this website and also more and more organizations have virtual clubs and fan pages.
	The user experience on the website depends on the interactions between members (not only one-to-one as on the other websites, but also the ability to watch the interactions between friends) and the groups where members can give and receive help to each other.
Number of users	750 Million
Target Audience	Anyone
Regional focus	World
Type of memberships	Free membership
Country of origin	USA
Remarks	• The third-party applications give Facebook added appeal and are probably the reason for its exponential growth. On the other hand, this might also become the reason why people will stop using it because they get too many invitations for time-consuming games and quizzes. • Has huge potential for professional interactions.

Ning

URL	www.ning.com
Description	Ning is a platform where people can create their own virtual community. Unlike other networking platforms where the user is the focus, here the community is central. The communities where members can give and receive help to each other provide the appeal for the user experience on the website.
Number of users	90,000 networks (approx. 67 million visitors/month)
Target Audience	Anyone
Regional focus	World
Type of memberships	Paid Membership for network owners (Mini, Plus, & Pro)
Country of origin	USA
Remarks	• Limited profile information obliges people to also have memberships on other sites. • Easy to create your own community.

Netlog

URL	www.netlog.com
Description	Netlog is an online platform where users can keep in touch with and extend their SOCIAL network. It is an online social portal, specifically targeted at European youth.
Number of users	79 million
Target Audience	Anyone, targeted at youth
Regional focus	World, mainly Europe
Type of memberships	Free
Country of origin	Belgium

Remarks	• Especially popular with youngsters • Easy directory with Members, Brands, Applications, and Events. • Multilingual user interface (34 languages) lowers the threshold to participate in this network for people who don't speak English well.

Hyves

URL	www.hyves.nl
Description	Hyves is the most popular SOCIAL networking site in the Netherlands.
Number of users	11.5 Million
Target Audience	Anyone
Regional focus	World, but primarily the Netherlands
Type of memberships	Free membership Gold membership (paid)
Country of origin	Netherlands
Remarks	• 9.3 million members are from the Netherlands. • Only available in Dutch and English.

Appendix B: Practical Tools

We love to share a list of practical tools. Most of them are even Genius Shortcuts. Many people lack the time to search for productivity tools or simple solutions that could make their lives easier. Here is a selection of helpful tools we discussed in this book. Although several alternatives exist for a number of these tools, we have verified and used all the below-mentioned tools ourselves.

> If you want to watch a small video about some of these tools, go to the "Video & Tools Library" at www.how-to-really-use-linkedin.com.

RSS

- Google Reader (http://bit.ly/li-book14): Google Reader is an online RSS feed reader. It allows you to subscribe to RSS and Atom feeds. You can manage feeds, label them, and even share your feed collection with others.

- NewsGator (http://bit.ly/li-book15): NewsGator is an RSS feed reader with different versions for different platforms. FeedDaemon is for Windows. NetNews-Wire is for Mac, iPhone and iPad.

- Netvibes (http://bit.ly/li-book16): Netvibes is more than just an RSS feed reader. It can also include newspapers, blogs, weather, email, search, videos, photos, social networks, podcasts, widgets and games. They are all brought together in one single page—your personalized dashboard.

URL Shorteners

- Tinyurl.com (http://tinyurl.com): TinyURL is a URL shortening service, a web service that provides short aliases for redirection of long URLs. A big advantage is that TinyURL lets you choose your own custom alias.

- Bit.ly (http://bit.ly): bit.ly is a URL shortening service, where you can also track the number of clickthroughs.

- Ow.ly (http://ow.ly): ow.ly is a URL shortening service, neatly integrated with HootSuite.

- Goo.gl (http://goo.gl): goo.gl is Google's URL shortening service. It shares statistics publically.

- Is.gd (http://is.gd): Is.gd is an ethical URL shortening service.

- Su.pr (http://su.pr): su.pr is Stumple Upon's URL shortening service. It integrates neatly with your Stumble Upon account.

- Lnkd.in (http://lnkd.in): lnkd.in is LinkedIn's URL shortening service. When you share your Status Update with a long URL, LinkedIn will replace it automatically with a short one.

Text Substitution

- Texter (http://tinyurl.com/texter): Texter is a small tool (for Windows) that allows you to replace chunks of text with what they call a "hotstring" (= a shortcut).

- TextExpander (http://tinyurl.com/textexp) is the alternative for Texter for Mac. It saves you countless keystrokes with customized abbreviations for your frequently used text strings and images.

Keyword Tool

- Google Ads Keywords Tool (http://bit.ly/li-book12): Use the Google Ads Keyword Tool to find synonyms or suggestions for alternative words. This tool is used primarily for Google ads, but you can also use it to find the right words for your Profile.

Social Media Dashboards

- HootSuite (http://bit.ly/li-book9): HootSuite helps you to distribute your Status Update to several Social Media platforms and can help you launch marketing campaigns, identify and grow audiences, and distribute targeted messages across multiple channels. HootSuite also integrates Ping.fm.

- Ping.fm (http://ping.fm): Making an update on Ping.fm sends the update to a number of different social websites at once. When using multiple social networks it allows you to update your status only once, without having to update it in all your social media individually.

- Tweetdeck (http://bit.ly/li-book10): With Tweetdeck you can consciously post your message to multiple networks at once.

- Google Alerts (http://www.google.com/alerts): Google Alerts give you updates on specific topics or people whenever something on the web is published about them.

Online Marketing/Business Tools

- KickStartCart (http://bit.ly/li-book27): KickStartCart integrates everything you need to do business professionally over the Internet—an Internet merchant account, a payment gateway, a secure online order form, autoresponders, Affiliate tracking, ad tracking, detailed reporting, etc. (Remark: look beyond the first outdated page).

- Aweber (http://bit.ly/li-book24): Aweber is an email-marketing tool to setup your opt-in marketing campaigns, email newsletters, autoresponders, etc. Aweber is a useful tool to build your database. It is an alternative to Kickstartcart.

- PayPal (http://bit.ly/li-book28): PayPal allows any business or consumer with an email address, to securely, conveniently and cost-effectively send and receive payments online.

- GoDaddy (http://x.co/Ycxt): GoDaddy is one of the biggest domain name registrars. You can easily order your domain names, email addresses, and web hosting.
- If you use Wordpress as platform for your website, look at Wishlist (http://bit.ly/li-book40) to set up a membership or community platform.

Email Tools

- Xobni (http://www.xobni.com): Xobni is an MS Outlook plugin that offers email management and quick access to important information in your email.
- SMTP2GO (http://bit.ly/li-book29): Simply use smtp2go.com as your outgoing mail server and never worry about problems sending emails ever again. Helpful for when you have to send emails from different locations (when traveling, for example).

Picture Editing Tools

- DrPic (http://bit.ly/li-book33): DrPic.com is probably the easiest free online picture editor. You can resize, crop (cut out a part of the image), rotate, insert text, etc. You can save it in JPG, GIF, PNG or BMP.
- Pixlr (http://bit.ly/li-book34): If you are looking for a more advanced free online image editor, look at Pixlr.com. You can even work with layers and be almost as creative as if you were working with Adobe Photoshop.

Video Editing Tools

- Camtasia (http://bit.ly/li-book32): Camtasia is a screen recording and video editing software program. Very handy to create your own (YouTube) videos. It runs on Windows and Mac.
- IShowU (http://bit.ly/li-book39): IShowU is a screen recording and video- editing tool for Mac.

Publishing Tools

- CreateSpace (http://bit.ly/li-book41): CreateSpace provides tools and services to help you complete a booklet, book or CD and self-publish it.
- Foto.com (http://bit.ly/li-book26): Foto.com is a specialized website in digital photo products like prints, personalized books, posters, calendars, stationery, etc.

Event Tools

- Eventbrite (http://bit.ly/li-book25): Eventbrite is a very practical online tool to create and to plan your own (offline) event(s), including website, tickets, payment, guest lists, badges, promo tools, etc.
- GoToWebinar (http://www.gotowebinar.com): With GoToWebinar you can conduct do-it-yourself webinars with up to 1,000 people.

Find Freelancers

- Elance (http://bit.ly/li-book43): For businesses wanting to outsource or staff a team on an hourly or project basis, Elance offers instant access to qualified professionals who work online and provide the skills to hire, view work as it progresses, and pay for results.

Location Based Social Networking

- Foursquare (http://4sq.com/li-book36): Foursquare is a web and mobile application that allows registered users to connect with friends and update their location.

- GoWalla (http://bit.ly/li-book37): GoWalla is a location-based social network and an alternative to Foursquare. Users log in at Spots in their vicinity, either through a dedicated mobile application or through the mobile website.

Computer Tools

- Box.net (http://bit.ly/li-book31): Box.net is an online content management and file storage business. The core of the service is based around sharing, collaborating, and working with files that are uploaded to Box.net.

- DropBox (http://bit.ly/li-book31): DropBox is a web-based file hosting service that uses cloud computing to enable users to store and share files and folders with others across the Internet. DropBox also enables file synchronization and is also practical for sharing files with colleagues.

- Mozy (http://bit.ly/li-book42): Mozy is an online backup service for both Windows and Mac users. The cloud service allows users to back up data continuously, manually, or schedule updates.

- Skype (http://bit.ly/li-book44): Skype is free telephone, teleconference and videoconference tool (if all participants are online). You can also call people on their landlines or mobile phones for a small fee.

- Parallels (http://bit.ly/li-book60): Parallels Desktop for Mac is a software program allowing you to install Windows on your Mac. This way, you can have the best of both worlds!

If you want more of these tools, go to the
"Video & Tools Library" at www.how-to-really-use-linkedin.com.

About the Authors
Jan Vermeiren & Bert Verdonck

Jan Vermeiren

Jan Vermeiren is the founder of Networking Coach and according to *HR Tribune* one of Belgium's top 10 speakers.

Jan and his team provide key note lectures, presentations, training courses and personal coaching about networking and referrals, and also advise organizations how to stimulate networking at their own events and how to integrate networking in their sales and recruitment strategy.

He is interviewed regularly about networking and referrals by different media like Belgian national television and radio (De Zevende Dag, Lichtpunt, Radio 1), newspapers and websites (Forbes), job sites (Vacature.com, Jobat) and the magazines of several Chambers of Commerce.

Jan is the author of the best-selling networking books: *Let's Connect!* and *How to REALLY Use LinkedIn*, the networking CD *Let's Connect at an Event!*, the *Everlasting Referrals Home Study Course*, and the *Network Box* (Home Study Course).

The US version of *Let's Connect!* reached the Amazon bestseller list on October 9, 2007 with second position in marketing books and ninth in management books. Jan is the first Belgian author to reach this position.

The first edition of *How to REALLY Use LinkedIn* was a best seller on Amazon as well with first position in the category "Sales & Selling". In the Netherlands, the Dutch version was the overall number 1 on www.managementboek.nl.

Jan and his team are hired by large international companies like Alcatel, Deloitte, DuPont, IBM, ING, Mobistar, Nike, SAP, and Sun Microsystems as well as by small companies and freelancers.

Jan is also a guest lecturer in the international MBA programs of Vlerick Leuven Gent Management School (Belgium) and RSM Erasmus University Rotterdam (the Netherlands).

Bert Verdonck

Bert Verdonck is an inspiring, enthusiastic and humorous speaker. He is master trainer at Networking Coach and a creative lifehacker.

Bert is an excellent example of the value of networking.

Bert teaches people how to be more comfortable when networking, and how to improve results from networking, whether online (on LinkedIn and other business networks) or offline (receptions, mixers, conferences, fairs, and other networking events).

As well as delivering practical networking training courses and personal coaching, Bert hosts the Networking Coach's webinars together with Jan.

Bert is the founder of Genius Shortcuts, his personal flavor of life hacking. Ever imagined what you could do with 2 hours extra per day? Bert already helped thousands of people to boost their productivity and saved them hours per day.

As a lifehacker Bert published 3 books in 1 year. He co-authored *Your Book in 100 Days*, *175 Lifehacking Tips* and *The Wealth Garden*. He created the Genius Shortcuts CD *How to Shorten Your Workday by 2 Hours?* And now he teamed up with Jan to co-author the second edition of *How to REALLY Use LinkedIn*.

In Belgium, Bert is already a prominent lifehacker and networking coach. Internationally, his reputation is growing rapidly. He has been on stage in the Netherlands, France, Hong Kong, India, Indonesia, New Zealand, the United Kingdom, and Switzerland.

Other Books and CD's

From the same authors

- Vermeiren Jan, *Let's Connect!* (http://bit.ly/li-book1)
- Vermeiren Jan, *Let's Connect at an Event* (CD) (http://bit.ly/li-book23)
- Vermeiren Jan, *Everlasting Referrals Home Study Course* (http://bit.ly/li-book23)
- Vermeiren Jan, *The Netwerk Box* (Home Study Course) (http://bit.ly/li-book23)
- Verdonck Bert, *How to Shorten Your Working Day by 2 Hours?* (CD) (http://bit.ly/li-book30)
- Verdonck Bert, & Gibbins-Klein Mindy, *Your Book in 100 Days* (http://amzn.to/li-book38)

Books that are mentioned in this book

- Alba Jason, *I'm on LinkedIn, now what?* (http://amzn.to/li-book20)
- Baker Wayne, *Networking Smart* (http://amzn.to/li-book5)
- Burg Bob, *Endless Referrals* (http://amzn.to/li-book6)
- Burg Bob, The Go-Giver (http://amzn.to/li-book13)
- Butow Eric and Taylor Kathleen, *How to Succeed in Business using LinkedIn* (http://amzn.to/li-book2)
- Covey Stephen MR, *The Speed of Trust* (http://amzn.to/li-book7)
- Elad Joel, *LinkedIn for Dummies* (http://amzn.to/li-book3)
- Fisher Donna, *People Power* (http://amzn.to/li-book4)

Other Products and Services of Networking Coach

Jan Vermeiren, Bert Verdonck and the team of Networking Coach have specialized in the topics of online and offline networking and referrals.

Products

- **Free online and offline networking e-course:** www.networking-coach.com
- **LinkedIn related:**
  - **Free LinkedIn Fundamentals Webinar:** an introduction to LinkedIn (see the calendar at www.networking-coach.com for the next session).
  - **LinkedIn Steps to Success Webinar Series:** in-depth webinar series for crafting an attractive Profile, how to build your LinkedIn network fast, personal & company branding, finding new customers, and using LinkedIn to get more out of live events (see the calendar at www.networking-coach.com for the next sessions or recordings).
  - **LinkedIn Dive in Deep Packages:** let us guide you to even more success with these packages including more self-assessments, worksheets, checklist, video tutorials, and much more (see www.how-to-really-use-linkedin.com).
- **Offline networking:**
  - **Network book and bestseller, *Let's Connect!:*** a practical guide for networking at events and on the web for every professional whether in sales or not" (free light version available at www.letsconnectbook.com).
  - **Network CD *Let's Connect at an Event*:** 30 immediately applicable networking tips to make every event a success" (free light version available at www.networking-coach.com).
- **Home Study Courses:**
  - ***The Network Box*:** home study course containing *How to REALLY Use LinkedIn, Let's Connect!, Let's Connect at an event*, a workbook, and follow up emails. Currently available only in Dutch. (www.networking-coach.com)
  - **Everlasting Referrals Home Study Course:** how to create a network of ambassadors that will bring in customer after customer so you don't ever have to call strangers again (www.everlasting-referrals.com).

Services

For individuals: workshops and training courses (open format and customized in-company versions):

- Introductory session on networking or referrals (half day)
- LinkedIn sessions:
  - o Link & Learn: 2-hour interactive introductory seminar
  - o Boost Your Business: half-day interactive workshop to attract more customers or new employees
  - o Catapult Your Career: half-day interactive workshop to find a new job
  - o Dive in Deep: one day hands-on training course
- What's Your Sticky Story©? (one half-day)
- Proactive Networker Training Course (2 days)
- Everlasting Referrals Training Course (2 days, for business owners and sales people)
- Smart Networking Training Course (3.5 days)

For organizations:

- **(Interactive) Presentations and Key Note Speeches,** some examples:
  - o "Everlasting Referrals, No More Cold Calls". What are the 7 main reasons that most organizations don't get (spontaneous) referrals and what to do about it?
  - o "Your Net Works". How to tap the Power of your Network.
  - o "What's your Sticky Story©?" How to answer "And what do you do?" in a way so you will be remembered.
  - o "Help, I need a new job": How to tap the power of your network to find a new job.
  - o "Oh no, another reception". How to network efficiently at a business cocktail party, conference, or any other event.
  - o "How to REALLY Use LinkedIn". How to find and get introduced to the people who can help you reach your goals (new customers, a new job, new employees, suppliers, partners or experts).
- **Corporate Programs, consisting of a mix of**
  - o Strategic consulting on how to integrate networking and referrals in a sales or recruitment strategy
  - o Advice on how to stimulate networking between the participants of a networking event
  - o Tactical sessions about how to use networking at an organizational level
  - o Workshops about LinkedIn, networking and referral in different formats: class room, webinars, teleseminars or a combination

All interactive presentations, keynote speeches and training courses are adapted to the audience, and the situation of the organization.

Detailed descriptions and the calendar of open training courses and seminars can be found at www.networking-coach.com

Generous Networkers

2012 will mark the beginning of a new project for entrepreneurs, called Generous Networkers. The project will start in Belgium and the Netherlands.

The central focus is how entrepreneurs can be (even more) generous towards themselves, towards the other participants and towards society (for example by supporting charities with money, time or expertise).

This is the mission of Generous Networkers:

"Generous Networkers invites entrepreneurs to join the experience of sharing their generous nature, co-creating sparkling magic and enjoying the habit of genuine giving while living their true passion."

The project consists of three parts: The Entrepreneurs Experience, The Generous Networking Training Program and The Generous Networking Circle.

You can already follow an e-course (only in Dutch for the moment) at www.generous-networkers.com and follow us on Twitter via @gnrs.

References

These are some of the **companies and professional organizations** the team of Networking Coach has worked for:

Accenture, Agoria, Alcatel, Belgacom, BIASS, BNP Paribas Fortis, Bosch, Colruyt, CTG, Deloitte, Delta Lloyd Bank, Dexia, Dupont, EDS, Ernst & Young, Euphony, Fortis, Gemeente Den Haag, Getronics, IBM, ING, Johnson & Johnson, Johnson Controls, KBC, Leaseplan, Mobistar, Nike, Partena, SAP, SD Worx, Securex, Siemens, Sun Microsystems, Telenet, TNT, Unisys, USG People, Chambers of Commerce and many small business owners and freelancers.

These are some of the **universities, alumni organizations and not-for-profit organizations** the Networking Coach team has worked for:

Aiesec, Ehsal Alumni, RSM Erasmus International MBA Rotterdam, Hogeschool Arnhem Nijmegen Alumni, GSS (Global Speakers Summit), JCI (Junior Chamber International), Karel De Grote Hogeschool, Markant, Palliatieve Zorgen Netwerk, NSA (National Speakers Association), Provinciale Hogeschool Limburg, PSA Holland (Professional Speakers Association Holland), Solvay Business School Alumni, University of Antwerp Management School and Vlerick Leuven Management School International MBA.

One tip from this book
can change your life dramatically.

Pay it forward
by making a donation for charity.

www.how-to-really-use-linkedin.com/
donate.html

Get even more out of LinkedIn:

LinkedIn Fundamentals Webinars

LinkedIn Steps to Success Webinars

LinkedIn Dive in Deep Packages

www.how-to-really-use-linkedin.com

Made in the USA
Lexington, KY
17 March 2013